The Biblical Seminar
63

DREAMS AND DREAM NARRATIVES IN THE BIBLICAL WORLD

DREAMS AND DREAM NARRATIVES IN THE BIBLICAL WORLD

Jean-Marie Husser

Translated by Jill M. Munro

Sheffield Academic Press

Originally published as 'Songe', in the *Supplément au dictionnaire de la Bible*, XII (Paris: Letouzey et Ané, 1996).

This first English edition published in 1999 by Sheffield Academic Press Ltd

Published by Sheffield Academic Press Ltd
Mansion House
19 Kingfield Road
Sheffield S11 9AS
England

Printed on acid-free paper in Great Britain
by The Cromwell Press
Melksham, Wiltshire

British Library Cataloguing in Publication Data

A catalogue record for this book is available
from the British Library

ISBN 1-85075-968-5

CONTENTS

PREFACE TO THE ENGLISH EDITION

This work is the English translation of an article published in 1996 in the *Supplément au dictionnaire de la Bible* under the heading 'Songe'. The translation does not modify the text, with the exception of the bibliography, which has been updated and adapted for English readership. I have simply added a few original texts in the chapter on Egypt, because in the French edition I referred directly to the monograph by Serges Sauneron, which is perhaps less accessible to the English reader. I am happy to be able to express my gratitude here to the publishers Letouzey et Ané who authorized this translation, and to my wife Dr Jill Munro, who, with much patience, used both her ability as a biblicist and her knowledge of French in order to bring it about.

In its present book form, the text displays a certain number of characteristics that are inherited from the form in which it was originally published, and concerning which it might be helpful to give a few explanations to the reader.

First of all, the very nature of an undertaking such as the *Supplément au dictionnaire de la Bible* is to present a subject related to the Bible and its cultural environment in its current state of research. Consequently, it is the Old Testament that is at the centre of this monograph on dreams and that occupies the greatest place therein. The section concerning Near Eastern texts does not claim to be as exhaustive as the latter and simply seeks to situate the subject in the wider context of the 'biblical world'. This Bible-centred approach is a choice that may be challenged, but which finds its justification in the editorial project of the *Supplément au dictionnaire de la Bible*. Specialists in different domains, Mesopotamian, Hittite or Egyptian, will no doubt find these chapters insufficient. I am aware of this, but am also the first to regret the absence of any monograph on the subject either of dreams or of their significance and function in the different civilizations of the ancient Near East, apart from that of A. Leo Oppenheim, which remains a remarkable synthesis to which scholars will continue to refer for a long time.[1]

Secondly, the specificity of a dictionary lies in its mandate to give an overview of the question in hand without entering into lengthy critical remarks on different aspects of the material. This allows the reader to get to the heart of the matter straightaway, rather than to lose his way among the meanders of source criticism, which is undoubtedly indispensable, but the subject of other publications. The way in which the texts are tackled here thus reflects the current state of research; no attempt is made to give a detailed account of the problems posed by each to source criticism. Of the numerous epigraphical, philological or literary questions, only those that relate directly to our subject are rapidly sketched. When they do give rise to discussion, I try to justify as succinctly as possible the options chosen and the hypotheses necessary to the interpretation of the texts, so as not to overload the presentation and to concentrate on its principal subject.

For the same reason, I have deliberately left aside the vast cumbersome apparatus of bibliographical references to which exegetes are used. Using the author–date style, the references in the text refer principally to the translation and edition of ancient texts, as well as to studies concerning different aspects of the subject in question. In order to provide the reader with a bibliography specific to dreams, there is at the end of each chapter an accompanying bibliography relating directly to the subject in hand. The bibliography for dreams in the Bible is to be found at the end of Chapter 6.

Strasbourg
15 May 1998

1. Butler's recent monograph (1998) unfortunately appeared too late for it to be taken into consideration.

ABBREVIATIONS

ÄAT	Ägypten und Altes Testament
AcOr	*Acta orientalia*
AfO	*Archiv für Orientforschung*
ALASP	Abhandlungen zur Literatur Alt-Syrien-Palästinas und Mesopotamiens
ANET	James B. Pritchard (ed.), *Ancient Near Eastern Texts Relating to the Old Testament* (Princeton, NJ: Princeton University Press, 3rd edn, 1969)
AnOr	Analecta orientalia
AnSt	*Anatolian Studies*
AOAT	Alter Orient und Altes Testament
AOS	American Oriental Series
BAGB	*Bulletin de l'association Guillaume Budé*
BASOR	*Bulletin of the American Schools of Oriental Research*
BBB	Bonner biblische Beiträge
Bib	*Biblica*
BWANT	Beiträge zur Wissenschaft vom Alten und Neuen Testament
BZ	*Biblische Zeitschrift*
BZAW	Beihefte zur *ZAW*
CS	W. Hallo and K.L. Younger, Jr (eds.), *The Context of Scripture. Canonical Compositions from the Biblical World* (Leiden: E.J. Brill, 1997)
CT	*Cuneiform Texts from Babyloian Tablets in the British Museum* (London: The Trustees of the British Museum)
CTH	E. Laroche, *Catalogue des textes hittites* (Paris: Klincksieck, 2nd edn, 1971)
DAPT	Deir 'Allah plaster text
EC	*Etudes classiques*
IBS	*Irish Biblical Studies*
IFAO	Institut français d'archéologie orientale
JAOS	*Journal of the American Oriental Society*
JCS	*Journal of Cuneiform Studies*
JNES	*Journal of Near Eastern Studies*
JQR	*Jewish Quarterly Review*
JSOT	*Journal for the Study of the Old Testament*
JSOTSup	*Journal for the Study of the Old Testament*, Supplement Series

KAI	H. Donner and W. Röllig, *Kanaanäische und aramäische Inschriften* (3 vols.; Wiesbaden: Otto Harrassowitz, 1962–64)
KAR	E. Ebeling, *Keilschrifttexte aus Assur religiösen Inhalts*, I, II (WVDOG 28, 34; Leipzig: Hinrich, 1915; 1923)
KBo	*Keilschrifttexte aus Boghazköi* (Volumes 1-22 belong to WVDOG, Leipzig: Hinrich, 1916–21; Berlin: Mann, 1922–).
KTU	M. Dietrich, O. Loretz and J. Sanmartin, *The Cuneiform Alphabetic Texts from Ugarit, Ras Ibn Hani and Other Places* (ALASP, 8; Münster: Ugarit Verlag, 1995)
KUB	*Keilschrifturkunde aus Boghazköi* (Berlin: Staatliche Museen, Vorderasiatische Abteilung, 1921–53)
LÄS	Leipziger ägyptologische Studien
LKA	E. Ebeling, F. Köcher and L. Rost, *Literarische Keilschrifttexte aus Assur* (Berlin: Akademie-Verlag, 1953)
MDAI	Mitteilungen des deutschen archäologischen Instituts
MVAG	Mitteilungen der vorderasiatisch- ägyptischen Gesellschaft
OBL	Orientalia et biblica lovaniensia
OBO	Orbis biblicus et orientalis
OLP	*Orientalia lovaniensia periodica*
Or	*Orientalia*
OTL	Old Testament Library
PL	J.-P. Migne (ed.), *Patrologia cursus completus...Series prima [latina]* (221 vols.; Paris: J.-P. Migne, 1844–65)
PRU	*Le palais royal d'Ugarit*
RA	*Revue d'assyriologie et d'archéologie orientale*
RB	*Revue Biblique*
REg	*Revue d'égyptologie*
RevQ	*Revue de Qumran*
RevScRel	*Revue des sciences religieuses*
RivB	*Rivista biblica*
SBL	Society of Biblical Literature
SR	*Studies in Religion/Sciences religieuses*
STT	O. Gurn, J.J. Finkelstein, P. Hulin, *The Sultantepe Tablets,* I, II (Occasional Publications, 3, 7; Ankara: British Institute of Archaeology, 1957; 1964).
TDNT	Gerhard Kittel and Gerhard Friedrich (eds.), *Theological Dictionary of the New Testament* (trans. Geoffrey W. Bromiley; 10 vols.; Grand Rapids: Eerdmans, 1964–)
TDOT	G.J. Botterwerk and H. Ringgren (eds.), *Theological Dictionary of the Old Testament*
UBL	Ugaritisch- Biblische Literatur
UF	*Ugarit-Forschungen*
UT	Cyrus H. Gordon, *Ugaritic Textbook* (AnOr, 38; Rome: Pontifical Biblical Institute Press, 1965)
VAT	Vorderasiatische Ton Tafeln (Berlin: Staatliche Museen)

VD	*Verbum domini*
VT	*Vetus Testamentum*
VTSup	*Vetus Testamentum*, Supplements
WVDOG	Wissenschaftliche Veröffentlichungen der Deutschen Orient-Gesellschaft
WZ(L).GS	*Wissentschaftliche Zeitschrift der Karl-Marx-Universität Leipzig. Gesellschafts- und Sprachwissenschaftliche Reihe*

Part I

THE ANCIENT NEAR EAST

Chapter 1

INTRODUCTION

The texts studied in the present book suggest other possible titles for the monograph, such as 'oneiromancy' or 'incubation' or even more generally 'dream experiences'. In other words, the subject tackled here under the heading 'dreams' involves a variety of aspects rarely clarified by the texts, aspects such as oneiromancy, incubation or dream experience, each of which must be defined as precisely as possible. Moreover, if we do not want to limit ourselves simply to a commentary of literary forms, it is indispensable to try to reach the real life dream experience lying behind the interpretation that the texts give of it. We must try, therefore, to distinguish between the expression—stereotypical though it may be—of the dream experience (ordinary dream, visionary dream, nightmare, etc.) and those more or less ritualised practices whose object it was to deal with such experiences (incubation, oneiromancy, magical conjuration, etc.). To these two fundamental aspects of the phenomenon, constituted by the subjective experience of the dreamer and the practices brought to birth by this experience, we must add a third: *aetiology*, the interpretative discourse concerning the recognized cause or origin of the different types of dreams, which justifies and gives rise to the different practices observed. It is, moreover, this interpretative discourse that implicitly upholds the use made of dreams as literature and the critical attitude expressed with regard to them.

French literary usage picks up the distinction already present in ancient Greek between ἐνύπνιον (*rêve*) and ὀνεῖρος (*songe*). The latter tends to be used of presages and of poetic or religious experiences, while the meaning of the former is more general, and is even occasionally derogatory. We shall soon discover that in the interests of clarity, given the diversity of oneiric experience and practice, we would benefit from a similar diversity of precise technical terms in order to be able to tackle the subject correctly. This, however, is a vocabulary that the ancient semitic texts, and the Bible in particular, did not possess. The result is apparent confusion, which is dissipated to some degree by the concepts elaborated by modern psychological or neurophysiological study into sleep and dreams.

1. *The Nature of the Sources*

Since there is not one single dream that is related directly by the subject supposed to have had the experience, we must allow for the intervention of one or more redactors unknown to the dreamer when considering the question of composition. These redactors wrote up events according to the literary schemas and compositional conventions of the time, thereby eliminating any real spontaneity from the dream accounts. Clearly, therefore, it is not the dreams themselves that are the object of study, but rather the more or less elaborate reports made of them. Consequently, it is worth remembering that the sources available to us do not give access to the personal dream experience of such and such a dreamer, but bear witness directly to the mythical, theological or naturalistic interpretations made of the phenomenon.

The question of the authenticity of the dream experiences related by the texts therefore arises, indeed all the more intensely given that literary criticism has clearly demonstrated the fictitious character of most of these reports. It is true that the question is posed differently according to the nature of the document (literary work, letter, practical manual, etc.), but it is nevertheless appropriate to distinguish here between historical and psychological authenticity.

Whatever the literary genre of the text in which the dream report appears, it is necessary, if the report is to be understood by the readers, that they should be able to recognize in the description an experience known to them. To the extent that the dream report, however fictitious, means something to the readers, it avoids being conditioned solely by literary forms and necessarily retains something of common psychological experience. In other words, the historical authenticity of the experience related in the dream report is less important to the reader than its psychological plausibility.

On the other hand and inversely, the strongly traditional character of the texts means that they unavoidably acted as paradigms. However stereotypical the dreams reports, they in turn determined to a certain degree, the actual dream experience of the individuals to whom they were addressed. Literary forms apart, it would appear possible, by reason of this inevitable and necessary collusion between author and reader, to assume a degree of formal analogy between the intimate dream experience of individuals and its stereotypical literary expression, however fictitious.

This question, evoked here in general terms, must of course be reconsidered in the context of each particular case, for the function of the dream narrative varies considerably according to the genre of the text in which it appears. At first sight, it is striking to note the diversity of contexts and literary genres in which a dream may appear. This impression is quickly modified, however, when one realizes that not every type of dream experience is attested in every type of document.

Thus it is that ordinary, everyday dreams in all their fantastic variety, apart from a few isolated ironical allusions in literary texts, are to be found exclusively in *practitioners' manuals*. Particularly well attested in Mesopotamia, but also in Egypt, these *dream books*, which give the key to one's dream, are presented in the form of interminable lists of presages. The rule of the genre, and above all the practical efficaciousness of the professionals which used them required that the greatest possible number of dream situations, from the most banal to the most incongruous, be described in the clearest and most concise manner possible. Lacking in any personal detail, these *dream books* are nevertheless the reflection of dreams as they were experienced in the environment that generated them. We also often find along with them collections of rituals aimed at averting the harmful effect of bad dreams.

Dream reports as such, either premonitory dreams with symbolic scenarios, divine visions or messages received from the gods, are proper to *literary texts*. Where epic or legendary works are concerned, their function may be essentially narrative; on these occasions the dream is important to the general structure of the narrative, contributing in some cases to the transformation and valorization of the hero.

A good number of dream reports are to be found in *royal inscriptions*, particularly under the last sovereigns of the Hittite empire, in Mesopotamia, during the neo-Assyrian and neo-Babylonian periods, and in Egypt, under the pharoahs of the New Empire. In biblical literature, Solomon's dream at Gibeon (1 Kgs 3.5-15), though it is not an inscription strictly speaking, finds its inspiration, at least in part, in this literary genre. This brings us into the realm of Near Eastern royal ideology according to which the sovereign enjoys a special and privileged relationship with the divinity, albeit with subtle differences according to the cultural context. The authenticity of the experience described in these royal dreams is never called into question in so far as the possibility of this kind of meeting between the king and the divinity is part of the ideology that they help to define. The dreams reported in this kind of text are often considered nowadays as instruments of political propaganda. This kind of interpretation should be handled with care; it should be remembered that a good number of inscriptions were not available for public readership and that the latter were the reserve of a very limited number of erudite scholars.

A certain number of dreams are reported in *letters*, the only surviving examples of which belong to the corpus of letters found at Mari, even if it is probable that their uniqueness is due solely to the chances of destruction and discovery. In spite of their exceptional character and their short time span, the immediacy of their testimony to events as they were experienced makes this kind of document particularly valuable.

2. *Practices Related to Dreams*

With the exception of *dream books* and magical rituals, whose practical purpose is fairly clear, the surviving texts make only scattered allusions as to the circumstances surrounding the reception of dreams. Although often not very explicit, the literary context does however, in certain cases, suggest the existence of more or less ritualized behaviour or practices designed to provoke dreams or to interpret their contents. In general, practices associated with dreams stem from belief in the ominous or specifically oracular significance of dreams and link up for the most part with divinatory practices.

The traditional distinction between inspired and deductive divination goes back to Plato (*Phaedr*. 244c-245b; 249d-e; 265b-c) and proves to be adequate even now:

> Divination manifests itself in two ways, from without or within: its presence is made known by external signs or internal illumination. Consequently, the variety of individual procedures and rituals attested may be reduced to two general methods; the method which the ancients call 'artificial' (ἔντεχνος, τεχνιτής, *artificiosa*) and which consists of making a conjectured interpretation of external signs; and the so-called 'natural' or spontaneous method (ἄτεχνος, ἀδιδάκτος, *naturalis*), according to which the soul passively allows itself to be directed by divine inspiration (Bouché-Leclercq 1963: I, 107).

In *inspired* divination (otherwise known as *intuitive* or *spontaneous* divination), ecstacies, visions or dreams put the individual into a frame of mind favorable to the manifestation of the divinity and to the reception of his or her message, without the former having to intervene in any way. This form of divination includes the range of prophetic manifestations and behaviour.

On the other hand, *deductive* divination (otherwise known as *artificial* or *conjectural* divination), by far the most widespread in Mesopotamia, depends upon the deliberate action of the individuals who seek to decipher the will of the gods as it is inscribed and made manifest in the world in which they live. This divinatory practice, at the crossroads between mythical and deductive thinking, depends upon a procedure that is both logical and rational, as has been amply demonstrated by A.L. Oppenheim (1964) and J. Bottéro (1974). The search for presages in all observable natural phenomena begins with the observation of coincidences (no doubt recurring) between these phenomena and specific historical events. Once accumulated, this empirical data may then be systematized to constitute lists of presages, a well-known form in which 'protasis–apodosis' are set logically against each other. The secular and scientific character of this divinatory technique has often been remarked, even though it depends upon a profoundly religious vision of the world, according to which the will of the gods is inscribed in natural phenomena.

Dream experiences give rise to practices drawing on both of these forms of divination. Collections of dream presages testify to what may be termed *deductive oneiromancy*. These were based upon ordinary dreams, which, by virtue of being comparable to all other natural phenomena, were likely to be considered portentous. As for dream experiences on a grand scale, that is, symbolic dreams or dream theophanies, these belong to the realm of inspired divination in so far as it is the divinity him or herself who takes the initiative to visit the sleeper in a dream in order to speak to him or her directly or to send a message in the form of undeciphered enigmatic images. It is then that *intuitive oneiromancy* becomes necessary; this is the science of seers or of inspired interpreters, whose task it is to communicate the enigmatic messages of the dreams in such a way as they might be understood. There was no *dream book*, no key to dreams, to guide this practice in ancient times, for as far as we know it depended solely on the wisdom and charism of the interpreter. It is noteworthy that this form of dream-criticism is attested in literary texts only. Consequently, it is difficult to have any real idea of the precise way in which it was practised.

Incubation appears to be another practice related to dreams. It makes use of both types of divination. According to the standard definition of historians of religion, it consists of preparing oneself ritually by means of diverse observances (fasting, purification, sacrifices) and of spending the night in a sanctuary or in a natural holy site, in order to receive either a visit or a message in a dream from the divinity invoked. Other sacrificial or purificatory rituals follow upon awakening. It is evident from the manner in which the visit from the divinity is asked for and ritually provoked that incubation is a deductive procedure, while the dream experience that usually accompanies it, namely the visit of the god in the dream, has certain similarities with inspired divination.

Much has been written on the subject of incubation in the ancient Near East and in Israel in particular, but it is less well attested than is often supposed, as we shall see. Texts that speak of it in unambiguous terms are rare before the Hellenistic period, and interpretation of any positive indice depends on the preliminary definition given to it. The reconstruction of the ritual of the type generally recognized is based essentially on Greek and Latin sources. They rarely predate the Hellenistic period and describe the practice of therapeutic incubation in the sanctuaries of healer gods (Asclepius, Pan, Sarapis, *et al.*).

Therapeutic incubation, widespread in the Mediterranean area from the fifth century BC onwards, should be distinguished from *oracular incubation*, although the former is the direct product of the latter. In ancient Greece, it was customary to use incubation to consult the oracles of chthonic divinities, such as that of Amphiaraus at Oropus in Attica (Paus. 3.36.6), or those of certain heroes. This was the case as regards Trophonius, who was consulted in the cave where he met with his death (called μαντεῖον or ἱερόν Τροωνιου) near Lebadea (Paus. 9.39.5). The preparatory rites were numerous, and included purification, fasting, ablutions, flagellation, unctions, dances and a variety of sacrifices, in order that the subjects might give themselves up to the κατάβασις. The aim of consulting these oracles by means of incubation was often to get rid of an illness. With the development of the cult of Asclepius, and then that of other thaumaturgic divinities, incubation became a central element in practices designed to bring about healing.

By contrast, the type of incubation to which the ancient Near Eastern texts preceding the Hellenistic period seem to refer is oracular in character. Taking into account also the cultural and chronological difference, we should therefore be cautious in using the Hellenistic model of this practice to interpret our sources. Nevertheless it is certain that forms of oracular consultation by means of dreams were practised thoughout the entire Near East, although the details of the rituals and techniques that were used escape us for the most part. Besides, it seems likely that we should allow for different forms of incubation, and distinguish between popular, royal, priestly and prophetic practices, each having a specific function and each accomplished according to their own particular observances. We will see, as regards Israel and the Aramaic world, that a form of prophetic incubation was certainly practised, although it probably corresponded more precisely to what we call today a *guided dream* than to the classic definition of incubation.

3. *Literary Forms and Dream Experiences*

Throughout this book, 'experience' should be understood as real life experience, the German *Erlebnis*. Even if the texts are rarely explicit about this, certain indications suggest that an effort was made to distinguish between the nature and provenance of dreams in order to assess their oracular value. Moreover, the practices I have just mentioned seem to correspond to specific forms of dream experience. We should therefore allow for a relative diversity of dream *states,* a diversity to be distinguished from the infinite variety that exists as regards *content*, the latter being the product of the imagination as it is exercised in the dream world or of the preoccupations of the redactors.

Artimedorus of Daldis in the second century AD gathered together in the five volumes of his *Oneirocritica* the sum total of efforts made to classify and interpret dreams in antiquity. He distinguishes between dreams that are simply natural phenomena having no revelatory function (ἐνύπνια) and dreams that alone are of divinatory value (ὄνειροι). The former are the product either of the body, testifying to the state of its organs, or of the soul, expressing its desires and fears. The latter, on the other hand, are 'a movement or polymorphic modeling of the soul, signifying good or bad events to come' (1.2). Consequently, someone whose body and soul are at peace does not dream ἐνύπνια but ὄνειροι. Artimedorus also distinguishes between theoromatic dreams, 'those which, when they are realised, mirror their contents exactly' (1.2), and allegorical dreams, 'which signify one thing by means of another' (1.2)

(Festugière 1975). In other words, he distinguishes between dreams that are immediately comprehensible and those requiring interpretation.

True to his stoic ideas, Artimedorus does not accept that dreams may have an origin external to the soul. This very 'materialist' position was not very widespread, and generally a third category of dreams is proposed, those of divine origin, described simply as *oracles* (χρηματισμός). 'We call a dream oracular in which a parent, or a pious or revered man, or perhaps or even a god clearly reveals what will or will not transpire, and what action to take or to avoid' (Macrobius, *Somn. Scip.* 1.3.8).[1]

Although it did not formulate them as systematically as the specialists of late antiquity, the Near East worked with the same basic distinctions in its practice of oneirocriticism. Ordinary everyday dreams, considered to be a natural phenomenon, and possibly of portentous value—and thus the object of oneiromancy—were treated differently from dreams of religious significance.

Taking up Artimedorus's distinction between theorematic and allegorical dreams, modern historical criticism defines two types of dreams, the one distinguishable from the other by virtue of their respective literary form:

Message-dreams are characterized by the sudden appearance in a dream of a divinity or of someone who communicates a message, the contents of which are immmediately intelligible to the sleeper. There is virtually no scenario, and the visual element is limited to a description of the figure who appears in the dream. Alternatively, it may even be absent altogether. Though auditory perceptions dominate this kind of dream, the dreamer does not necessarily remain passive, for sometimes a dialogue opens up between the dreamer and the figure who appears in the dream. Apart from its obvious literary function, the psychological significance of this dream dialogue is of interest to us. We will tackle this question later.

Allegorical or *symbolic dreams* also transmit a message from the gods, but by means of a coded language made up of images, pictures and events, whose significance escapes the dreamer. Visual perception is dominant here but what is perceived is not intelligible straightaway; these dreams require to be interpreted on the dreamer's awakening. Allegorical dream reports therefore usually first relate the dreamer's

1. English translation and commentary by Stahl (1952).

vision, followed by the interpretation made of it by a third party, who may or may not be a specialist.

However pertinent from a literary point of view, and though it probably does group together dream states with analogous characteristics, such as auditory dreams and visual dreams, the typology proposed above is inadequate to the task of defining and classifying the relative diversity of the dream reports available to us. Several of them are a mixture of visual allegory and speech; others are entirely symbolic, without being enigmatic; finally, others act as veritable oracles, in so far as the message in the dream is not meant for the dreamer but for a third party informed by the latter. These may be termed *prophetic dreams*.

Moreover, by reason of the nature of our sources, the dream reports, in the literary form they take, give expression above all to dream experiences of religious significance, dream experiences thought to transmit messages, either seen or heard, hailing from the realm of the divine. It is therefore difficult to accede by this means to other kinds of dream experiences, which, not having their own specific literary form, might nevertheless sometimes find expression in borrowed forms. Noteworthy is the example of the *nightmare*, which is never acknowledged as such in the texts, but which I suspect sometimes constitutes at least part of the experience evoked in the classical form proper to message or allegorical dreams.

To this economy of form as regards literary expression there corresponds a relative poverty of vocabulary in west Semitic languages: one single root *ḥlm*, with its nominal derivatives, denotes dream experiences or states, the variety of which is difficult to evaluate. Nevertheless, we can assume that the texts always refer to a type of experience known to the reader, and that there are enough indications to enable him or her to identify it. It is therefore vital to claim for *ḥlm* a semantic field wide enough to cover the range of—or at least the most important—oneiric manifestations, if we are to avoid attributing to biblical authors an unlikely degree of inconsistency in their attitude towards dreams.

On the whole our modern languages suffer from a similar indigence of terms when it comes to describing the plurality of oneiric states rediscovered in recent years by diverse scientific disciplines. In addition to the simple alternation of wakefulness/sleep, neurophysiological research into sleep encourages us to distinguish three states: wakefulness/sleep/ dreaming. The latter is characterized by a specific electro-encephalographic graph (EEG) that is both rapid and of low amplitude, giving evidence of brain activity comparable to that of wakefulness; this phase of sleep is known as rapid eye movement sleep (REM sleep).

REM sleep thus appears to constitute a break in the cycle of sleep phases, being close both to wakefulness by virtue of accelerated brain activity and to deepest sleep by reason of the way in which it impedes sensory and motory centres. This phase of REM sleep is accompanied by characteristic physiological manifestations (REM, a general fall in temperature, increased consumption of oxygen and glucose by the brain, the erection of the penis in men—and its clitoral equivalent in women).

If we can be sure of a correlation between REM sleep and ordinary oneiric activity, it appears that dreaming is not limited to these periods, for *slow wave sleep* too is characterized by a degree of mental activity in the course of its different constituent phases: 50–60 per cent of subjects woken at this point affirm that they have dreamt, but are not able to reconstitute the sequence of the scenario.

> Compared with memories of periods of REM sleep, mental activity during slow wave sleep is generally poorer in memories, nearer to thoughts than to dreams, less lively, less visual, more conceptual, subject to greater control of the will, more closely related to everyday life, for it is produced by sleep which is lighter, less subject to the emotions and more pleasant (Jouvet 1992: 113).

It has been recognized for a long time that there are two kinds of *oneiric consciousness* in the dreamer, both of which have now been confirmed by observations made in the laboratory: (1) an inner awareness of events experienced in the dream accompanied by the certainty that it is not a dream but reality; (2) an inner awareness on the part of dreamers at a second level, and much less frequently, that they are dreaming and even, in certain cases, that they are able to direct their actions within the oneiric situation: these are called *lucid dreams* (Jouvet 1992: 130-32). We can safely suppose that a conscious capacity such as this, accompanied by the mastery of lucid dreams, is the background to some of the dream reports in our sources.

Finally, a variety of modern methods of psychotherapy have developed techniques designed to stimulate a state in which the subject may have *day dreams*. These dreams operate in the same way as *hypnic dreams*, except that the former may be guided or induced by external factors. This state of wakeful dreaming is objectively defined by means of an electro-encephalographic graph revealing alpha waves, the formation that characterizes all other states of diffused wakefulness, sometimes termed 'altered consciousness'. The alpha rhythm also accompanies relaxation and meditation.

The rapid evocation above of these less habitual aspects of one's dream life may seem to digress from our subject, but their relevance will become apparent when, in the course of our study, we try to answer the following question: why did the prophets in Israel never speak positively of dreams, when at the same time their nights were full of 'visions'?

4. *Selected Bibliography*

Arnold-Forster, M., *Studies in Dreams* (New York: Macmillan, 1921).

Bottéro, J., 'Symptômes, signes, écriture en Mésopotamie ancienne', in J.-P. Vernant *et al.*, *Divination et rationalité* (Paris: Le Seuil, 1974), pp. 70-197.

Bouché-Leclercq, A., *Histoire de la divination dans l'Antiquité* (4 vols.; Brussels: Culture et civilisation, 1963 [1879–82]).

Caillois, R., and G.E. von Grunebaum (eds.), *The Dream and Human Societies* (Berkeley: University of California Press, 1966).

Freud, S., *The Interpretation of Dreams* (ed. and trans. J. Strachey; Standard Edition, 4–5; London: Hogarth Press, 1978).

—*On Dreams* (trans. J. Strachey; London: Hogarth Press, 1952).

Green, C., *Lucid Dreams* (Oxford: Institute of Psychological Research, 1968).

Hobson, J.A., *The Dreaming Brain* (New York: Basic Books, 1988).

Jouvet, M., *Le sommeil et le rêve* (Paris: O. Jacob, 1992).

Jung, C.G., *Dreams* (The Collected Works, 4, 8, 12, 16; Bollingen Series, 20; Princeton, NJ: Princeton University Press, 1974).

Killborne, B., 'Dreams', in M. Eliade (ed.), *The Encyclopedia of Religions* (16 vols.; New York: Macmillan, 1987), IV, pp. 482-92.

LaBerge, S., *Lucid Dreaming* (New York: J.P. Tarcher, 1985).

Marjash, S., 'On the Dream Psychology of C.G. Jung', in R. Caillois and G.E. von Grunebaum, *The Dream and Human Societies* (Berkeley: University of California Press, 1966).

Chapter 2

MESOPOTAMIA

Given the vast ensemble that constituted ancient Mesopotamia, it would seem appropriate to distinguish more precisely than I do here between the different periods and cultural eras of which it is composed: Sumer and Babylon in the south, western Elam to the east and Assyria to the north-west. It is no doubt significant that all the major dream reports known to us of dreams that are symbolic or that have a pronounced visual component belong to the literary works of the Sumero-Babylonian world (the dreams of Gilgameš, Gudea, Sargon, Dumuzi, of the righteous sufferer in *Ludlul bēl nēmeqi*, *et al.*). Literary and mythological developments occupy an important place in all these texts. The Assyrian world, on the other hand, with its royal inscriptions and divinatory literature, seems to have paid more attention to the oracular character of dreams, whether they be everyday dreams or the exceptional opportunity for the visit of a god. Mari, even nearer the west Semitic world, expresses a similar interest in the prophetic letters of its royal archives. Lack of information, however, advises caution as regards an over-systematic reconstitution of the Mesopotamian scene. That is why it is the nature of the documents rather than their cultural origin that determines the organization of this presentation.

1. *Dreams and Divination*

In the considerable effort made by the ancient Mesopotamians to decipher destinies with the aid of the science of divination in the multiple forms in which it developed there, dreams only occupy a very modest place. For example, of the estimated 1500 tablets, of which Assurbanipal's library was originally composed, without counting the numerous duplicate copies of each of these, more than 300 are devoted to texts of presages, while epic and mythical literature only constitute around 40 of the total. Of all the divinatory texts in this collection, the famous canonical Babylonian *Dream Book* only occupies 11 tablets.

Furthermore, there is no evidence of a specific group of professionals solely devoted to oneiromancy among the specialists in divination. The *šā'ilu* and *bārû*, whom we see involved in the interpretation of dreams, are seer-priests competent in all domains of divination. The *bārû* are seers who are particularly expert in scholarly divination. Their task is to apply deductive oneiromancy to lists of presages. The *šā'ilu*, on the other hand, who are mentioned much less frequently and among whom there are numerous women (*šā'iltu*), seem to be rather more oriented towards divinatory forms such as libanomancy, necromancy and oneiromancy; their interpretation tends to be more intuitive, and we encounter them mainly in the context of the interpretation of symbolic dreams.

Certain terms in the Akkadian vocabulary express very clearly the close link between dreams and night or sleep. The habitual word for 'dream', *šuttu* (poetic *šunatu*), comes from the same root as *šittu*, 'sleep' (*wšn*, which we meet again in the Hebrew *yšn* and in the Arabic *wsn*, 'to doze'). This semantic relationship is verified by another, less frequently used term, *munattu*, derived from the root *nwm*, 'to sleep' (attested in Hebrew and in Arabic), whose usual meaning is 'early morning', but which, in certain cases, must be translated by 'sleep' or 'dream'. Oppenheim (1956: 225) cites an unpublished fragment of Sumero-Akkadian lexicography in which the entries are arranged in semantic groups; there, *šuttu*, *ḫiltu* and *munattu* are presented as synonyms for 'dream'. In cases of poetic parallelism, the synonym for *šuttu* is *tabrīt mūsi*, 'vision in the night' (*tabrītu* comes from *burrû*, 'to show'), which, in Sumerian, is translated by MAŠ.GE$_6$. Another Sumerian term commonly used to refer to dreams is MA.MÚ, 'product (?) of the night'.

Akkadian, like Sumerian, has no verb 'to dream'. One simply says 'to see', using the verbs *amāru* or *naṭālu* or less frequently *naplusu*. In the Mari letters, a distinction is made between dreams that are simply 'seen', *amāru*, and those which a hepatoscopic examination has proved oracular, and in association with which the verb *naṭālu* is used thereafter. When the dream is provoked by a divinity, the verb *šubrû*, 'to show', is used. A dream is therefore something that is seen at night, but which one is careful to distinguish from a vision, *bīru*.

On the other hand, the interpretation of dreams is designated by a specific verb, *pašāru*, a verb of equal semantic complexity to that found in Sumerian, where its equivalent, BUR, is used. The expression *šutta pašāru* refers equally well to three distinct moments in the interpretative process and may mean either: (1) to tell someone one's dream, (2) to interpret a dream, or (3) 'to undo' a dream, by which it is meant that the harmful consequences of the dream for the dreamer are diverted or destroyed by the interpretation itself or/and by varied magical techniques. The semantic richness of *pašāru* confirms the cathartic function of interpretation, a function that is also suggested by certain details both in the texts and in the rituals. As long as a dream remains unexplained, it retains its harmful hold on the dreamer. This same verb gives rise to the expression *mupaššir šunate*, 'he who accomplishes the *puššuru* of dreams', the Sumerian equivalent of which is LÚ SAG-ŠÈ NÁ A, 'the man who sleeps at a person's head'. The significance of this function is clarified by a passage in Cylinder A of Gudea (xx.7-11), to which I will return later in Section 6.

Everyday dreams are termed 'pleasant' (*šunāte damqāte)* or 'bad' (*la-ṭābu*), according to the impression they leave upon the dreamer. This does not, however, prejudge their ominous value in any way, for a pleasant dream may be a bad omen, or vice versa. Two aspects of the dream are therefore to be noted: its ominous character and its value as symptomatic of the psychosomatic state of the dreamer. The latter aspect is illustrated by a private letter in old Babylonian, in which a merchant on a journey writes to his family: 'I am well [*šalmāku*], the boss is well [*šalim*], and my dreams are extremely pleasant [*šunātūa mādiš damqa*].' In the following paragraph we will look at the various precautions taken to thwart the effect of a bad dream whose content is never disclosed in the text for apotropaic reasons.

As in the science of divination as a whole, it is Šamaš who presides over dreams and who holds in his possession knowledge of the messages they transmit. Nevertheless, with the exception of dreams in which the gods communicate a message directly, dreams, good and bad alike, are considered to be demoniac powers or beings, and for this reason are placed under the authority of the god of dreams (*ilu ša šunāte*). In Sumerian, his name is simply *Dream* (^{d}MA.MÚ). Divinity lists situate Mamu in Šamaš's entourage, and the development of a late school even makes him her daughter. In the AN = *Anu* lists of Assurbanipal's library (*CT* XXIV 31 iv.84-86; XXV 26 19-21) are the following entries: ^{d}MA.MÚ = DUMU.SAL.^{d}UTU.KE_4 ('Mamu = daughter of

Šamaš') and ᵈSI.SI.IG = DUMU.ᵈUTU.KE$_4$ ('Sisig = son of Šamaš'). The Sumerian ᵈSI.SI.IG corresponds to ᵈ*zaqīqu*, the god of dreams in Akkadian, whom theological constructions place alongside Mamu as the child of Šamaš.

Etymology relates Zaqīqu (also Ziqīqu) to the verb *zâqu*, 'to blow (of a storm)', and its diminutive form suggests the idea of a gentle breeze or zephyr. In numerous texts, the verb *zâqu* describes the activity of nocturnal demons as they pass like draughts through the finest of cracks in houses to attack those who sleep or who are ill. These parallels attest to the demoniac character of the god of dreams, and the meaning 'spirit' or 'demon' for *zaqīqu* is confirmed in several texts. The term is sometimes even used to describe the spirits of the dead (*Gilg*. 12 84: '...and the spirit [*utukku*] of Enkidu, like a breath of air (*kima zaqêqu*), came out of hell'). Likewise, one last name for the god of dreams, AN.ZA.QÀR, is associated, in certain lexical lists (ERIM.HUŠ = *anantu*: *CT* XVIII 48r i.30), with nocturnal demons who wander about in desert places and attack travellers.

2. *Deductive Oneiromancy*

This form of oneiromancy aims to decipher the messages contained in ordinary, everyday dreams, messages thought to presage future events in the life of the dreamer. The experience gained from this long-standing practice led to the constitution of lists of oneiric presages that are formulated in exactly the same way as other lists itemizing oracles arising from other natural phenomena. In these collections, the *omens* are consistently composed of two propositions, protasis and apodosis; the protasis proposes a typical example presented in the form of a hypothesis, while the apodosis responds with its interpretation. The vertical wedge (DIŠ) that marks the beginning of each omen in these lists was interpreted by scribes, from the middle Babylonian period onwards, as an element of syntax meaning 'if'. Sometimes they even replaced it by BE, to read *šumma*, 'if', or by UD.(DA), 'when'. Indeed, it appears that the presages in divinatory lists use the structure proper to legislative collections, and that the now classic expression 'if a man, in his dream...' is an adaptation of the formula used in casuistic laws.

The most ancient example of an *omen* drawn from oneiric experience is to be found in a small collection of oracles, dated around 1700 BCE, and comprising around 60 cases. These oracles are based upon the observation of physionomy and of human behaviour:

If a man while he sleeps [dreams that]
 the town falls again and again upon him
and he groans and no one hears him:
the [protective spirits] Lamassu and Šedu are attached
 to this man's body.

If a man while he sleeps [dreams that]
 the town falls again and again upon him
and he groans and someone hears him:
an evil Šedu-demon to his body is attached.
(VAT 7525 iii.28-35; Köcher and Oppenheim 1957–58: 67)

This text invites us to make several remarks: first, it is the only known case of a presage that explicitly describes a nightmare. Secondly, as was pointed out above, in spite of the disagreeable impression left by the dream, it may in fact presage something favorable: here, in a general atmosphere of terror, we see this characteristic process of reversal at work in so far as the least catastrophic situation (the call for help that is answered) is a bad omen, and vice versa. Finally, the dream is not explicitly referred to in the text; the mention of sleep alone is enough to suggest that it is an oneiric presage. An analogous situation arises in a tablet of presages found at Susa and dated around the second half of the second millennium BCE: in it there is no indication that the presages refer to dreams, but the context of the majority of them (about one hundred) leaves us in no doubt (Oppenheim 1956: 256-60).

Collections of presages such as these were gradually compiled to eventually form the large canonical Babylonian *Dream Book*, the main copies of which survive from the library at Nineve.[1] It is composed of eleven tablets: the first and the two last tablets contain exorcisms, the eight others each contained four to five hundred presages of which only a fifth survives. The series begins with the invocation of the god of dreams: [EN *Zi*]*qīqu ziqīqu* ^{d}MA.MÚ *ilu ša* [*šunāte*], '[Lord Zi]qiqu, gentle breeze, O Mamu, god of [dreams]...' Here, explicit reference is made to the oneiric context at the head of the first omen of each tablet: DIŠ.NA *ina* MÁŠ.GE$_6$-*šu*, 'if a man, in his dream...'

Each dream contains an example of a typical oneiric situation. Concrete, personal details are absent and the central motif in the dream serves as the entry by means of which the presages may be grouped

1. Edition, translation and commentary by Oppenheim (1956: 261-344; 1969: 153-65).

together in small thematic series. The entry is sometimes the verb that characterizes the main action in the dream, all the variations of which are then envisaged according to object and circumstance; for example, 'to give (to drink)': 'If <in his dream> he is given water...; beer...; wine...; river water...; water from a well...; water from an oil well...; water from a ditch...; water from a canal...; etc. (to drink)'. Here is a short example of presages and their interpretation:

> If <a man in his dream> he eats the meat of a [do]g: rebellion, not obtaining of (his) desire.
> If he eats the meat of a beaver: rebellion.
> If he eats the meat of a gazelle: (the disease) saḫal šêri.
> If he eats the meat of a wild bull: his days will be long.
> If he eats the meat of a fox: (an attack of) saḫal šêri, for an unfortunate person: good (luck).
> (Tab A ii.4'-7'; Oppenheim 1956: 270)

The apodosis is not always as abstract as the protasis. The final example in the above demonstrates that interpretation allowed for the fact that the meaning of the same dream might differ according to the situation of the dreamer. A small series in the fragments of Tablet II (= C) contains presages in which the oracle is more fully developed:

> If <in his dream> he takes off and flies (once) for an important (person) his good (luck), for a commoner: his bad (luck) will leave him; [if] he is thrown in jail: he will leave the jail, he will see the light, if he is sick: he will become well (again) (Oppenheim 1956: 287).

Finally, we should mention that, among all the possible oneiric situations envisaged by the *Dream Book*, provision is made for the appearance of a god in a dream, apparently in the form of his or her cultic statue; the oracles unfortunately have been lost:

> If the god stands before the man and [
> If the god remains without moving upon his pedestal: [
> If the god changes (his attitude) upon his pedestal: [
> If the god walks toward the man: [
> If the god jumps toward the man: [
> If the god sings in front of the man: [
> (Tab C, fgt 1; Oppenheim 1956: 289)

Identical thematic groups also gather together dreams of going up to heaven, or dreams about descending into hell.

The specialist in this type of oneiromancy is the *bārû*, whose name reminds us that he was originially associated with haruspication.[2] He puts his knowledge to work in every domain of divination. The *bārû* together constitute an organized corps of high officials (the *mar bārû*, 'sons of *bārû*'), the titles of whose senior members are known to us (*šāpir bārê*, 'commander of the *bārû*', for example). The principles underlying their interpretations are difficult to discern and seem in any case to be of a variety of types (Bottéro 1987: 150-54). The relationship between signifier and signified is sometimes based upon common day-time experience, upon the symbolic value of the oneiric motif, upon a play of words or upon assonance, or even upon a learned reading of pictograms, playing upon the multiplicity of phonetic or ideographic values present there. It is noteworthy that oneiric situations that infract moral laws or taboos are generally favorable: 'If he drinks the urine of his wife, this man will enjoy (lit. eat) abundance' (Oppenheim 1956: 266).

Tablets I, X and XI of the series contain *namburbû* rituals and conjurations designed to 'dissolve' or 'efface' the consequences of bad dreams. Series such as these are attested elsewhere[3] and a list of the texts with which the apprentice *bārû* had to familiarize himself (*KAR* 44) mentions, after a lengthy series on the subject of exorcism *Maqlû* and *Šurpû*, a work entitled 'How to make bad dreams good'. First of all, one can try to avoid bad dreams by reciting a formula of the following type: 'May the dream that I see be pleasant, may the dream that I see be worthy of credence, (O gods) make the dreams that I see good dreams.' In the event of a bad dream, conjuratory formulas are addressed to Sin and/or to Šamaš:

> Shamash, you are the judge—judge my case!
> You are the one who makes the decisions—decide my case!
> Change the dream I had into a good one!
> (*KAR* 252 iii.4-6; Oppenheim 1956: 300)

Recourse was also made to magical practices:

> If a man had a 'wrong' dream, he shall (in the morning) without (?) breakfast tell the dream [to], he shall burn (it) in fire [and the evil (?) consequences] will not impede him (Oppenheim 1956: 303).

2. From the verb *bārû*, 'to examine, inspect, observe', in Sumerian MÁŠ.ŠU GÍD.GÍD, 'he who puts his hand to the kid'.
3. *KAR* 53, 252 ; *LKA* 132.

> If (a man) had a dream (and) cannot remember (it) or the dream is…he shall throw seven grains of the PI.TA.PI.PI-plant into fire and place (the plant itself) upon his forehead and he will be fine (Oppenheim 1956: 304).

It is noteworthy that a forgotton dream is as formidable as a bad dream, for it may have been bad, but even more importantly, it will not have been 'exorcised' by interpretation *(pašāru).*

3. *Intuitive Oneiromancy*

With this form of oneiromancy we come to the question of the interpretation of *symbolic dreams* and we leave the realm of real life experience for that of literary fiction. All the symbolic dreams known to us are in fact reported in literary texts, and the majority of them are to be found in the *Gilgameš Epic* (cf. Dalley 1989). Even if this quasi-exclusivity is in part due to the chance conservation and discovery of certain texts, such a concentration of dreams in the same work is nevertheless remarkable. We should no doubt beware of attributing this to a particular predilection for dreams on the part of the author of the Babylonian version, since the Sumerian episodes of the same legend already included a good number.

Two initial dreams appear on the first tablet. They are experienced on the same night by Gilgameš, while the courtesan charms Enkidu in the steppe. Gilgameš recounts his dreams to his mother, who interprets them: using the symbolic images of a block fallen from the sky or of a hatchet placed in the city, his dreams herald the arrival of a powerful and loyal companion sent by the gods. The interpreter does not have recourse to any divinatory technique; the text simply underlines her wisdom and her knowledge (*Gilg*. 1.216-63).

A second series of dreams is recounted in the course of the journey of the two heroes towards the forest of cedars (*Gilg*. 4); the text has numerous lacunae, but enough remains to suggest that the journey is undertaken in six stages, and that in the course of each of the first five stages, Gilgameš has a dream that he recounts to Enkidu, who interprets it. In the Ninevite version, these dreams are provoked by an incubation ritual to which we will return later. As I have already said, the passage contained five dream reports in the Ninevite version, each followed by its interpretation; the text as it survives contains the first, the third and bits and pieces of the fourth dream. Two fragments of the Babylonian version, conserved in the Iraqi Museum in Bagdad, transmit three of the dreams belonging to the same episode, but with different contents. Each of these dreams describes perilous situations that Gilgameš finds terrifying and considers to be bad. Enkidu, however, interprets them favourably, recognizing them to be promising presages as regards the outcome of the journey. Here again, the interpreter needs no key to understand or interpret the dreams. His hermeneutical principle seems simply to consist in a reversal of values, changing a negative signifier into a positive signified.

As far as we can tell, the Sumerian cycle of legends about Gilgameš also recounted a certain number of dreams, but in episodes that were not included in the Babylonian epic.[4] It seems therefore that the hero was always associated with dreams, but, in the case of the epic, they are clearly a literary creation of the Babylonian author and appear partly as elements of compositional procedure. In general, they heighten the dramatic tension of the text by means of delay and help to emphasize the superhuman character of the heroes and their adventures; it is in his early dreams that Gilgameš discovers the heavenly origin of the one who will be his double in both an antithetical and complimentary sense. We may ask ourselves whether Enkidu's capacity to interpret dreams is due to his origin (he was created by the gods, not born of woman), or due to the wild, instinctual side of his nature. In any case, it is clear, above all in the Ninevite version, that the gift of interpretation is accompanied by a ritual know-how is that efficacious in the provocation of dreams (*Gilg*. 4; see Section 6).

Furthermore, Enkidu himself is present in a dream at the council of the gods, at the moment when his death is decided (*Gilg*. 6),[5] and a little further on (*Gilg*. 7.4.14-54), still in a dream, he experiences his own death and descent to the nether world. These two dreams do not fit the usual typology and literary artifice is particularly obvious here: to be present at the divine council in a vision may be understood as the imitation of a prophetic pattern, while the motif of descent into the nether world in a visionary dream will have a bright future in world literature.[6] Nevertheless, the fact that provision is made for this oneiric theme among the titles of the neo-Assyrian *Dream Book* (which

4. See Kramer (1944; Tigay 1982).
5. Only preserved in the Hittite version; see Section 4
6. The *Vision of the Nether World* is similarly introduced as a 'night vision' in an Assyrian text from the seventh century BCE (*ANET*: 109-10).

attributes around fifteen oracles to it) shows a strong cultural influence upon individual psychology (Oppenheim 1956: 327; Tab. C i.71-85).

Previous to *Gilgameš*, two important examples of symbolic dreams are related by Sumerian sources. The *dreams of Gudea*, prince of Lagash (2143–2124 BCE), belong to a long narrative recounting the building of the temple of Ningirsu (Wilson 1996). Not understanding the meaning of a dream in which the god appears to him as regards its construction (Cyl. A i.7–ii.3), Gudea sets off by boat for Nin, the city of the goddess Nanshe, to ask her to interpret the dream for him. After preparing himself ritually, he tells his dream to Nanshe, entitled 'ENSI of the gods' (= *šā'iltu*). The dream, moreover, is not strictly speaking symbolic, but rather a sort of theophany in which several characters appear with their attributes, characters whom Gudea is unable to identify. The goddess oneiromancer then explains the dream to the king figure by figure (Cyl. A iv.7–vi.14). Nothing allows us to tell from the text that the dialogue with the goddess takes place in a dream. If this had been the case the dream would have qualified as an incubatory dream. It is more probable that the interpreter is a priestess from the sanctuary of Nanshe, a priestess thought to be inspired by the goddess in the exercise of the art of oneiromancy. Gudea then asks for a sign; the latter is given in the form of a genuine message-dream (Cyl. A ix.6–xii.11) in the course of which Ningirsu appears to him a second time and speaks to him at length.

Dumuzi's dream appears at the beginning of an integral narrative of 267 verses, treated as an episode of the Ishtar cycle. It recounts the death of one of her lovers (Alster 1972). The literary function of the dream is very clear: having announced, from the start, the death of the hero by means of several symbolic images, the narrative hastens to the realization of this initial prophecy and by means of inclusion ends with images of the dream now realized. In order to elucidate the dream, Dumuzi calls upon his sister Geštinanna, a wise woman, expert in song and in writing, 'who knows the meaning of dreams':

> 'In the ominous dream, my dear sister–
>   in the ominous dream,
>   in the midst of my ominous dream,
> rushes rose for me
>   rushes grew up for me,
> and a lone reed was shaking the head in grief [for me].

Of twin reeds
    one was taken away from me.
In the forest a tall tree
    was uprooted for me all by itself
On my pure embers
    water was poured in my presence,
the owner's marks of my pure churns
    had been removed,
my pure cups that hang on pegs
    had been taken d[own] from the pegs,
and I had lost my staff.

An owl had caught
    a lamb in the sheepcote,
a falcon had caught a sparrow
    in the reeds of the fence.
My bucks and goats were dragging, to my (horror,)
    their lapis lazuli beards in the dust,
my rams, to my (horror,) were raking the ground
    with their big horns.
    The churns lay on their sides,
    poured out no milk,
the cups lay on their sides,
    Dumuzi lived there no more,
the winds only swept the fold.'

Geshtinanna replied to it
    to Dumuzi.
'My dear brother, your dream bodes no good,
    nor may it be propitiated.
Dumuzi, your dream bodes no good
    nor may it be propitiated...'

(Jacobsen 1987: 30-31)

Noteworthy is the role of women in dream interpretation in the majority of the texts; if it is generally men who dream, it is women who interpret their dreams. Like Geštinanna, Nanshe, who elucidates Gudea's dream, is entitled 'ENSI of the gods', the Akkadian equivalent of which is *šā'iltu*. The seer *šā'ilu* (root *ša'ālu*, 'to question') is frequently mentioned alongside *hārû* in profane or religious texts; he is 'the one who questions' gods and destinies, but by contrast with *hārû*, it is often the feminine form of the noun, *šā'iltu,* that we encounter. Little is known of the techniques used by the *šā'il(t)u* and their exact social status, their role in dream interpretation is attested essentially by literary texts recounting symbolic dreams. This no doubt suggests a practice of a more intuitive nature than that of the highly technical *bārû*, a practice depending upon an innate personal gift, or even a form of inspiration. This probably also explains the apparently inferior social status of the *šā'iltu*; they are to be found exercising their gift of divination outside the official scene, and specialize in more popular practices, such as necromancy. A passage from a hymn to Šamaš evokes the function of the *šā'ilu*:

> In the seer's bowl with cedar-wood apurtenance,
> You enlighten the dream priests and interpret dreams.
> (Lambert 1960: 128.53)

4. *Message-Dreams*

This type of dream is essentially found in royal inscriptions, but what remains of them is very unevenly distributed in the course of history. In fact, two periods in particular are represented: the reigns of Assurbanipal (668–627 BCE) (no dream of this kind is mentioned in the numerous inscriptions of his predecessors Sargon II, Sennacherib and Asarhaddon), and of Nabonidus (555–539 BCE), the last neo-Babylonian king. Here, too, the absence of evidence may be due to the potluck aspect of discoveries made, but it does seem probable that dreams did not arouse equal interest in all sovereigns.

The most ancient evidence, however, goes back to the pre-Sargonic period. It is to be found in the Sumerian inscription upon the *Vulture Stela*, an inscription that celebrates the victorious war waged by the king of Lagash against Umma.[7] King Eanatum I (*c.* 2454–2425 BCE) is reassured by the god Ningirsu as to the outcome of the war:

> [...] He followed after him. Him who lies sleeping, him who lies sleeping—he approaches his head. Eanatum who lies sleeping—[his] be[loved] master [Ningirsu approaches his head. (3 cases broken)]. 'Kish itself must abandon Umma, and being angry, cannot support it. The sun-(god) will shine at your right, and a ... will be affixed to your forehead. O Eanatum [(7 cases broken)] you will slay there (vi.26–vii.11; Cooper 1986: 34)

A recently found fragment of the Sumerian *Legend of Sharrumkin* (Sargon of Akkad, 2334–2279 BCE), written in palaeo-Babylonian, recounts the dream Sharrumkin had when he was cupbearer in the ser-

7. Text and translation by Jacobsen (1976) or Cooper (1986).

vice of Urzababa, king of Kish.[8] The dream frightens Sharrumkin who cries out and wakes up; Urzababa runs to his side and asks him to tell him his dream:

> At that time, the cupbearer, in the temple of Ezinu,
> Sargon, lay down not to sleep, but lay down to dream.
> Holy Inana, in the dream, was drowning him (Urzababa) in a river of blood.
> Sargon, screaming, gnawed the ground.
> When king Urzababa heard those screams,
> He had them bring him (Sargon) into the king's presence.
> Sargon came into the presence of Urzababa, (who said):
> 'Oh cupbearer, was a dream revealed to you in the night?'
> Sargon replied to his king:
> 'Oh my king, this is my dream which I will have told you about.
> There was a single young woman, she was high as the heaven, she was broad as the earth,
> She was firmly set as the [bas]e of a wall.
> For me, she drowned you in a great [river], a river of blood.'
>
> (Cooper and Heimpel 1983: 77)

It was thus that the king learned that his cupbearer would take his place! This example reveals the inadequacy of dream typology as it is usually presented, for this dream is neither symbolic nor a 'message' dream, but contains a clear visual message that does not require interpretation. The vision of the goddess is comparable to the one in Gudea's 'symbolic' dream and to the theophanies in typical message-dreams.

Assyrian and Babylonian *royal inscriptions* containing a number of message-dream narratives attest to the astonishing diversity of styles proper to each particular sovereign. Whether dedicatory stela, rupestrian inscriptions, consecratory nails or bricks, or votive objects, these inscriptions were not normally designed to be read by anyone but the gods or future kings. If we take this fact into consideration in our appreciation of the dream reports, the latter would appear to reflect a genuine aspect of the king's personal piety rather than to be motivated by the more immediate needs of propaganda. Moreover, they are not bound by stereotypes and evidence remarkable freedom in their formulation. In so doing they contribute to the literary originality of each reign (translation in Oppenheim 1956: 249-50).

8. Text and translation by Cooper and Heimpel (1983).

First of all, among the neo-Assyrian annals of Assurbanipal, there is the rare example of a collective dream in which Ištar appears to the entire army to assure the soldiers of her support of the king and to encourage them to cross a river in spate: one night during the Elamite invasion, Assurbanipal, prostrate at the foot of a statue of Ištar in her temple, beseeches the goddess who then speaks comfortingly to him (it is not stated that a dream is involved here). The inscription continues: 'During the night in which I appeared before her, (50) a *šabrû* priest lay down and had a dream. He awoke with a start and then Ishtar caused him to see a nocturnal vision (*tabrit muši… ušabrûšu*). He reported to me as follows…' There follows a description of the goddess, dressed as a warrior, who orders the king to stay where he is while she goes to fight his enemies (*ANET*: 606).

Here we have a sort of double dream: the king, in the temple, hears words of comfort, while the priest, at home, receives the actual oracle by means of an oneiric theophany. The priest appears to be the direct witness of a dream that is in fact destined for the king. The text suggests that the priest's oneiric vision was provoked by the king's prayer, suggesting a kind of incubation by transfer or delegation. It is noteworthy that an analogous situation is evoked by the words of the young girl who appears in *Ludlul bēl nēmeqi*'s third dream (III: 36-37, cited below): 'She said: "Be delivered from your very wretched state, whoever has had a vision during the night…"' It is possible that there are echoes of a specific incubatory practice here (see p. 48 below), but we should be careful about applying the concept of incubation as such.

Among the numerous royal neo-Babylonian inscriptions, only those from the reign of Nabonidus (555–539 BCE) relate dreams, though these are fairly numerous. As in the case of the Hittite king Hattušili, it was not uncommon for a usurper to legitimate his power in this way. Two of his dreams, of which the first was seen by the mother of Nabonidus, are typical examples of apparitions made by divinities to kings in order to ask them to reconstruct a sanctuary: Marduk and Sin make a request on behalf of the É.HÚL.HÚL at Harran, Šamaš on behalf of the temple at Sippar:

> During my lawful rule, the great Lords became reconciled with this town and (its) temple out of love for my kingship; they had mercy (upon the town) and they let me see a dream in the very first year of my everlasting rule: Marduk, the Great Lord, and Sin, the luminary of heaven and earth, stood (there) both; Marduk said to me: 'Nabonidus, king of Babylon,

> bring bricks on your own chariot (drawn by your own) horse, (re)build the temple É.HÚL.HÚL and let Sin, the Great Lord, take up his dwelling there!'
>
> I said to the Ellil of the gods, Marduk: 'The Umman-manda (the Medes) are laying siege to the very temple which you have ordered (me) to (re)build and their armed might is very great!' But Marduk said to me: 'The Umman-manda of who you spoke, they, their country and (all) the kings, their allies, shall cease to exist!'
>
> (And indeed) when the third year come to pass, he (Marduk) made rise against them Cyrus, king of Anshan, his young servant... (Oppenheim 1956: 250).

The same command from the gods to rebuild the É.HÚL.HÚL at Harran is repeated in two other dreams, of which the first was seen by the mother of Nabonidus, reported on the stelae of Harran (H 1.B: ii 5-11; H 2.A: i 7-14; Gadd 1958). But the most interesting dream is related on a basalt stela and tells of his accession to power (*ANET*: 308-10); this came about following a revolt that eliminated Nebuchadnezzar II's youngest son, Labashi-Marduk. The purpose of the entire text is obviously one of self-legitimation; Nabonidus presents himself as the 'executor' (*našparu dannu*), that is, the appointed continuator of Nebuchadnezzar and Neriglissar, his royal predecessors:

> vi)... With regard to the impending constellation of the Great Star and the moon, I became apprehensive (but in a dream) a man came to my assistance, saying to me: 'There are no evil portents (involved) in the impending constellation!' In the same dream, when my royal predecessor Nebuchadnezzar and one attendant (appeared to me) standing on a chariot, the attendant said to Nebuchadnezzar: 'Do speak to Nabonidus, that he should report to you the dream he has seen!' Nebuchadnezzar listened to him and said to me: 'Tell me what good (signs) you have seen!' (And) I answered him, saying: 'In my dream I beheld with joy the Great Star, the moon and Marduk (i.e. the planet Jupiter) high up on the sky and it (the Great Star) called me by my name!' (Oppenheim 1956: 250; *ANET*: 309-10)

This dream has several particularities: it is the only example among the texts of the Near East of the apparition of a dead person in a dream, though his role here is clearly to express how the transfer of power from Nebuchadnezzar to Nabonidus came about. The message in the dream thus operates at several levels, for in addition Nebuchadnezzar interprets a previous dream that had remained enigmatic, and whose message—unfortunately lost—we suppose was along the same lines. It is noteworthy that the possibility of encountering a 'dream' that itself was 'recounted and interpreted (*pašāru*) in a dream' is allowed for among the cases requiring exorcism in the *Dream Book*, Tab. X (Oppenheim 1956: 305 n. 229).

In literary works, message-dreams are relatively rare, but the Babylonian poem *Ludlul bēl nēmeqi* describes an impressive oneiric experience of this kind, experienced in the course of three successive dreams by the righteous sufferer, who has reached the point of dire agony:

I gro[an] day and night alike,
Dreaming and waking [I am] equally wretched.
A remarkable young man of extraordinary physique,
Magnificent in body, clothed in new garments—
Because I was only half awake, his features lacked form.
He was clad in splendour, robed in dread—
...
A second time [I saw a dream].
In the dream I saw [at night],
A remarkable purifier [...]
Holding in his hand a tamarisk rod of purification,
'Laluralimma, resident of Nippur,
Has sent me to cleanse you'.
He was carrying water, he po[ured it] over me,
He pronounced the resuscitating incantation, he massaged [my] bo[dy].
A third time I saw a dream,
In my dream I saw at night:
A remarkable young woman of shining countenance,
Clothed like a person (?), being like a god,
A queen among peoples [——]
She entered upon me and [sat down]
She ordered my deliverance [...]
'Fear not!' she said, I [will]
Whatever one sees (?) of a dream [——].
She ordered my deliverance, 'Most wre[tched] indeed is he,
Whoever he might be, the one who saw the vision at night.'
In the dream Ur-Nindinugga, a Babylonian (?)
A bearded young man wearing a tiara,
He was an exorcist, carryinig a tablet:
'Marduk has sent me.
To Shubshi-meshre-Shakkan I have brought a sw[athe],
From his pure hands I have brought a sw[athe]'.

(*CS*: I, 489-90)

This passage, which has so much in common with the vision in Gudea's first dream, is marked to a great extent by the creativity of the artist. In it are gathered together all the characteristic traits of oneiric theophanies, traits used more sparingly elsewhere. The layout of the poem suggests that these dreams come in response to the terrifying dreams that are mentioned, but never described, to which Shushi-meshrê-Shakkan, in common with other sick people of his kind, had fallen victim and which had contributed to his suffering (Tab. I: 54). In this triple vision, he witnesses the decisive, and in the end successful, intervention of divine healing and of magical powers to rid him of his ailments.

In a quite different literary genre, allusion is made to a message-dream, when, in the *Epic of Gilgameš*, Ea denies having revealed to Utanapištim the gods' plan as regards the flood: 'I did not disclose the secret of the great gods, I just showed Atrahasis a dream, and thus he heard the secret of the gods' (*Gilg.* 11.186-87; Dalley 1989: 115). We know, however, from lines 19-31 in the same tablet that this dream was in fact a message murmured by the god in whispering tones through the reed walls of his house.

Noteworthy too is the relatively atypical dream of Enkidu. This is a dream that gives him access to a meeting of the gods, in the course of which he learns of his impending death. Since the Ninevite version of the text is now lost, it is known only in the Hittite version. It is possible that the dream was transposed from Sumerian reports that attributed the dream to Gilgameš and informed the hero that after his death he would become 'Judge of the Dead' (Kramer 1944). The theme of visionary or oneiric participation in the deliberations of the gods united in council is perhaps only a piece of ingenious literary fiction, for it is also found in west-Semitic prophetic circles: there, it is not the god who comes to speak to the sleeper, but the latter who finds himself as it were transported to the very threshold of the world of the gods.

To close this section, a curious indication at the conclusion of the *Epic of Irra* provides us with further evidence of the inadequacy of the traditional typology as regards dream reports. This work is rather unusual, as much on account of its literary qualities as on account of its contents and apotropaic function. It is, however, essentially a long poem celebrating in epic style the destructive exploits of Irra, another name for Nergal, god of the underworld:[9]

9. Text and translation by Cagni (1969); English translation by Foster (1993).

> The one who put together the composition about him
> was Kabti-ilani-Marduk, son of Dabibi.
> (Some god) revealed it to him in the middle of the night,
> and when he recited it upon waking, he did not miss anything out
> Nor add a single word to it.
>
> (v.42-44; *CS*: I, 415)

This text distances us somewhat from the usual typology of message-dreams, for it is the work of Kabti-ilâni-Marduk as a whole, which is presented here as the fruit of divine revelation during the night. There is certainly no explicit reference to a dream, but absence of the word is not enough to free the form of inspiration that the poet-theologian claims for himself from the oneiric atmosphere that pervades throughout. Although this is an isolated reference, it probably was not simply a compositional convention, but attests to the way in which Babylonian poets accounted for the inspiration that fired them. Analogous situations are to be found in the west Semitic world, in particular in the inscription from Deïr ʻAlla (see pp. 82-84 below), where a similar description of an upheaval in world order is reported to the prophet *in a night vision*.

5. *Prophetic Dreams*

These are also message-dreams, since their content is clearly expressed by a divinity or some other character. The dreamer, however, is not the person to whom the message is ultimately addressed, but only its mediator. We have noted that message-dreams are always addressed to important people, heroes, priests or kings; prophetic dreams are also addressed to them, although someone else, usually of considerably lower social status, dreams in their stead. Dreams of this type are well documented in the *Mari letters*. In this abundant epistolary corpus, more than thirty tablets recount oracles, and seventeen prophetic dreams. The interest of this type of text, apart from the fact that it provides evidence of a period little documented up till now (eighteenth century BCE), lies in its very special proximity to real events. These are not works of literary fiction or of propaganda, and, even if the dreamer is occasionally mistaken, his discourse is entirely plausible to his contemporaries, who nevertheless do not for one moment suspend their critical judgment as regards his dreams (Durand 1988: 453-82).

What is new about the documentary material of the ancient Near East is that the dreamers are as likely to be women as men; some belong to the royal family, some are priestesses, but many, men and women alike, are of humble origin. In the batch (no. 225 plus 224?), there are one (or perhaps two) royal dreams. The dreams reported in these letters are all of oracular value and concern either the king directly or some aspect of life in his kingdom. Indeed it is this political dimension which accounts for their being written down and preserved. The writer is not usually the dreamer himself, but a local official who transmits to the king the message related to him by a seer, except if the latter belongs to the royal family (nos. 237 and 239).

Mention is made several times of the consultation of a *haruspex* in order to test the oracular value of the dream. On the basis of this examination, the seer decided if the dream should be considered 'seen' (*naṭlat*) or 'not seen' (*ūl naṭlat*), depending on whether it contained an genuine oracle or not. Another factor in this decision might also be the time of night when it occurred: dreams during the first half of the night were discounted as having no oracular significance. There is also frequent mention made of a 'strand of hair' or 'dress string' being taken from the dreamer for examination. In this respect, oneiric oracles are treated in the same way as oracles derived from *āpilum* and *muḫḫum*.

In these dreams it is not only gods or their statues who speak, but also human beings, either anonymous characters (nos. 230, 233, 239) or the deceased, as in the case of the high priest of Annunitum:

> (1) Speak to my lord: Thus Kibri-Dagan your servant. (5) Dagan and Ikrub-El are safe and sound; the ci[ty of Terqa and] the district are safe and sound. (A badly preserved line and a break of about six lines.) (rev.) He saw the following (dream): 'You (pl.) shall not (re-)build this deserted house. If this house is (re)built, I will make it collapse into the river.' (5') The day he saw this dream, he said nothing to anyone. The next day he again saw the following dream: 'It was a god. You (pl.) shall not (re)build this house. (10') If you (re)build it, I will make it collapse into the river.' I now hereby (15') dispatch to my lord the fringe of his garment and a lock from his head. From that day [this] servant has been ill (M.13841 = Durand 1988: no. 234; *ANET*: 623)

Here is another example:

> Speak to my lord: Thus Addu-duri. Iddin-ili, the priest (5) if Itur-Mer, saw a dream. Thus he (spoke): 'In my dream Belet-biri stepped up to me and (10) spoke as follows. Thus she (spoke): is [his] ki[ngsh]ip and the rule is his permanent possession. (15) Why does he keep going up again and again to the family house? Let him guard himself.' Now my lord must not be negligent in guarding himself (A.122 = Durand 1988: no. 238; *ANET*: 631).

Oneiric oracles such as these must certainly have been known elsewhere other than at Mari and at other periods. One survives in neo-Assyrian annals, more than a millenium after those at Mari. At the beginning of the civil war against his brother Šamaššumkin, king of Babylon, Assurbanipal receives an oracle in this way. It announces the defeat of his adversary:

> In these days a man went to bed in the middle of the night and had a dream as follows: Upon the pedestal (*kigallu*) of (the image of) Sin was written (here a variant adds: the god Nabu, the scribe of the world, (in) his divine function was standing there and reading again and again the inscription of the pedestal of Sin): 'Upon those who plot evil against Aššurbanipal, king of Assyria, and resort to (actual) hostilities, I shall bestow a miserable death, I shall put an end to their lives through the quick iron dagger of (war), conflagration, hunger, pestilence (literally: the disease of Irra)! This (dream) I (Aššurbanipal) heard and put my trust upon the word of my lord Sin' (Rawlinson V 2 iii 118-27; Oppenheim 1956: 249)

More so than with message-dreams that are addressed to kings directly and in which the personal piety of the king is as important as royal ideology, with prophetic dreams we find ourselves immersed in the realm of inspired divination. None appears to have been solicited by an incubation ritual or to have taken place in the context of the professional practice of divination.

6. *Incubation*

Oppenheim (1956: 190) puts forward the hypothesis that the typical message-dream, with its impressive theophany sometimes marking the entrance of the god into the dream, is the literary transposition of the experience of the dreamer in the context of an incubation ritual. According to his theory, the size and appearance of the statue of the divinity in the temple *cella*, and the ritual conditioning of the incubant prostrate at its feet, may well have structured the dreamer's oneiric perceptions so as to function in the above manner. The hypothesis is plausible, but not easily verifiable, all the more so in so far as the disposition and appearance of the divine image may effectively have been enough to provoke theophanic, oneiric images without any ritual preparation whatsoever beforehand. On the other hand, sanctuaries were not the only places where sometimes very simple forms of incubation were practised. We will therefore restrict ourselves to a very minimal definition of incubation, taking care not to seek to reconstitute, in every case, the relatively complex and well-known ritual pattern of Hellenistic sanctuaries.

The most ancient evidence available to us thus far is no doubt a very fragmentary incantatory text found at Mari, a text belonging to a batch of pre-Sargonic tablets contemporary with the archives at Ebla (TH 80.111) (Bonechi and Durand 1992). The text speaks of a woman 'who, for a dream, has lain down', and of the interpretation of the dream. In addition to this allusion to a dream that is actively sought, the text mentions a 'seer' (IGI-DU_8) who, in order to interpret the dream, 'sits at the head of the woman lying down' (SAG MUNUS NÚ-A). This phrase is often related to the expression used of a professional oneiromancer on Cylinder A of Gudea (xx.7): LÚ ŠAG-ŠÈ NÁ A. By contrast with its Akkadian translation, *mupaššir šunāte*, 'dream interpreter', the Sumerian phrase is literally 'he who lies down at the bedside of'. It refers directly to a technique practised by specialists in oneiromancy. In this fragment from Mari, therefore, the oneiromancer, sitting in an appropriate position at the sleeper's bedside, interprets the dream of someone who has deliberately (?) gone to sleep in his presence.

If we return to the message mentioned in Cylinder A of Gudea (xx.7-11), we note that the latter 'lies down and sleeps (like) a LÚ ŠAG-ŠÈ NÁ A (Oppenheim 1956: 224) or, according to another interpretation, 'makes a LÚ ŠAG-ŠÈ NÁ A lie down (beside him)' (Falkenstein 1966: 55), in order to receive some final instructions before beginning the construction of the temple at Ningirsu. The text then recounts a dream sequence in which the temple is described in minute detail. However we interpret it, this passage clearly suggests that, as at Mari, the figure 'who lies down at the bedside' is a special kind of oneiromancer, a sort of professional dreamer-sleeper, capable either of dreaming on request, or of provoking a dream in someone else and of interpreting it afterwards. It is probably a LÚ ŠAG-ŠÈ NÁ A that is represented on a cylinder seal of the same period (printed on the cover), studied by Asher-Greve (1987): a woman in a dress is lying on a bed whose feet are decorated with bull's hooves; her eyes are open and she has her arm over her face. A man is kneeling at the foot of the bed and seems to be touching the woman's feet, there are two people standing at the head of the bed, a man and a woman, whose hands are raised as if she were an orant. The woman lying down could be a LÚ ŠAG-ŠÈ NÁ A who interprets the dream of the person kneeling at her feet, before two witnesses.

In the palaeo–Babylonian period, an as yet unpublished letter from the archives at Mari[10] recounts a case in which recourse is made to an oracle from the god Aštabi-El so as to be able make a decision in a matter concerning calumny. The instruction given by the king is as follows: 'The god Aštabi-El should take his place on his couch and should be questioned so that his *seer* may speak...' (lines 13-14). This 'seer' is thereafter designated 'the one who makes' the god Aštabi-El 'lie down'. Here we would seem to be dealing with a oneiromantic practice which consists in placing a statue of the divinity on a 'couch' or 'bed' while his 'seer' lies down and sleeps (beside him, at his bedside, in an appropriate place?). The statue is questioned as regards the matter in hand and the 'seer-sleeper' receives the reply from the god (in a dream?). What is remarkable about this practice is that it implies a *double* incubation: that of both the statue of the god and that of the seer.

Some have wanted to see evidence of incubation in the dream of Ištar's priest recounted on an inscription belonging to Assurbanipal (see pp. 37-38 above; *ANET*: 606), in spite of the fact that nothing in the text says that it took place in a sanctuary. It is true that the dream appears to be provoked by the shouts, prayers and beseeching of the king who is present before the statue of the goddess, but then we have to be careful about the meaning we give to the word 'incubation', for in this case the ritual is accomplished by one person—the king—and the oneiric revelation is received by another, without any apparent concertation beforehand: here we are back to the pattern of the prophetic dream, though this time it is actively sought by the person for whom it is destined.

An unequivocal description of incubation is found on Nabonidus's stela referred to above (p. 41); on it is related the dream in the course of which another of the king's dreams is interpreted by Nebuchadnezzar. Nabonidus then feels the need to have his dream confirmed by the gods: in spite of a break in the text, it would seem that he prepares a base on which to set up images of the celestial bodies to whom he addresses an intercessory prayer, destined for Marduk. After that he lies down and sleeps; he then sees the goddess Bau make a gesture which confirms the interpretation of the preceding dream.

The *Gilgameš Epic* also gives us a relatively precise description of an

10. A.747, kindly conveyed to me by J.-M. Durand.

incubation ritual. It is accomplished five times in all, at each stage in the journey towards the forest of cedars:

> At twenty leagues they ate their ration.
> At thirty leagues they stopped for the night.
> Fifty leagues they travelled during the day.
> The distance (took from) the new moon to the full moon,
> then three days more: they came to Lebanon.
> (There) they dug a pit in front of Shamash.
> They [refilled] their waterskins (?).
> Gilgamesh went up to the mountain,
> And made his flour-offering to [——]:
>
> 'O mountain, bring me a dream, a favorable one!'
>
> Enkidu arranged it (?) for him, for Gilgamesh.
> A dust-devil passed by, and he/it fixed (?) [——]
> He made him lie down inside the circle and [ ]
> [——] like wild barley [——]
> blood (?) [——].
> Gilgamesh sat down with his chin on his knees.
> Sleep, which spills out over people, overcame him.
> In the middle watch he finished his sleep.
> He rose up and said to his friend:
>
> 'My friend, didn't you call me ? Then why am I awake?
> Didn't you touch me? Why am I so upset?
> Didn't a god pass by? Then why is my flesh so feeble?
> My friend, [I had a dream (?)]
> And the dream that I had was extremely upsetting.
> At the foot of the mountain [——]
> [——] fell/hit [——]
> We were like flies (?) [——].'
>
> [He who] was born in open country, an [——]
> Enkidu explained the dream to his friend.
>
> (*Gilg.* 4.1.4-32'; Dalley 1989: 67)

The rite is practised in the open air, but the place is rendered sacred both by virtue of its site (a mountain), and by the magic circle traced by Enkidu around Gilgameš. Noteworthy is the well dug in order to make libations of fresh water to Šamaš, the use of perfume, *maṣhatu*, or scented flour recalling the use of incense by the *ša'ilu* in the interpretation of dreams, and finally the position adopted by Gilgameš, resting his chin on his knees. It must be emphasised, however, and this limits yet further the hypothesis of an original link between incubation and message-dreams, that the dreams received by Gilgameš in the course of these five nights of incubation are all *symbolic*, and all have to be interpreted by Enkidu.

Apart from these rather complex priestly or royal practices, there was a much simpler popular practice, sometimes consisting simply of a prayer addressed 'to the gods of the Night', asking them for a good dream. An example of this kind of practice is found on one of the Sultantepe tablets (*STT* 73; see Reiner 1960): 'Let me, your worshipper, speak with my god and goddess so that, until I carry out my plan, they may give me a favorable decision, or, (until) I get up (in the morning? = *tebâku*), they may give me a favorable sign.' We cannot call this 'incubation', however, without forcing the meaning of our terms. But this same Sultantepe tablet (*STT* 73), which gives us evidence of private divinatory techniques not found in the canonical omen literature, also includes a whole section (lines 61-70) with the prayers and details of a real domestic incubation ritual. This ritual consists in sweeping and sprinkling the roof with clean water, drawing a circle and offering incense and flour ground by a virgin boy. After which, the text says, '[Y]ou recite the incantation three times, and, without speaking to anybody (afterwards), you go to sleep and will see a dream.' Here is the text of the incantation:

> 'Divine Wagon, heavenly Wagon, whose yoke is Ninurta, whose pole is Marduk, whose axles are (the two) heavenly daughters of Anu! It rises toward Assur, it is bent toward Babylon. In order that NN, son of NN may live (?), entrust him with [...], so that he may see a dream' (Reiner 1960: 27).

The two last lines of the section interpret the dream seen by the petitioner in the style of the professional *dream books*. It is noteworthy that this ritual may be used for different purposes, and that the interpretation is adapted accordingly:

> If they give him something (in his dream), the sick man will get well; if they do not give him anything, the sick man will die.
> If you perform this to foretell the success of an enterprise, if they give him something, he will have success; if they do not give him anything, he will fail (Reiner 1960: 27).

7. *Selected Bibliography*

Asher-Greve, J.M., 'The Oldest Female Oneiromancer', in J.-M. Durand (ed.), *La femme dans le Proche-Orient antique* (XXXIIIe Rencontre Assyriologique Internationale, Paris: Recherches sur les civilisations, 1987), pp. 27-32.

Alster, B., *Dumuzi's Dream: Aspects of Oral Poetry in a Sumerian Myth* (Mesopotamia, 1; Copenhagen: Akademisk Forlag, 1972).

Bonechi, M., and J.-M. Durand, 'Oniromancie et magie à Mari à l'époque d'Ebla', *Quaderni di Semistica* 18 (1992), pp. 151-59.

Bottéro, J., 'Symptomes, signes, écriture en Mésopotamie ancienne', in J.-P. Vernant *et al.*, *Divination et rationalité* (Paris: Le Seuil, 1974), pp. 70-197.

—'L'oniromancie en Mésopotamie ancienne', *Ktema* 7 (1982), pp. 5-18; reprinted in J. Bottéro, *Mésopotamie, l'écriture, la raison et les dieux* (Paris: Gallimard, 1987), pp. 133-56.

Butler, S.A.L., *Mesopotamian Conceptions of Dreams and Dream Rituals* (AOAT, 258; Münster: Ugarit Verlag, 1998).

Durand, J.-M., *Archives épistolaires de Mari*, I.1 (Paris: Recherches sur les civilisations, 1988), pp. 455-82.

Follet, R., 'Šunatua damqa', *VD* 32 (1954), pp. 90-98.

Lambert, M., 'Le rêve de Gudea et le cylindre BM.N 89115', *RA* 41 (1947), pp. 185-200.

Leibovici, M., 'Les songes et leur interprétation à Babylone', in *Les songes et leur interprétation* (Sources Orientales, 2; Paris: Le Seuil, 1959), pp. 63-86.

Oppenheim, A.L., *The Interpretation of Dreams in the Ancient Near East* (Transactions of the American Philosophical Society, 46.3; Philadelphia: American Philosophical Society, 1956).

—*Ancient Mesopotamia: Portrait of a Dead Civilization* (Chicago: Chicago University Press, 1964), pp. 206-27.

—'Mantic Dreams in the Ancient Near East', in R. Caillois and G.E. von Grunebaum, *The Dream and Human Societies* (Berkeley: University of California Press, 1966), pp. 341-50.

—'New Fragments of the Assyrian Dream-Book', *Iraq* 31 (1969), pp. 153-65.

Reiner, E., 'Fortune-Telling in Mesopotamia', *JNES* 19 (1960), pp. 23-35.

Saporetti, C., 'Paronomasia nell'oniromanzia assira', *Egitto e Vicino Oriente* 18 (1995), pp. 193-211.

Sasson, J.M., 'Mari Dreams', *JAOS* 103 (1983), pp. 283-93.

Silva, A. da, 'Dream as Demonic Experience in Mesopotamia', *SR* 22 (1993), pp. 301-10.

Tfinkdji, J., 'Essai sur les songes et l'art de les interpréter (onirocritie) en Mésopotamie', *Anthropos* 8 (1913), pp. 505-25.

Chapter 3

THE ḪATTI

1. *Dreams and Divinatory Practices*

The Hittite kingdom always preferred active divinatory techniques, such as spells (KIN), the observation of bird flight (MUŠEN) or hepatoscopy (SU) to the simple observation of natural presages. Traditionally, therefore, the long lists of presages characteristic of the *bārû* are of no interest here. However, the period of the Cassite dynasty, following Mursili I's raid on Babylon (1595 BCE), and then that of the New Empire, particularly the eighth century, were two periods when Mespotamian divinatory practices did penetrate the Hittite world, thanks to the mediating influence in both cases of the Hurrians. Arriving late in terms of the evolution of its institutions, these divinatory techniques never seem to be fully integrated into the life of the kingdom. Lists of Akkadian presages constitute only a tenth of the entire body of divinatory texts found at Bogazköy.[1] Among these very fragmentary lists, covering most aspects of Mesopotamian divination, but in particular astrology, only one is devoted to oneiric presages (*KUB* XLIII 11 and 12).

The exceptional character of this text reveals both the little interest that this form of divination held for the Hittites, and the element of fashion that no doubt accounts for its presence in the capital during the reign of Hattušili III (1280–1255 BCE). It is under this usurper sovereign, on the eve of the brutal decline of the empire, that all sorts of forms of divination enjoy unprecedented favour, and that particular interest is paid to dreams. Indeed, the word for a dream appears in Hittite documents only from the New Empire onwards (fourteenth century). Equivalences begin to appear from the reign of Muršili II (1334–1306 BCE): *tešḫaš* = *zašḫai* = U = MA.MÚ, and lexicographical lists

1. *CTH*, nos. 531-56, 560, 774.

mention: *tešḫaš* = *šuttu* = MÁŠ (*KBo* I 42: v 14). From the two synonyms for 'dream', *tešḫaš*- and *zašḫai*-, the expression *tešḫaniya*-, 'to appear in a dream', evolves.

Even if dreams and oneiromantic practices were never given institutional status, they nevertheless played a considerable part in the personal piety of the sovereigns of the New Empire—the texts speak principally of the royal family—who recognized them to be a means by which the gods made known their will clearly and directly. Since it is message-dreams alone to which they refer, there is consequently never any mention in the texts of any kind of more or less inspired interpreter, or of any sophisticated technique of oneiromancy, or finally of any clergy specializing in the subject. A document dating from the reign of Muršili II speaks of a commander of border troops who takes the citadel of Ištahara following a dream (*KBo* II 5: i 13-17). This detail is exceptional enough to be noteworthy, for traditionally war oracles are sought by other means.

When struck by illness, the prince and high priest Kantuzzili prays to the sun god Ištanu to restore his health and to reveal to him the error that has caused this manifestation of divine wrath:

> [Now] may god freely open his heart and his soul and t[ell] me my sins, so that I may know them. May my god either speak to me in a dream—indeed, may my god open his heart to me [and] tell [me] my [sin]s, so that I may know them—or may a prophetess speak to me or may a seer of the Sun god tell me (my sins) from (inspecting) a liver. Indeed may my god freely open his heart and his soul and tell me my sins, that I may know them (*KUB* XXX 10: 24-28; Beyerlin 1978: 169).

This kind of highly developed prayer may be considered a defence speech *(arkuwar)*. In it, a variety of forms appear, including the hymn, the lamentation and the negative confession. Kantuzzili's prayer served as model for many other official prayers, and among them that of Muršili II composed on the occasion of a pestilential epidemic that had ravaged the country for 20 years. It is addressed to the storm god, patron of the Hittite kingdom:

> But if the dying continues for any other reason, may I see (this) in a dream or may it be [established] through an oracle or may an ecstatic announce it to me, or may all the priests find out by incubation what I have asked of them. Weather god of Ḫatti, my lord, save me! And may the gods, my lords, show their divine power! Let someone see it in a dream. And may the reason why dying continues be established (*KUB* XIV 10; XXVI 86: 8-18; Beyerlin 1978: 174)!

In these two texts, three suggestions are made to the god as to how he might make his thoughts known: by means of a dream *(zašḫeya)* addressed to the suppliant directly, through the mediation of a female diviner (^{sal}ENSI) or by means of a hepatoscopic oracle. To these three divinatory techniques, Muršili II, apparently hard-pressed by the gravity of the situation, adds *collective incubation*. He recommends incubation to priests in order to discern the will of the gods as it is revealed in the dreams that are part of the incubation process. This is one of the few clear references to this practice, and it allows us to conclude by virtue of the contrast between them that the oneiric revelation requested in the first part of the two prayers mentioned does not refer to incubation. It is also important to remember that recourse to these diverse oracular practices is mentioned in the prayers only after all other means of investigation and exoneration have been tried, and have failed to raise a response from the gods.

Another defence speech is addressed as a prayer to Tešub and to the gods of Kummanni by Muwatalli (1300–1280). In it, the king promises to make amends for all the misdeeds and sins of omission that have offended the gods. He also asks Tešub to help him to identify these errors:

> If someone has overthrown the throne of Tešub (or) a sacred stone, or if someone has blocked up a sacred spring, then, [whatever I find…] I will repair, but whatever I do not find, (or) whatever I do not find in hieroglyphics on a wooden tablet (GIŠ.HUR)[… may] the great magician (šalliš^{lu}ŠU.GI) inform me, O god, make your word clear thanks to a dream *(tešḫit parkunut)* (*KBo* XI 1: 41-43; translated from Lebrun 1980: 302).

To the important evidence which Muršili II's prayer gives as regards the practice of incubation in priestly circles, we might add another document concerning a therapeutic practice. An incubation ritual designed to cure male impotence is described in minute detail in a text from Arzawa: offerings will be presented to the goddess on a table, a bed will be placed in front of the latter on which will be laid out the clothes of the incubant, made holy by contact with the offerings. Then,

> the sacrificer will lie down, (to see) whether he will experience the bodily presence of the deity in his dream, coming to him and sleeping with him. During the three days on which he is entreating the deity he tells all the dreams which he has, whether the deity appears to him and whether the deity sleep with him. (*KUB* VII 5+ 8+ IX 27: iv 1-10; *ANET*: 350).

A votive offering is prescribed, an object, stela or statue, if the patient is healed. This Luwite text is not clearly dated (fourteenth–thirteenth century), but it appears to be the oldest evidence we have of therapeutic incubation in the western Mediterranean.

A ritual describing practices accompanying the birth of a child stipulates that the priest *patili* should carry the parturient to the birthing chair 'if the dream is "pure"' (*KUB* XIX 22: iii 30). No doubt what is meant here is that the woman is declared pure by her dream. Other ritual texts refer to bad dreams whose ill effects should be averted, either by cross-examination using other oracular methods (bird flight, hepatoscopy) (*KUB* V 20; XVIII 56), or by magical practices. One text prescribes an offering should a dreamer see one of the deceased night after night in his dream (*KUB* XXXIX 61: i 1-2). Another tablet transmits a ritual entitled '[When a man] sees the "black god" in his dream *(zašḫiya)*' (*KUB* VII 71: verso 7-12). All these documents belong to fourteenth–thirteenth century BCE.

2. *Dreams in Personal Piety*

A number of texts (*KUB* XV 1-30) instance solemn vows *(malteššar)* pronounced by the king or queen. Among them, certain tablets (nos. 1, 3, 5, 12, 29) mention the apparition of a divinity in a dream. These are always message-dreams, occurring among members of the royal family, and all begin almost in the same way: 'Dream of His Majesty' or 'Dream of the Queen'. These documents were probably written up by members of the clergy in temples which benefited from royal gifts (golden statues, jewels, arms, sacrificial animals). Several of these vows were made by Queen Puduhepa, wife of Hattušili III, in return for the aid of such and such a divinity in restoring the health of the ailing king:

> A dream of the queen…the queen has made a vow in her dream to the goddess Hebat of the town Uda as follows: 'If you, goddess, my lady, will have made well again His Majesty and not have him given over to the "Evil", I shall make a statue of gold for Hebat and I shall make her a rosette of gold. They shall call it "Rosette of Hebat". And I shall make a pectoral of gold for your breast. They shall call it "Pectoral of the goddess"' (*KUB* XV 1: i 1-11; Oppenheim 1956: 254).

> When the god Gurwashu said to the queen in a dream (as follows): 'As to that matter which is on your heart concerning your husband (I promise): He will live, I shall give him 100 years!' The queen made a

> vow in (her) dream as follows: 'If you do thus for me and my husband remains alive, I shall give to the deity three *haršialli*-containers, one with oil, one with honey and one with fruits' (*KUB* XV 1: iii 8-16; Oppenheim 1956: 254).
>
> A dream of the queen: Somebody said again and again to me in a dream: 'Make a vow to the goddess Ningal as follows: "If that (disease) Fire-of-the-Feet of His Majesty will pass quickly I shall make for Ningal ten (?) talla (oil-flasks) of gold set with lapis lazuli!"' (*KUB* XV 3: i 17-20; Oppenheim 1956: 255).

These dreams are not always only auditory, and among these accounts two mention the consecration of statues fashioned in such a way as to resemble the divinity when he or she appeared in the dream:

> Concerning the god Iyarri, who in the dream was standing on a lion and looking as if he were the storm god, and (concerning) somebody who was saying in the dream to His Majesty: 'Here is the father of His Majesty!', (the priestess) Hepa-SUM said: 'We must make this statue exactly as (we have seen it) and give it to the Great Divinity' (*KUB* XV 5: ii 39-43).

3. *Message-Dreams*

Hittite message-dreams are much more sober than their Mesopotamian counterparts in the evocation of oneiric theophanies. Apart from the above-mentioned dream in which a votive offering is prescribed, there is not a single description of a divinity who appears in a dream, the latter being essentially auditory. Most of the dream accounts appear in what is called the *Apology* of Hattušili III. This long autobiographical text, of which several copies were made, relates the events that led to his seizure of the throne after the deposition of his nephew Urhi-Teshub. Several abridged versions exist in which there are sometimes supplementary details (see Goetze 1925). By contrast with Assyrian royal inscriptions, the apologetic character and propagandist function of these texts are undeniable. They contain no less than five dream accounts; they punctuate the principal stages in his life and in his seizure of power with as many divine interventions.

In this *Apology*, Hattušili presents himself above all as a pious servant of Ištar of Samuhaš, to whose clergy he belongs. The first of these dreams recounts the origins of his consecration to Ištar:

> (Now,) Ištar, My Lady, sent Muwatalli, my brother to Muršili, my father, through a dream (saying): 'For Hattušili the years (are) short, he is not to live (long). Hand him over to me, and let him be my priest, so he (will) live.' My father took me up, (while still) a boy, and handed me (over) to the service of the goddess, and as a priest I brought offerings to the goddess (*KUB* I 1: i 13-17; *CS*: I, 199).

We might hesitate here in our interpretation of the text: either Muwatilli receives the message from the goddess in a dream, and then transmits the contents to his father, according to the model of prophetic dreams evidenced at Mari, or else Ištar appears in Muršili's dream in the guise of his son who speaks to him. The apparition of a divinity in the guise of a person known to the dreamer is a feature of Homeric poems. Given the geographical and cultural situation of the Hittite kingdom, the choice of one or other of these solutions (both of which are grammatically correct) depends to a degree on our own understanding of the Hittite world.

Among the five dreams of this autobiography, only one is directly seen by Hattušili. It occurs at a moment when he is assailed by all kinds of attacks and slander:

> My brother, Muw[at]alli summoned me 'to the wheel'. But Ištar, my Lady, appeared to me in a dream and through the dream she said this to me: 'To the deity (of the process) I will leave you, so do not fear!' and through the deity I was aquitted (*KUB* I 1: i 36-39; *CS*: I, 200).

It is also in a dream that Ištar orders him to take as his wife Puduhepa, herself a priestess of Ištar of Lawazantia and the daughter of a priest of Ištar. When Hattušili launches his coup d'état against the king, his nephew, Ištar intervenes once more:

> Because Ištar, My Lady, had already early (fore)told kingship for me, Ištar, My lady, appeared at that moment to my wife in a dream (saying): 'I will march ahead of your husband and all of Hattuša will turn to (the side of) your husband. Since I elevated him, I never exposed him to an evil trial (or) an evil deity. Now too, I will lift him and install him in priesthood for the sun goddess of Arinna, and you must worship me as Ištar *parašši*!' Ištar, my Lady, backed me, and as she promised me, it happened too (*KUB* I 1: iv 7-23; *CS*. I, 203).

We should note that, in this last example, it is a collective dream that is described, an example of which we have already remarked in an inscription ascribed to Assurbanipal.

It is not necessary to insist upon the concern for legitimation that is evident in these texts. Noteworthy is the fact that these dreams are intimately linked to the piety of the king: devoted apparently exclusively to Ištar, it is she alone who appears in the dreams that concern him. Dreams seem to be perceived as an essential element in his relationship with the divinity, almost as if they were the pledge of a particular intimacy with her. The precision with which Hattušili shows how his whole life has been guided by the divine will is probably partly apologetic, but we find that the same conviction underpins every act of divination. This being so, dreams are the instrument used by the gods to bend human behaviour to conform to their divine will, much more so than the means employed by men to discern the designs of the gods.

4. *Selected Bibliography*

Goetze, A., *Hattušiliš: Der Bericht über seine Thronbesteigung nebst den Paralleltexten* (MVAG, 29.3; Leipzig: Hinrich, 1925).

Hout, Th. P.J. van der, 'Träume einer hethitischen Königin: KUB LX 97 + XXXI 71', *Altorientalische Forschungen* 21.2 (1994), pp. 305-27.

Kammenhuber, A., *Orakelpraxis, Träume und Vorzeichenschau bei den Hethitern* (Texte der Hethiter, 7; Heidelberg: Carl Winter, 1976).

Vieyra, M., 'Les songes et leur interprétation chez les Hittites', in *Les songes et leur interprétation* (Sources Orientales, 2; Paris: Le Seuil, 1959), pp. 87-98.

Chapter 4

EGYPT

1. *Dreams and the Awakening of Consciousness*

Egypt did not develop a divinatory system as complex as that of Mesopotamia. Little evidence exists there of any interest in knowing the future, and there is none at all concerning deductive divination, either by the simple observation of natural phenomena or by liturgical manipulation. In the consultation of oracles, attested from the 18th Dynasty onwards, these are always addressed to the gods and pass by the mediation of the clergy in the sanctuaries concerned, principally that of Amon at Thebes. The expected response is of the type 'yes' or 'no' and usually concerns choices to be made, disputes to be settled and, more and more frequently, judiciary decisions. Dream interpretation is, however, well attested, but it is not an integral part of a divinatory system of which it is one of numerous techniques; rather, it seems to be related to magic, for '[t]rue indeed is the dream; it is beneficial to him who places it in his heart but evil for him who does not know it' (conclusion of the 'Dream stela' of Tantamati, 25th Dynasty). Dreams are therefore not considered to be ordinary natural phenomena, liable to be deciphered as such. Rather, they open up perspectives upon another world.

By contrast with Akkadian, which insists upon the relationship between dreams *(šuttu)* and sleep *(šittu)*, the Egyptian word for a dream, *rswt*, is derived from the root *r(j)s*, 'to keep watch, be awake'; dreams seem therefore to be perceived more as a kind of awakening. The latter is thought to be favoured by a headrest, a stone or wooden pillow in the form of a half-moon garnished with a cushion, which keeps the head in line with the vertebral column when the incumbent is lying on his side. The word for 'headrest' is another derivative of the same root *r(j)s*, in the intensive form *wrs*, and may be translated by 'that which keeps awake', that is, that which facilitates dreaming.

Etymologically, therefore, the accent is upon the special state of consciousness constituted by dreaming, an emphasis all the more significant given that the sleeper is often associated with the dead and the inhabitants of the nether regions. Conversely, the deceased is likened to a sleeper. Indeed, the 'bedside formula' in the *Book of the Dead* (ch. 166) begins thus: 'The swallows waken you, you who sleep, they lift your head towards the mountain on the horizon.' The awakening of the dead is here compared to the awakening of a sleeper and to the movement of the solar disc rising behind the mountains on the horizon, a comparison corroborated by the iconography of certain sarcophagi. The 'bedside formula' is sometimes inscribed at the base of headrests left among other funerary objects (Falgayrettes 1988). When, each night, the sleeper awakens into the dream world, he enacts the awakening of the dead into the world beyond, just as the head of the sleeper on his headrest evokes the motif of the sun rising each morning on the horizon in order to recreate the world.

The sleeper's wakefulness is, moreover, a risky business, for it may put him or her in touch with the demons and dark forces of the uncreated world of the night. Magical formulas or representations of the evil spirits to be warded off are inscribed on the base of the headrests for protection against these forces. Other magical formulae may be recited on awakening, if, in spite of these precautions, the sleeper has been troubled by bad dreams. The end of the *Dream Book* transmitted by one of the Chester Beatty papyri (see below) is concerned with an incantation of this order addressed to Isis. It takes the form of a dialogue between the goddess and her son Horus. The latter is presented as the prototype of every dreamer; he asks Isis to purify his dreams of any ill effects caused by Seth:

> *To be recited by a man when he wakes in his (own) place.* 'Come to me, come to me, my mother Isis. Behold, I am seeing what is far from me in my city.' 'Here am I, my son, Horus, come out with what thou hast seen, in order that thy afflictions throughout thy dreams may vanish, and fire go forth against him that frighteneth thee. Behold, I am come that I may see thee and drive forth thy ills and extirpate all that is filthy.' 'Hail to thee, thou good dream which art seen <by> night or by day. Driven forth are all evil filthy things which Seth, the son of Nut, has made. (Even as) Re is vindicated against his enemies, (so) I am vindicated against my enemies.'

> *This spell is to be spoken* by a man when he wakes in his (own) place, these having been given to him *pesen*-bread in (his) presence and some fresh herbs moistened with beer and myrrh. A man's face is to be rubbed therewith, and all evil dreams that [he] has seen are driven away (Gardiner 1935: 19).

2. *Royal Dreams*

These are fairly typical *message-dreams*, written on stelae. Almost all of them are attributed to pharaohs as early as Sesostris I (12th Dynasty) up to Ptolemy V (c. 187 BCE), the latest as far as we know. Throughout eighteen centuries the literary forms of the genre changed little, and in the messages addressed by the divinity to the pharaoh the themes remain much the same. There are essentially three themes: (1) the announcement of victory (the dreams of Amenophis II, of Merneptah and of Ptolemy IV, the latter on papyrus), (2) a request to look after a sanctuary or a statue (the dreams of Sesostris I and of Thutmosis IV), (3) the promise of kingship (the dreams of Thutmosis IV and Tantamanati).

The earliest of these oneiric revelations known to us is the dream of Sesostris I (1962–1928 BCE), recounted on the dedicatory inscription of the Temple of Satet in the Elephantine. The text of the inscription is very badly damaged and indeed the explicit reference to a dream has had to be restored by the editor in order to cohere with the general interpretation of the fragment (Schenkel 1975): the goddess Satet asks the king in a dream to go to a city (Elephantine) to look after the cult in her honour there. This is probably one of the elements of the foundation account of the sanctuary:

> 1' [...] in a dream (?) ... [...]
> 2' [...] city, in order (?) that you might prepare the sacrifice: incense on the flame and an offering of hip pieces; that thus the Great might find favour in it [...]
> 3' [...decorated] with ochre and all kinds of precious stones, on the occasion of which she (= Satet?) found the two countries feasting and rejoicing [...] (translated from Schenkel 1975).

Similar in theme is the often cited and much commented upon *Stela of the Sphinx* at Gizeh, which recounts one of Thutmosis IV's (1425–1417 BCE) dreams:

> One of these days it happened that the King's Son Thut-mose came on an excursion at noon time. Then he rested in the shadow of this great god. Sleep took hold of him, slumbering at the time when the sun was at (its) peak. He found the majesty of this august god speaking with his own mouth, as a father speaks to his son, saying:
>
> 'See me, look at me, my son, Thut-mose! I am thy father, Harmakhis-Khepri-Re-Atum. I shall give thee my kingdom upon earth at the head of the living. Thou shalt wear the southern crown and the northern crown on the throne of Geb, the crown prince (of the gods). Thine is the land in its length and its breadth, that which the Eye of the All-Lord illumines. Provisions are thine from the midst of the Two Lands and the great tribute of every foreign country. The time is long in years that my face has been toward thee and my heart has been toward thee and thou hast been mine. Behold, my state was like (that of) one who is in need, and my whole body was going to pieces. The sands of the desert, that upon which I had been, were encroaching upon me; (but) I waited to let thee do what was in my heart, (for) I knew that thou art my son and my protector. Approach thou! Behold, I am with thee; I am thy guide.'
>
> When he had finished these words, then this king's son awoke, because he had heard these [words...] and he understood the speech of this god... (*ANET*: 449).

It is the most detailed account found in an inscription, and A. Hermann (1938) relates it to a particular literary genre, the *Königsnovelle*, attested in inscriptions from the Middle Empire up to the Ptolemaic period. Extremely diverse in content, texts belonging to this literary genre have in common the fact that they recount and celebrate a royal act (a military expedition, the foundation or restoration of a sanctuary, the digging of a well, etc.) that is included in a brief biographical account. On these grounds, the dream of Thutmosis IV has been likened to that of Solomon at Gibeon, which some critics claim to be an imitation of the Egyptian *Königsnovelle*.

This literary genre has similarities with another dream account, namely that of the last Ethiopian prince, Tantamani (664–656 BC). It is unique in so far as it is the only symbolic dream to be transmitted by this kind of inscription. The symbolism of the dream is not very sophisticated, but mention is nevertheless made of an interpretation rendered by the king's servants, and about which the text tells us nothing. In the *Dream stela*, Tantamani tells how he regained power from the Saitic Pharaoh Nekao:

> Year 1 of his installation as king… His majesty saw a dream in the night: two serpents, one on his right, the other on his left. His majesty awoke, but he did not find them.
>
> His majesty said: 'Why has this happened to me?' Then they declared to him: 'Upper Egypt belongs to you; take for yourself Lower Egypt (also). the Two Goddesses (have) appeared on your head. The land is given to you in its length and (in) its breadth. There is no other to share it with you!'
>
> When his majesty appeared on the throne of Horus in this year, his majesty came forth from the place in which he had been, as Horus came forth from Chemmis. When he came forth from…a million came to him and a hundred thousand followed after him. Then his majesty said: 'True indeed is the dream; it is beneficial to him who places it in his heart but evil for him who does not know it' (Oppenheim 1956: 251).

Let us take as examples two royal dreams that are veritable war oracles. First, there is that of Amenophis II (1450–1425 BCE), the father of Thutmosis IV, dreamed during his second military campaign in Syria and inscribed on a stela in Memphis (see Badawi 1943):

> Year 9, 3rd month of the first season, day 25. His majesty proceeded to Retenu on his second victorious campaign, against the town of Apheq (…). Thereupon his majesty rested. The majesty of this august god, Amon, Lord of the Thrones of the Two Lands, came before his majesty in a dream, to give valor to his son, Aa-khepru-Re. His father Amon-Re was the magical protection of his son, guarding the Ruler. His majesty went forth by chariot at dawn, against the town of Iteren, as well as Migdol-yen… (*ANET*: 246)

And, secondly, once more among the sovereigns of the 18th Dynasty, there is the example of Merneptah (1212–1202 BCE), who, while fighting the Libyans and Sea Peoples, finds renewed courage in a dream in which he has a divine vision:

> Then his majesty saw in a dream as if it were the image of Ptah standing in the presence of the Pharaoh, (and) he was standing as high as [...] (And) he said to him: 'Take now', giving to him the sword, 'and banish from yourself your troubled heart!' (And) Pharaoh said to him: 'Indeed [...] (Oppenheim 1956: 251).

We notice that the dreamer does not see the god Ptah himself but his cultic statue, just as in the Sphinx stela it is the statue that addresses Thutmosis IV. This is, therefore, not a theophany strictly speaking, for these inscriptions seem deliberately to avoid describing a direct apparition of the divinity in a dream. It is difficult to say whether they had a particular goal in mind, for it is not systematic. This precaution disappears totally in more recent texts, such as, for example, the Sehel stela in Upper Egypt, generally known as the *Famine stela* (Barguet 1953). It is a pseudepigraphical document—no doubt that of Ptolemy V—that attributes an apparition of the god Khnum in a dream to Pharaoh Djoser (3rd Dynasty). The dream is the god's response to all the attempts made by the king both to find out which divinity is responsible for the flow of the Nile in view of the fact that the country had been suffering from drought for seven years, and to gain his favour:

> As I slept in peace, I found the god standing before me.< I >propitiated him by adoring him and praying to him. He revealed himself to me with kindly face; he said:
> 'I am Khnum, your maker.
> My arms are around you,
> to steady your body,
> to safeguard your limbs.
> […]
> I shall make Hapy gush for you,
> No year of lack and want anywhere,
> Plants will grow weighed down by their fruit;
> With Renutet ordering all,
> All things are supplied in millions!
> I shall let your people fill up,
> They shall grasp together with you!
> Gone will be the hunger years,
> Ended the dearth in their bins…'
> I awoke with speeding heart. Freed from fatigue, I made this decree on behalf of my father Khnum.
>
> (*CS*: I, 133)

The theme of this dream is rather different from those examined up till now, and the text has often been linked with the biblical Joseph story. However, the idea that the text should be attributed to Djoser, thereby making it plausible that the same famine was at the origin of the two accounts, is now definitively excluded, and the question remains as to the aim of using pseudepigraphy in a royal inscription.

A funerary inscription at Thebes dating from the Ramesside period stands out from the above-mentioned inscriptions by its (thus far) exceptional character: it is the account of how an ordinary person receives a visit from the goddess Hathor, the patron of the western necropolis in Thebes, in a dream, and of how she gives him clear instructions as to where exactly he should build his tomb. The man acted accordingly and considered his dream to be a good sign for the rest of his life (Assmann 1978).

3. *Dream Interpretation*

By playing on the etymology of *rswt,* a passage in the *Instruction for Merikare* (10th Dynasty) alludes to the link mentioned above between magic and dreams in so far as both are capable of predicting the future: 'He made for them magic as weapons / To ward off the blow of events, / Guarding (*rsi*) them by day and by night.'[1] Here, night vigilance is not the direct equivalent of a dream (*rswt*), but refers to it at a second degree as the means whereby one might discern in advance those happenings that, in the event, magic would be able to avert. Confidence in the ominous value of dreams is constant throughout the entire history of Egypt up until the Ptolemaic period, when it is particularly strong. This confidence is expressed in a saying in the *Insinger pap.* (32.13), a demotic copy from the first century CE of a Ptolemaic *Instruction*: 'He [the god] created the dream to show the way to the dreamer in his blindness' (i.e. during sleep).

Dream interpretation was the business of specialists in sacred writing, specially appointed *ḫery-ḥeb ḥery-tep*, of which the Hebrew *ḥarṭom* and Assyrian *ḫarṭibi* are reminiscent. The word is made up of *ḫry-ḥb*, 'he who is underneath', that is, 'he who bears the *ḥeb*', the 'ritual', and *ḥery-tep*, 'he who is at the head'. These 'priest-readers in chief' were members of the House of Life *(per-'ânḫ)*, which transmitted, taught and cultivated all the sciences that were necessary for the life of the sovereign and the gods, living and departed: theology, ceremony, astronomy, medicine, magic, the plastic arts, etc. The title 'reader' *(ḫery-ḥeb)* came as a result to designate all the members of the House of Life, and certain texts identify them as 'scribes of the divine book' *(seš meḏ'at neṯer)* or as 'scribes of the House of Life' *(seš-per-'ânḫ).* This expression is found in the Coptic term *sphranḫ*, used of the dream interpreter in the Joseph story. The *ḫery-ḥeb* is above all a specialist in magic and religious writings and in certain texts we see him scrupulously oversee the execution of ceremonial rites. It is fairly natural that the term eventually came simply to designate 'magician'.[2]

The earliest known *Dream Book* is to be found in a hieratic papyrus

1. *Hermitage pap.* 135; *CS*: I, 61-66.
2. See Vergote 1959; Quaegebeur 1987; Goedicke 1996.

belonging to the Chester Beatty collection (no. III, recto 1-11), put in writing at the Ramesside period, but possibly composed in the Middle Empire period (Gardiner 1935). Eleven pages of the document are reasonably well preserved. As regards each of the first ten, a vertical line gives the introductory phrase common to each of the presages on the page: 'If a man sees himself in a dream…' Each page contains twenty-five to twenty-eight dream types with their interpretation; *omens* invariably have the same structure: '(If a man sees himself in dream), in the middle of doing such and such: good/bad, it means that…' The oracle is first of all expressed clearly in terms of a simple alternative good/bad followed by a small explanatory development. The presages succeed each other without any apparent concern for classification, apart from the fact that pages 1-6 gather together 'good' omens, and pages 7-10 'bad' omens. Here are two extracts:

If a man sees himself in a dream…	
sitting in an orchard in the sun:	good; it means pleasure.
dislodging a wall:	good; it means absolution from all ills.
[eating] excrement:	good; eating his possessions in his house.
having connexion with a cow:	good; passing a happy day in his house.
eating crocodile [flesh]:	good; [acting as] an official among his people.
directing (a jet of) water:	good; it means prosperity.
plunging in the river:	good; it means absolution from all ills.
spending the night upon the ground:	good; eating his possessions.
	(5: 13-20)

If a man sees himself in a dream…	
entering into the temple of a female divinity:	bad; […] him […]
eating notched sycamore figs:	bad; it means pangs.
copulating with a female jerboa:	bad; the passing of a judgement against him.
drinking warm beer:	bad; it means suffering will come upon him.
eating ox flesh:	good (!); it means something will accrue to him.
munching a cucumber:	bad; it means words will arise with him on his being met.
walking on a […]:	bad; it means the starting upon words with him.
eating a *na'r*-fish that has been split open:	bad; his being caught by a crocodile.
munching *d3is* (= herb):	bad; it means hostility (*d3is*).

removing one of his legs: bad; judgement upon him by those yonder.
seing his face in a mirror: bad; it means another wife.
the god making his tears cease for him: bad; it means fighting.
(7: 1-12; Gardiner 1935: 14, 16)

The absence of thematic classification must have made it difficult to consult the collection. As indicated above, the list of good and bad presages ends with an incantation addressed to Isis by the dreamer, who is likened to Horus. From page 11 onwards, however, a new list of omens begins, of which only a few lines remain, concerning 'the dreams of the followers of Seth'. The text that contains the description of Seth's followers is badly damaged, but it is clear that they constitute a vast range of individuals, grouping together all those who are afflicted with a moral vice or a psychological weakness. The value of a dream is therefore determined by the appurtenance of the dreamer to one or other of the two categories into which humanity is divided—the followers of Horus and the followers of Seth—which means that in the interpretation of the dream the psychological make-up of the dreamer was taken into consideration.

Numerous *dream books* from the Ptolemaic period are attested, but all survive in a rather fragmentary state; notable, in particular, are the *Carlsberg papyri* XIII–XIV (Volten 1942) and the *Bologna papyri* 3171 and 3173 (Tait 1977: nos. 16-17, pp. 56-61). The presages there are classified according to theme, as in Assyrian collections, thereby showing a real concern for practicality, and no doubt revealing foreign influence. The presages in the *Carlsberg papyri*, for example, are grouped in series, each of which is preceded by a title indicating the general theme of the dreams interpreted in the list that follows: 'The kinds of sexual intercourse dreamt about [if a] woman dreams of that' (XIII, b, 2.14); 'The kinds of beer a man dreams of' (XIV, a, 1); 'What [happens to someone who] dreams [that there is a snake in front of him]' (XIV, a, 16); etc. Here are some examples of presages taken from the *Dream Book* in the *Carlsberg papyri*:

The different kinds of sexual intercourse about which one can dream, [if a] woman dreams about it:

If [a woman] is married to her husband: she will be destroyed.
If she embraces him, [she] will have sorrow.
If a horse has intercourse with her, she will be violent with her husband.

If a donkey has intercourse with her, she will be punished for a serious crime.
If a billy goat has intercourse with her, she will die quickly.
If a ram has intercourse with her, Pharaoh will be good to her.
(XIII, b, 2, 14-20; translated from Volten 1942: 87)

What it means for a woman to dream that she gives birth to such and such an animal:

If she gives birth to a cat, she will give birth to many children.
If she gives birth to a dog, [she] will give birth to a son.
If she gives birth to a donkey, she will give birth to a mad child.
If she gives birth to a shrew, [——] from her towards God.
If she gives birth to a wolf, [——].
If she gives birth to a crow, [she will give birth to a child who is] mad.
If she gives birth to a crocodile, [she will give birth] to many [children].
(XIV, f, 1-8; translated from Volten 1942: 99-101)

The principles according to which everyday dreams are interpreted seem fairly varied and are not always identifiable. Recognizable, however, is the association of ideas, based on very often fanciful etymologies, on assonance or on paranomasia. The symbolic value of objects or of beings seen in dreams also occupies an important place in the effort to elucidate their meaning, but the latter is often difficult for us to grasp; the references may be mythological, social or psychological. Even if we can thereby discern certain principles, we notice that they are not applied systematically.

The archives of a priest of the Memphis serapeum in the second century CE, Hor of Sebennytus, have yielded more than 50 demotic ostraca bearing the texts of letters, some of which mention dreams, which perhaps originated in incubatory experiences (Dray 1976). In this same sanctuary, and dating from the same period, a lengthy Greek papyrus recounts a series of dreams carefully collated by a certain Ptolemy (Wilken 1927: 353), whose spontaneity of expression is remarkable; each dream is precisely dated and none is commented on. Everything in the document suggests that this collection is a tool of the trade belonging to an oneirocritic practising in the sanctuary. The presence of interpreters offering their services to visitors is well attested in these documents; in them we find once again, in demotic, the title *ḥr- tbw* mentioned above, the equivalent of the Greek ἐνύπνιοκριται. They either belonged to the temple staff or worked independently, as is born out by a stela found within the serapeum of Saggara: 'I interpret dreams, having been commissioned by god; good luck; the interpreter present here is Cretan' (Roeder 1960: 192; Dunand 1997: 72).

4. *Incubation*

Parallel to this passion for knowledge of dreams, the Ptolemaic period witnessed the development of the practice of incubation in sanctuaries dedicated to healing gods. The most frequently solicited divinity in this context is Isis, by reason of her links with magic since time immemorial:

> As for Isis, the Egyptians say that she was the discoverer of many health giving drugs and was greatly versed in the science of healing; consequently, now that she has attained immortality, she finds her greatest delight in the healing of mankind and gives aid in their sleep to those who call upon her, plainly manifesting both her very presence and her beneficence towards men who ask her help... For standing above the sick in their sleep she gives them aid for their diseases and works remarkable cures upon such as submit themselves to her; and many who have been despaired of by their physicians because of the difficult nature of their malady are restored to health by her, while numbers who have altogether lost the use of their eyes or of some other part of their body, whenever they turn for help to this goddess, are restored to their previous condition (Diod. 1.25).

As in the various Greek sanctuaries of a similar kind, dreams were provoked by diverse techniques or ritual practices, including the following, noted by Plutarch (*Isis and Os.* end): he gives a detailed list of the perfumes burnt in the Egyptian temples and comments on the function attributed to them: in the evening, the *kyphi*, composed of sixteen ingredients, was designed to incite rest, 'to calm the over vivid impressions experienced during the day, but also to render the imagination, the seat of dreams, clearer and purer'. Therapeutic incubation was practised essentially in the sanctuaries of Sarapis at Canope and at Memphis.

But other sanctuaries were also reputed for the quality of sleep and of the dreams received there, for example at Abydos, where one can read the Greek graffiti left by pilgrims in the oratory consecrated to Bes (see Dunand 1997). This divinity is called ὀνειροποδότης, 'the one who gives dreams', in several of these inscriptions (Perdrizet and Lefèbvre 1919: nos. 489; 492, 493; 500; 503), among which is the following written by a pilgrim from Galilee: 'I have slept here several times, and I have seen truthful dreams, I, Harpocras, inhabitant of the holy city of Panias, and priest, the dear son of the priest Copreias. To Bes, the great god of prophetic voices, infinite gratitude' (Perdrizet and Lefèbvre 1919: no. 528). At Karnak, an ostracon from the Brooklyn Museum, dated the twentieth year of the reign of Ptolemy,[3] describes the request of a certain Thothertaïs, the aged and now blind servant of the temple of Amon. He asks for attention from the medical staff of the temple, and describes a dream he had while in incubation:

> 8) ...] said: 'I slept in the courtyard 9) of Amonrasonter, since my eyes were poorly 10) and I could not see, so that someone else had to show 11) me the way. [...] 18) I prayed before Amon and said: 'Allow me 19) to be sent to a place where I might be given medical treatment, so that it might be brought about.' I lay down to sleep 20) on the aforesaid night, and I saw myself in a dream, whilst a priest [...] (translated from Volten 1962: 129).

The abundant documentation available from papyri and ostraca belonging to this period, in addition to the numerous testimonies of Greek authors, in comparison with the near silence of earlier Egyptian sources, led to the formerly widely held conclusion that incubation was introduced into and developed in Egypt under the influence of Hellenism. The truth of the situation is no doubt more complex. Several popular tales mention incubations: of the three tales presenting Setni-Khaemousas, Ramses II's son, the two tales recounted in papyrus no. 604 of the British Museum describe incubation dreams (Griffith 1900). The papyri do indeed date from the Ptolemaic period, but the material of the tales may well be older. One of the dreams is dreamed by the wife of Setni as she sleeps in the temple in the hope of being cured of her sterility; the other comes to a magician to whom Thot reveals the hiding place of a book of magic spells that Thot himself has written. Magic occupies a very large place in all these tales.

Another important piece of evidence is a small funerary stela of unknown provenance, but which palaeography enables us to date around the second half of the first Intermediary Period, contains the first known allusion to incubation in Egypt. It concerns a message addressed by a certain Merirtyfy to his deceased wife:

> A communiction by Merirtyfy to Nebetiotef: 'How are you? Is the West taking care of you [according to] your desire. Now since I am your beloved upon earth, fight on my behalf and intercede on behalf of my name. I have not garbled [a spell] before you when I perpetuated your

3. Text and translation by Malinine 1960; new translation by Volten 1962.

> name on earth. Remove the infirmity of my body. Please become a spirit for me [before] my eyes that I may see you fighting on my behalf in a dream. I will (then) deposit offerings for you [as soon as] the sun has risen and outfit for you your offering-slab' (Wente 1975–76: 595).

Since the stela would have been situated near to where the funerary cult of the deceased took place, we might suppose that, on the basis of the text, Merirtyfy sometimes spent the night there in the hope of seeing his spouse in a dream. This form of incubation is rather different from that revealed by Ptolemaic texts. We are here in the context of a private funerary cult; the content of the request also recalls a form of necromancy, though the aim is not to ask the deceased about a specific problem or to know the future. This text seems to confirm the remark made at the beginning of this chapter, that dreams and the diverse uses to which they were put in Egypt, belong more to the realm of magic than to divination.

Both as regards incubation and dream interpretation, the conceptions and practices of the Egyptians must have undergone a profound transformation as a consequence, no doubt during the Saitic period, under both Greek and Aramaic influence. A fifth-century BCE Aramaic ostracon, originating in a colony of mercenaries in Elephantine, bears witness to the importance accorded oneiric presages by the oriental population living in Egypt:

> Now, behold, I have seen a dream, and from that time on I have been exceedingly feverish. An apparition appeared. Its words: 'Peace!'
>
> Now, if you will sell all of my bundles (of grain), the small children may eat; for, lo, there is no remainder of coins (Levine 1964: 19).

No doubt the beliefs and practices of Asiatic mercenaries, settled in Egypt from the seventh century onwards, little by little reorientated ancient notions so as to make them correspond to what we observe from the Hellenistic period onwards, that is the association of oneiric experience with divination and with healing cults.

5. *Selected Bibliography*

Assmann, J., 'Eine Traumoffenbarung der Göttin Hathor', *REg* 30 (1978), pp. 22-50.
Goedicke, H., '*ḥarṭummim*', *Or* 65 (1996), pp. 24-30.
Israelit-Groll, S., 'A Ramesside Grammar Book of Technical Language of Dream Interpretation', in S. Israelit-Groll (ed.), *Pharaonic Egypt, the Bible and Christianity* (Jerusalem: Magnes Press, 1985), pp. 71-118.
Levine, B.A., 'Notes on an Aramaic Dream Text from Egypt', *JAOS* 84 (1964), pp. 18-22.

Parlebas, J., 'Remarques sur la conception des rêves et sur leur interprétation dans la civilisation égyptienne antique', *Ktema* 7 (1982), pp. 19-22.

Quaegebeur, J., 'La désignation (P*3*-)ḤRY-TP: phritob', in J. Osing and G. Dreyer (eds.), *Form und Mass* (Festschrift G. Fecht; AAT, 12, Wiesbaden: Otto Harrassowitz, 1987), pp. 368-94.

Sauneron, S., 'Les songes et leur interprétation dans l'Egypte ancienne', in *Les songes et leur interprétation* (Sources Orientales, 2; Paris: Le Seuil, 1959), pp. 18-62.

Vergote, J., *Joseph en Egypte* (OBL, 3; Louvain: Publications universitaires, 1959).

Vernus, P., 'Traum', *Lexikon der Ägyptologie* (1986), pp. 745-49 (in French).

Volten, A., *Demotische Traumdeutung. Pap. Carlsberg XIII und XIV verso* (Analecta Aegyptiaca, 3; Copenhagen: Akademisk Forlag, 1942).

—'Das demotische Ostracon im Brooklyn-Museum (Inv. No. 37.1821 E)', *AcOr* 26 (1962), pp. 129-32.

Wente, E.F., 'A Misplaced Letter to the Dead', in P. Naster, H. de Meulenaere and J. Quaegebeur (eds.), *Miscellanea in honorem J. Vergote* (OLP, 6.7; Louvain, 1975–76), pp. 595-600.

Zibelius-Chen, K., 'Kategorien und Rolle des Traumes in Ägypten', in H. Altenmüller and D. Wildung (eds.), *Studien zur altägyptischen Kultur*, XV (Hamburg: H. Buske-Verlag, 1988), pp. 277-93.

Chapter 5

SYRO-PHOENICIA

There has been little evidence up till now of documentation on the subject of dreams in the north-western Semitic world outside Israel. Only two domains allow us to make a few observations, themselves as different in time and space as in literary genre: Ugarit, for the Canaanite world of the Late Bronze age, and Deïr 'Alla for the Aramaeans of the eighth century BCE. Apart from these two, it seemed opportune to complete this dossier with a rapid consideration of Homeric literature, given the numerous commercial and cultural relations well attested by archaeology that linked the different peoples of the eastern Mediterranean. We will note undeniable similarities between oneiric representations in Archaic Greece and those in the north-western Semitic world.

1. *Ugarit*

The alphabetic tablets discovered at Ras Shamra and Ras Ibn Hani have up till now shown little trace of divinatory texts. Several examples of engraved clay livers and of lungs testify to the practice of hepatoscopy (*KTU* 1.141-144; 155) according to the Mesopotamian model. An isolated fragment (*KTU* 1.140) and several others allow us to reconstitute part of a tablet of presages concerned with monstrous births (*KTU* 1.103; 1.45). They testify to the influence of the Babylonian dream book *šumma izbu* in its Hittite version.[1]

A badly damaged tablet (*KTU* 1.86) may, according to Ch. Virolleaud, be the fragment of a dream book (*PRU* V: 189). It reads: [...].*ḥlm* . *ulp* . *šnt* . *w* [... (line 1). Recognizable here is the plural of *ḥlm*, 'dream', and *šnt*, 'sleep' (?), also attested in line 5, and in line 2 in the dual form (*šntm*); line 28 reads: *bḥlm* [..., 'in a dream [...'. Moreover the tablet mentions several animals' names, but since there is not

1. See Pardee 1986; Dietrich and Loretz 1990.

one phrase that is complete, the hypothesis must remain unverifiable. The latter becomes even more tenuous when we recognize that it is more likely that the semantic value of *ḥlm* is 'to be strong' and that of the noun *šnt* is 'year(s)'.[2] Should we attribute this relative silence to the chances of discovery given that the documentation is irremediably incomplete, or should we interpret it as an indication that the people of Ugarit, like the Hittites, did not attach the same importance as the Assyrians to deductive oneiromancy? We will leave this question aside for the present.

Literary texts contain two complete dream accounts. If neither speaks of dream interpretation, El's dream in the myth of *Baal and Mot* may make an allusion to oneiromancy:

> [For dead is Valiant Baal,]
> for perished is the Prin[ce, Lord of the earth!]
> But if V[aliant Baal] should be alive,
> and if the Prince, Lo[rd of the earth] should exist
> in a dream of the Compassionate, the god of mercy,
> in a vision of the Creator of Creatures,
> let the skies rain oil,
> let the wadis run with honey
> And I shall know that Valiant Baal is alive,
> that the Prince, Lord of the earth exists!
>
> (*KTU* 1.6: iii 1-9; Wyatt 1998: 136)

This passage follows the disappearance and death of Baal, consequent upon his confronation with Mot. The syntactical structure of the text is typical of the formulation of presage lists: 'If the heavens rain down fat...then Baal is alive.' In fact, this basic structure is developed by the text according to the perspective proper to myths; it reads '*If* Baal is alive, *then* the heavens will rain down fat, *so that* I will know that Baal is alive'. This oneiric presage is in fact intended for El, and even if it is not surprising that a god should dream, the myth takes El's function in the Ugaritic pantheon into account. El is the wise god *par excellence*, it is he who fixes destinies, and he who by virtue of this role retains a certain mastery over presages. In ordinary divination, the signified is deduced from the signifier *a posteriori*. This is possible thanks to empirical observations or to other kinds of supposed analogies between

2. In the translation of this text he publishes in *CS* I: 293-94, Pardee considers it as 'a rough catalogue of items that may be seen in dreams along with an interpretation by items or by category'.

presage and the thing presaged. In the mythical account, El himself defines *a priori* what exactly are to be the terms of the relation between protasis and apodosis. This explains the logical inversion: *if* Baal is alive, *then* such a presage will make it known.

In Ugaritic, there are two synonyms for the noun *ḥlm*, 'dream', used in poetic parallelism *hdrt* and *ḏrt* (*ḏhrt* in its full form).[3] The first, *hdrt*, is related to the Hebrew *hādār*, 'brilliance, glory, majesty', frequent in the psalms (cf. Ps. 29.2; 96.9; 1 Chron. 16.29) where it designates the splendour or supernatural brilliance that emanates from divinities or royalty. On the only attested occasion of its use, it intervenes parallel to *ḥlm* at the very moment when Keret wakens up and becomes aware of El's visit in his dream (*KTU* 1.14: iii 50-51: *krt yḫt wḥlm/'bd il whdrt*); *hdrt* seems to refer to the revelation of divine majesty, rather than to a particular characteristic of the dream.[4]

As for *ḏrt/ḏhrt*, derived from the root *dr*, it has been explained in at least five different ways: on the basis of the Hebrew *šwr* I, 'see, look at'; with reference to the Aramaic *šhr*, 'keep watch' (and Arabic *šahira*, 'to keep watch all night'); the Arabic *zawr*, 'a figure seen in a dream', from the root *zāra*, 'visit'; the Akkadian *šāru*, 'wind, breath', the equivalent in the lexicographical lists of *šēḫu*, 'ecstatic spirit', and *zaqīqu*, 'wind, breath, spirit, god of dreams'; and once more the Hebrew *zhr*, 'shine'. On the three occasions on which it is used in the *Keret Epic* (*KTU* 1.14), it is always in the same context, that of El's oneiric theophany, but on a fourth occasion (*KTU* 1.6: iii 4-5), it appears in the context of the ominous visual dream cited above, a dream announcing Baal's return to life. To explain the term exclusively in terms of a visit from a divine being in a dream does not therefore hold good in this last case. Preferable, therefore, is a more general translation, induced from links with the Hebrew *šwr* I or Aramaic *šhr*, something like 'a vision in the night'.

The other dream account is to be found on the first of the three tablets of what survives of the *Keret Epic* (*KTU* 1.14; 15; 16). It extends over almost three of its six columns. It is a typical message-dream received by a king. In it El appears to give a detailed account of how the serious crisis brought about by the sudden disappearance of all the royal

3. *ḥlm // hdrt* in *KTU* 1.14: iii 50-51; *ḥlm // ḏrt* in *KTU* 1.6: iii 4-5; 1.14: i 35-36, iii 46-47; vi 31-32.

4. *UT* (p. 389, no. 752) notes that 'the semantic connection may be: (divine) majesty > theophany > dream'; see also Tropper (1996).

descendants will be overcome. The following are the opening lines, at the point where Keret mourns the annihilation of his family:

> He went into his chamber (and) wept;
> redoubling his lamentations, he sobbed.
> His tears poured out,
> like shekels to the ground,
> like five-shekel weights onto his bed.
> As he wept he fell asleep;
> as he cried slumber (came).
> Sleep overpowered him and he lay down;
> slumber, and he curled up.
> And in his dream El came down,
> in his vision the Father of Man,
> and he drew near, asking Keret:
> 'What ails Keret that he weeps,
> the gracious one, heir of El, that he groans?
> Does he desire the kingship of bull, his father
> or domin[ion] like the Father of Man?
>
> (*KTU* 1.14: i 26-43; Wyatt 1998: 183-84)

There follows a long description of the expedition that Keret must undertake to obtain Hurray, the daughter of the king Pabil, as his new wife. The dream ends with the hallowed formula *krt.yẖt.wḥlm/ 'bd.il.w hdrt*: 'Keret looked about and it had been a dream, the servant of El, and it had been a vision' (*KTU* 1.14: iii 50-51). Keret's awakening constitutes the symetrical axis of the episode; it is followed by the account of his expedition to Udum, which takes up word for word the terms of instruction received in the dream, with a few additional developments.

The *Keret Epic* exceeded the three tablets known to us today. Organized into episodes, its epic structure has been highlighted. The third tablet ends with an episode that has scarcely begun. Literary criticism reveals the compositional techniques by means of which these originally independent episodes came to be linked one to another. In the two episodes that may be read in their entirety, the respective themes are shown to alternate between two successive phases: trials–restoration, an alternation that seems characteristic of the work as a whole. Running through these two phases and taking shape therein is a reflection upon kingship. This reflection highlights on the one hand the weakness and vulnerability of the king himself and on the other the unfailing support he, and consequently the royal institution also, receives from El. In the first episode (*KTU* 1.14: i 1–15: iii 25), the succession of the dynasty is endangered by the disappearance of both Keret's children and his wife; in the second episode (*KTU* 1.15: iii 25–16: vi 38), it is the power of royalty that is threatened by Keret's illness; the third episode is scarcely begun (*KTU* 1.16: vi 39 [?]), it perhaps deals with the rebellion of one of Keret's sons and the usurpation of the throne.

The function of the dream in the first episode appears to be multiple. First, from a literary point of view, it is a good example of the symmetrical structure that it can create in a text; one part takes place in the dream, the other after the subject has awoken, his awakening being what constitutes the main articulation in the narrative. Here, the symmetry is not only formal but also thematic, in so far as events seen in the dream are picked up after awakening, and also by virtue of the fact that the epilogue relates to the prologue by means of antithesis. In addition, and in accordance with the general orientation of the work, the dream recalls the privileged filial relationship that exists between El and the king by showing the close confidence between them. The god's oneiric visit is one of the means whereby he is able to come to the aid of the king and save the institution.

Numerous authors want to see a description of the practice of *incubation* in this text and link it with a passage in the *Aquat legend* particularly renowned for that. There is, however, no justification for reading the Keret text thus, since there is no reference whatsoever to any ritual. As for the beginning of the first tablet of the *Aquat legend* (*KTU* 1.17: i 1-19), it is Oberman's study (1946) that has oriented interpretation in this direction. His interpretation is, however, based upon a reading of the text and restitutions therein that are no longer acceptable today.

The text does indeed describe a long ritual of supplication, extending over seven days. It includes wearing a liturgical loincloth *(mizrt)*, making both offerings to the gods *(ilm ylḥm)* and libations *(yšqy bn qdš)*. It also involves being ritually naked during the night, a night that Danil perhaps spends on the terrace of his house: 'He cast down his cloak, went up, and lay down, cast down his girded garment so as to pass the night (there)' (*yd ṣth y'l wyškb/yd mizrt pyln*). On the seventh day 'Baal approached, having mercy on him' ([w]*yqrb b'l bḥnth*), and intercedes with El so that Danil might obtain the birth of a son. The words 'dream' or 'vision' never appear in the text, and the internal logic of the narration in columns I and II preclude any such allusion. This is strictly a supplication ritual, such as is evoked in 2 Sam. 12.16, and if it includes ritual sleep, it is not accomplished in the aim of receiving an oneiric revelation. It is therefore inappropriate to talk of incubation as regards these texts (see Margalit 1989: 260-66; Husser 1996).

2. *Homeric Literature*

The picture of dreams that emerges from Homeric poems is fairly characteristic, although not lacking in nuance, as the marked evolution from the *Iliad* to the *Odyssey* shows. Well-defined, this literary corpus also appears to be isolated and without antecedant, for the texts in linear B do not speak of this subject at all. As regards its successors it is equally isolated, for we must wait three centuries before we find, in the writings of Aeschylus (*Perses* 176-200), a dream account analogous to those in this epic literature. This literature is renowned for its ignorance of incubation, but the value of an argument *e silentio* is a doubtful one, and we could cite in favour of the practice the obscure allusion to the cult of Dodona in Achilles' invocation of Zeus Naïos, when he sends Patrocles off to fight:

> 'Zeus, thou king, Dodonaean, Pelasgian, thou dwellest afar, ruling over wintry Dodona,—and about thee dwell the Selli, thine interpreters, men with unwashen feet that couch on the ground…' (*Il.* 16.233-235).

The temple of Dodona was thought to be the oldest in the Greek world (hence the title 'Pelagian' given to Zeus here), and the oracle that the 'interpreters' of the god (ὑποφῆται) consulted there was well known. The latter also slept on the ground (v. 235: σοὶ ναίους ὑποφῆται ἀνιπτόποδες χαμαιεῦναι), and this contact with the earth is attested, in numerous forms, in the context of the cults of chtonic divinities. This detail is no doubt reminiscent of the fact that the oracular sanctuary of Dodona was originally consecrated to such a divinity. At the same time, it may indicate that incubation practices did persist there for some time. This hypothesis is however not mentioned in G. Rachet's otherwise well-documented article (1962).

That the practice of oneiromancy existed is beyond doubt, although the references are not very explicit. At the beginning of the *Iliad*, while the plague ravages the camp of the Achaeans, Achilles proposes that they consult the gods by means of the mediation of a number of specialists:

> 'Nay, come, let us ask some seer or priest, yea, or some reader of dreams —for a dream too is from Zeus' (*Il.* 1.62-63).

Three types of divination are enumerated here, including the practice of ὀνειροπόλος. The term appears to be ambiguous: does it refer to a dream interpreter, or to someone inspired by the gods by virtue of the dreams he receives? The root of the verb ὀνειροπολεῖν means simply 'to dream' (Plat. *Rep.* 534c; *Tim.* 52b; Aristoph. *Nu.* 16), and usually has nothing to do with dream criticism. Herodotus, however, seems to use the noun in the sense of 'interpreter' (Herod. 1.128; 5.56), although in his day ὀνειροκρίτης would have been the appropriate technical term (Vinagre 1996). At the risk of reading too much into this passage of the *Iliad*, it is noteworthy that none of the Achaeans had previously had any dreams that necessitated interpretation. Henceforth the ὀνειροπόλος was duty bound to receive a dream, either provoked or asked for of the gods, before speaking.

Iliad 5.148-50 is about the two sons of the Trojan Eurydomas, 'the old dream specialist' (ὀνειροπόλοιο γέροντος) who, the day they went off to be killed in combat, 'did not interpret dreams' (τοῖς οὐκ ἐρχομένοις ὁ γέρων ἐκρίνατ' ὀνείρους). The ὀνειροπόλος certainly knew how to be an ὀνειροκρίτης, but would he have interpreted his own dreams or those of his sons? The text is too allusive to answer the question with any certainty. Nevertheless, noteworthy is the presence in the Achaean army, as in the Trojan camp, of ὀνειροπόλοι who have the ability to speak of hidden things with the aid of dreams.

The end of v. 1.63 cited above summarizes well the basic way in which dreams were viewed in Homeric poems: καὶ γάρ τ'ὄναρ ἐκ Διός ἐστιν, 'the dream too comes from Zeus!' The *Iliad* contains four detailed dream accounts: the dreams of Agamemnon (2.1-41), of Rhesus (10.494-97), of Achilles (23.58-107), of Priam (24.677-95). The *Odyssey* too contains four dreams: the dreams of Penelope (4.794-841; 19.535-81; 20.87-90) and of Nausicaa (6.15-50), to which we should add Ulysses' imaginary dream, a pastiche of Agamemnon's dream (14.482-98), and two nocturnal apparitions of Athena in a kind of wakeful dream (15.1-56; 20.30-55). All these dreams are initiated by a divinity and, apart from Penelope's single *symbolic dream* (*Od.* 19.535), all speak of the arrival of an individual who clearly and unambiguously directs a message to the dreamer. These are therefore essentially *message-dreams*.

The reference dream is that of Agamemnon (*Il.* 2.1-41), in which all the characteristics of the genre are to be found. The oneiric situation usually takes the form of a visit paid to the sleeper by a solitary oneiric character, either a god or the dream messenger in person, Ὄνειρος. It is noteworthy that if ὄνειρος can designate the oneiric experience itself (cf. *Il.* 22.199), the word more commonly denotes a character. If it is a god who is the instigator of dreams, Oneiros is his messenger: Διὸς δέ τοὶ ἄγγελός εἰμι (*Il.* 2.26). He is a member of a numerous people, the φῦλον ὀνείρων, born of the Night along with Death and Sleep (Hes. *Theog.* 211-12), and whose dwelling, beyond the gates of the sun, is next to that of the dead (*Od.* 24.10-14). Besides, Oneiros is as elusive, as unsubstantial as a shadow or the soul of the dead (*Od.* 11.204-22). He may be a form, an εἴδωλον, specially made by the divinity for the occasion (*Od.* 4.796: εἴδωλον ποίησε), or alternatively the divinity may himself come, in the guise of someone known to the dreamer (*Od.* 6.20-24), or else undisguised, as in the case of Hermes when he appears to the elderly Priam (*Il.* 24.677-88).

This oneiric figure comes through the lock into his room and settles himself down at his bedside (στῆ δ'ἄρ ὑπὲρ κεφαλῆς), before addressing him in the following manner: 'You're asleep!' (Εὕδεις!). This pronouncement is a way of wakening him and may well signify, as in Egypt, a kind of awakening of consciousness during sleep. A dialogue follows, at the end of which the oneiric figure disappears in the same way as he came. Though sometimes with a few variants, a stereotypical formula introduces the contents of the dream: 'He therefore stands above his head and says...' (στῆ δ'ἄρ ὑπὲρ κεφαλῆς καί μιν πρὸς μῦθον ἔειπεν). There is only one case in which the oneiric character is not a god or his messenger, but someone who is dead, namely Patrocles, who appears to Achilles (*Il.* 23.65: ἦλθε δ'ἐπὶ ψυχὴ Πατροκλῆος). The soul of the deceased behaves in exactly the same way as the divine messenger. This way of representing dreams is not peculiar to Homer; subsequent literature attests to the persistence of this pattern.

There is evidence of a clear evolution between conceptions such as they are expressed in the *Iliad* and in the *Odyssey*. In the *Iliad*, the oneiric event has an almost cosmic dimension (cf. *Il.* 2.1; 24.677) and the emphasis is on its sacred character. In the vision of things peculiar to the epic, where the world of men and of that of the gods interact constantly one with the other, men and gods alike are subject to the same rhythm of night succeeding day. Men and gods both sleep; only the divinity preoccupied with a plan that he wishes communicate to men stays awake: this is true of Zeus as regards Agamemnon (2.1-6) and of Hermes as regards Priam (24.677-81). Rather than corresponding to the awakening of an individual in his sleep, dreams are therefore above all the fruit of a god's insomnia!

If in the *Iliad* it is the gods who address the hero, in the *Odyssey*, on the other hand, it is only women who dream, only they who are visited by the goddess Athena. There, more importance is accorded the dreamer, her mood, the premonitory character of the dream, and all this in a more familiar, intimate atmosphere. It may be surprising that Ulysses never had a dream, but he himself journeys in an intermediary world, a world distinct from the human world, to which it is precisely sleep, and the rapid vessels of the Phaeacian boatmen, that give him access.

One senses therefore the beginning of a growing interest in the psychological dimension of dreams, a tendency that will go as far as to deny their divine origin. This is never questioned in Homeric poetry, and Penelope's question to the oneiric figure who speaks to her, 'if your being is divine, then your message is divine' (*Od.* 4.831), is only a display of rhetoric. Her attitude of quiet confidence contrasts with the positivism of Artemidorus of Daldis, who speaks at length of the almost thousand-year-old evolution of Greek thought on this subject:

> Dreams on the other hand which come unsolicited, and which predict either something good or bad, are said to be 'sent by the gods'. However, at the moment I do not understand 'sent by the gods' to have the same meaning as that described by Aristotle, whose interpretation raises the problem of knowing whether the cause of the fact of dreaming lies in some exterior cause and comes from a god, or whether there is something in us which predisposes our soul in such a way that what happens happens naturally (Artem. *Oneir.* 1.6).

Even though they are sent by the gods, dreams can nevertheless be fallacious. The Greek epic, however, copes with the possibility of the gods' deceitfulness very well: Agamemnon's dream is a deliberate piece of trickery calculated by Zeus. Penelope's erotic dreams are qualified as bad and attributed to an unknown divinity, a δαῖμων, rather than to her own desires and frustrations (*Od.* 20.87. αὐτὰρ ἐμοὶ καὶ ὀνείρατ' ἐπέσσευεν κακὰ δαίμων). The existence of two doors, allowing dreams to escape (*Od.* 19.560-69), one in ivory for those that do not come true, and the other in horn for those that do, is another way of explaining the existence of misleading dreams without denying their divine origin. This mythical affabulation is the logical reply to the question raised by dreams whose messages are not realized. From the exile onwards, prophetic milieux in Israel will explain the origin of false prophecy in an analogous way (cf. 1 Kgs 22.20-23; Ezek. 14.9).

There are several similarities between the Homeric corpus and Ugaritic literature. First, we should note the royal character of all the dreams: only kings or people of royal status dream. Dreams are always provoked by a god who either appears or sends a messenger on his or her behalf. At any rate, the dreamer remains passive. As in Hebrew or in Ugaritic, the Greek terms used to describe the comings and goings of the oneiric character are very varied but none is specific to dreams or to religious vocabulary: the verbs used are προιέναι, πέμπειν, ἐλθεῖν, βαίνειν, ἰέναι, or else vocabulary that suggests a leap, a jump or a slip: οἴχεσθαι, ἐπισσεύειν, ἀποπτάμενος. No fear or alarm is experienced by the dreamer during this encounter that includes a dialogue. The divinity who comes to visit the dreamer is never described, his or her coming is discreet and is not accompanied by any manifestation of the extraordinary.

3. *Aramaean Kingdoms*

Two or three indications fairly scattered in time and space allow us to suppose that, in the diverse Aramaean kingdoms, dreams were regarded in a way fairly similar to that which we observe in Israel. In the text of the treaty between the kings of Arpad and Kašku (*ktk*) (Sfire stela I, mid eighth century BCE), dreams are used as a term of comparison in the maledictions invoked against anyone who might dare to break the treaty: 'May his kingdom be like a kingdom of sand, like a kingdom of dreams which Assur rules' (*KAI* 222 A: 25: *thwy mlkth kmlkt ḥl mlkt ḥlm zy yml 'šr*). This is the reading proposed by Dönner and Röllig, but the consonantal group *kmlktḥlmlkt ḥlmzy* is susceptible to other divisions, all of which imply that the stone carver is guilty of dittography. To associate dreams with all that is ephemeral or fragile is also characteristic of Isa. 29.5-7 and Ps. 73.20. This does not, however, mean that the entirety of oneiric manifestations were considered illusiory.

The Deïr 'Alla plaster text (DAPT), dated by palaeography and by archaeological evidence in the first half of the eighth century BCE, is an important element in the dossier, even though the term 'dream' does not actually appear there:

> (1) [...the bo]ok of [Ba]laam, [son of Beo]r. He was a seer of the gods. *And the gods came to him at night and he saw a vision (2) like an oracle of El. They said to [Balaa]m, son of Beor:* (the text is unintelligible) (3) *And Balaam arose in the morning [...] he called [...] and for two days he was not ab[le to eat. And he fast]ed, while he was weeping* (4) *grievously. And his people came to him and they said to Balaam, son of Beor: 'Why do you fast? [And wh]y do you weep?'* (5) *Then he said to them: 'Sit down! I shall tell you what the Šadd[ayin are...ing.] Now come and see, what the gods are about to do! (6) The go[d]s gathered, while the Šadday deities met in assembly and said to Ša[mš:] ...* (DAPT I: 1-6)[5]

We shall return later to Balaam's visionary capacity such as it has been interpreted by the biblical tradition of Numbers 22–24 and integrated into a more general reflection on prophetic inspiration. Sticking strictly to the text in the inscription, Balaam's function is defined by the three words contained in the title (written in red in the original): *'š ḥzh 'lhn h'*, 'a man who sees the gods (he was)', or 'a visionary of divine things'. Here we find, condensed in a single formula, two titles given to prophets in the ancient traditions of the Bible, *ḥozeh* and *'îš ha'elohîm*. The word *'îš*, in the construct case, expresses belonging to an ethnic or socio-professional group, and we should understand *'š ḥzh 'lhn* to be a specialist in divine visions, a member of a cast of seers. Specialists such as these are also mentioned on the Aramaic stela of Zakkur, king of Hamat, which is contemporary with DAPT. This stela puts visionaries and diviners side by side (*KAI* 202: 12: *byd ḥzyn wbyd 'ddn*). Both are specialists in oracular consultation.

DAPT gives the account of an oracle of doom, announcement of which the prophet received in a revelation during the night. The highly literary character of the text, however, is evident from the observation of certain details: the presence of a title, the meticulous calligraphy and layout that reproduces a leather or papyrus scroll, and finally the narration as a whole, written in the third person. This account, whose aim it is to introduce into the text the very words of the prophet, words that appear only in line 5, is close in literary genre to stories about the prophets or the prophetic apophthegm. Its narrative structure consists of four elements: (1) a divine word received by the visionary; (2) a

5. This text raises a lot of epigraphic questions because of its very bad state of conservation. The bibliography concerning DAPT is very large; see Hoftijzer and van der Kooij (1989).

symbolic act accomplished by him; (3) a request for an explanation on the part of the people; (4) an oracle that is uttered by the visionary. This literary schema is found in Ezekiel (Ezek. 24.15-21; 37.15-28) and seems to correspond to specifically prophetic behaviour.

This literary form also highlights the fact that the oracle transcribes the verbal formulation of the prophet and not the *perception* that he received directly from the gods. This perception is described in terms of 'a vision', 'an oracle' and 'words'. What exactly happened, however, we do not know: 'and he saw a vision like an oracle of El, and they said (to him)' (DAPT I: 1-2: *w]yḥz.mḥzh/kmś'.'l.wy'mrw*).[6] The words that follow are divine *words* (written in red in the text of the inscription), words whose gravity provokes the seer to fast and shed tears, though no satisfactory translation of the text has as yet been proposed. This is in part due to the poor state of the text, but also to the difficulty of elucidating a formulation that is deliberately obscure, designed to evoke the mysterious character of the divine revelation and to underline the necessary effort of interpretation, which is the task of the prophet in his role as mediator of the divine word.

The seer's 'vision' appears at first, at the moment of its perception, to be the auditory revelation, during the night, of an obscure divine word; then, at the moment of its proclamation, it resembles oracular speech by virtue of its numerous images and metaphors. There is talk of a decision taken by the council of the gods that will provoke an upheaval on the earth. The visionary does not attend the deliberations of this council, but is informed of the decision by heavenly beings who 'come to him in the night' (line 1: *wy'tw.'lwh.'lhn.blylh*). This formula is found four times in the Old Testament (Gen. 20.3; 31.24; Num. 22.9, 20), of which twice in the context of the precision *baḥ*^{a}*lôm*, 'in a dream' (Gen. 20.3; 31.24). The absence of any explicit reference to a dream may be explicable here by reason of the fact that the nocturnal visionary experience of the prophets was related to a form of dream experience distinct from that usually denoted by *ḥ*^{a}*lôm*. We will return to this point in connection with the prophets of Israel (p. 152 below), but we should just say here that what is designated by *vision* (*mḥzh*) describes a perception in reality more 'auditory' than 'visual'. It included a particular kind of consciousness during sleep, which one avoided calling a *dream*.

6. According to a restoration of the text proposed by several scholars which puts a fragment into the lacuna. Others simply read *w[ymllw.'lw]h / kmś.'l*, 'and spoke to him according to the utterance of El'.

4. *Selected Bibliography*

Byl, S., 'Quelques idées grecques sur le rêve, d'Homère à Artémidore', *EC* 47 (1979), pp. 107-23.

Caquot, A., 'Les songes et leur interprétation selon Canaan et Israël', in *Les songes et leur interprétation* (Sources Orientales, 2; Paris: Le Seuil, 1959), pp. 99-124.

Casevitz, M., 'Les mots du rêve en grec ancien', *Ktema* 7 (1982), pp. 67-74.

Husser, J.-M., *Le songe et la parole* (BZAW, 210; Berlin: W. de Gruyter, 1994), pp. 29-62.

—'The Birth of a Hero: Form and Meaning of KTU 1.17 i-ii', in N. Wyatt, W.G.E. Watson and J.B. Lloyd (eds.), *Ugarit, Religion and Culture: Proceedings of the International Colloquium, Edinburgh, July 1994* (UBL, 12; Münster: Ugarit Verlag, 1996), pp. 85-98.

Kessels, A.H.M., 'Ancient Systems of Dream-Classification', *Mnemosyne* 4 (1969), pp. 389-424.

—*Studies on the Dream in Greek Literature* (Utrecht: Hes, 1978).

Levy, E., 'Le rêve homérique', *Ktema* 7 (1982), pp. 23-41.

Lieshout, R.G.A. van, *Greeks on Dreams* (Utrecht: Hes, 1980).

Oberman, J., *How Daniel Was Blessed with a Son: An Incubation Scene in Ugarit* (JAOSSup, 6; New Haven: American Oriental Society, 1946).

Olmo Lete, G. del, 'Antecedentes cananeos (ugariticos) de formas literarias hebreo-biblicas', *Simposio Biblico Español, Salamanca, 1981* (Madrid: 1984), pp. 84-114.

Tropper, J., 'Ugaritic dreams. Notes on Ugaritic *ḏ(h)rt* and *hdrt*', in N. Wyatt, W.G.E. Watson and J.B. Lloyd (eds.), *Ugarit, Religion and Culture: Proceedings of the International Colloquim, Edinburgh, July 1994* (UBL, 12; Münster: Ugarit Verlag, 1996), pp. 305-14.

Vinagre, M.A., 'Die griechische Terminologie der Traumdeutung', *Mnemosyne* 49 (1996), pp. 257-80.

Part II

OLD TESTAMENT

Chapter 6

GENERALIA

1. *The Different Meanings of* ḥlm

Hebrew, like Ugaritic and the various Aramaic dialects, uses only one root, *ḥlm*, with its nominal derivatives, to describe different kinds of dreams. Arabic, on the other hand, reserves *ḥulm* for ordinary dreams, for nightmares and for more unusual dream experiences, while the word for a divine revelation in a dream is *ru'ya* or *manam*. The affirmation '*ru'ya* comes from God, but *ḥulm* comes from Satan' is a common place in Muslim tradition.

While there is no doubt at all that it means 'to dream', the etymology of *ḥlm* is unclear. There exists, however, an extension of the semantic field of *ḥlm,* organized around the basic meaning 'to be strong', attested in Hebrew, in respect of animals (Job 39.4: *yaḥlᵉmû bᵉnêhem*, 'their young grow strong'), and also in Syriac (*ḥelim*, 'strong') and Arabic (*ḥalama*, 'to become a man', sexually speaking). Consequently, some scholars argue that *ḥlm* corresponds to two distinct roots, while others opt for the following semantic evolution: 'to be strong', 'to reach puberty', 'to have erotic dreams' and finally 'to dream'. As such, the explanation seems rather forced, but we should remember that the erection of the penis is one of the physiological characteristics of paradoxical sleep at every age in life. The correlation between seeming sexual arousal and dreams may well have been established at a very early period. It could well have led to a semantic link between dreams and virility, without necessarily taking into account the sexual content of dreams.

The Hebrew noun *ḥᵃlôm* is a nominal form with a long second vowel of the *qᵉtôl* type. What the form might originally have been, however, we do not know (*qutal* or *qital*). Nor is it certain that the nominal form is derived from the verbal root; the opposite is actually more likely if we consider how each is used. In Ugaritic, only the noun is attested; in

Hebrew, verbal and nominal forms appear in fairly stereotypical syntactical constructions. 'To dream', or 'have a dream', is expressed thus:

ḥlm	(Gen. 28.12; 41.1, 5; Isa. 29.8; Jer. 23.25)
ḥlwm ḥlm	(Gen. 37.5, 9; 40.5, 8; 41.11, 15; Deut. 13.2, 4, 6; Judg. 7.13; Dan. 2.1, 3)
ḥlwm 'šr ḥlm	(Gen. 37.5, 6; 42.9; Jer. 29.8)
bḥlwm	(Gen. 20.3; 28.13; 31.11; 40.9, 16; 41.17, 22; Num. 12.6; 1 Sam. 28.6; 1 Kgs 3.4; 9.2; Job 7.14; 33.16)
r'h bḥlwm	(Gen. 31.10; 41.22)

The most common way of saying 'to dream' is to use the internal object *ḥlwm ḥlmty*, 'I dreamed a dream'. This expression is, however, only used of symbolic dreams. Message-dreams are simply introduced by the formula *bḥlwm*, 'in a dream', preceded by the verb describing the way in which God intervenes. The latter differs according to the context.

In general, therefore, the verb is rarely used on its own; in most cases (and in message-dreams in particular) the noun is enough to designate the occurrence of a dream. More precisely, *ḥ*^{a}*lôm* defines the framework in which something takes place. This happening occurs 'in a dream', as if the latter were an objective reality, a space, or an organ, in which something is likely to happen. On the other hand, when it comes to 'telling a dream', and here we are in the realm of symbolic dreams, the hallowed expression *spr ('t) ḥlwm*[1] assumes that *ḥ*^{a}*lôm* refers to the contents themselves of the oneiric experience.

If in Ugaritic, poetic parallelism suggests two synonyms for *ḥlm,* namely *hdrt* and *ḏ(h)rt*, the first designating an oneiric theophany, and the second simply a vision in the night (see p. 75 above), in Hebrew, the only synonym for *ḥ*^{a}*lôm* is *ḥ*^{a}*zôn lay*^{e}*lāh* (Isa. 29.7), or *ḥezyôn lay*^{e}*lāh* (Job 20.8; 33.15), 'vision in the night'. Its usage in these three instances seems to be governed more by poetic parallelism than by the desire to describe the nature of the oneiric experience accurately. We know, from the use made of it in prophetic texts, that *ḥzh* never designates a vision as such, but rather a 'revelation', the 'vision' of God's word. In spite of the primary meaning of *ḥzh*, therefore, when *ḥ*^{a}*lôm* and *ḥāzôn* exist in parallel, it is not so much in order to underline the visual character of the dream, as to draw attention to the capacity that

1. Gen. 37.9; 40.9; 41.8; Judg. 7.13,15; Jer. 23.28, and once *hgyd*: Gen. 37.5.

dreams have of making extra-sensorial perceptions during sleep.

If we concentrate on texts that are explicitly concerned with dreams, these are, in most cases, associated with night and with sleep. Thus it is that we find *ḥlm*/*ḥlwm* associated with:

> *lāyᵉlāh* (night) in Gen. 20.3; 31.24; 40.5; 1 Kgs 3.5;
> *škb* (to go to bed) in Gen. 28.11;
> *yšn* (to sleep) in Gen. 41.5; Dan. 2.1;
> *qyṣ* (to wake up) in Gen. 28.16; 41.7; 1 Kgs 3.15; Ps. 73.20.

The association of *ḥᵃlôm* with *tardemāh*, 'torpor, lethargy, deep sleep', is notable for its rarity: the combination appears only once (Job 33.15) out of the seven occurrences of the noun in the Old Testament. Apart from Genesis 15 and Job 4.13, where this torpor seems favourable to a vision, everywhere else it is on the contrary the cause of a complete absence of perception. The same observation is valid for the verbal forms of the root *rdm*, which does not appear any more frequently than the noun *tardemāh* as a technical term in visionary language. Of seven occurrences of the term, only two are situated in the context of a vision: Dan. 8.18; 10.9; the expression *nirdamtî 'al pānay 'ārṣāh* does not however describe the beginning of the vision, but rather a momentary interruption of the latter due to a crisis of lethargy. We cannot therefore say, as it is sometimes affirmed, that this torpor—sometimes provoked by God (Gen. 2.21; 15.12; 1 Sam. 26.12; Isa. 29.10)—presents the most opportune circumstance for a dream.

A rapid survey of the texts that either recount a dream narrative or that simply make an allusion to it allows us to draw up a relatively rich catalogue for the semantic field of *ḥlm*. The latter designates the following:

joy beyond compare	(Ps. 126.1)
something illusiory	(Isa. 29.5-7; Ps. 73.20)
an ordinary dream	(Isa. 29.8; Eccl. 5.2)
a nightmare	(Job 7.13-14; 33.14-18)
a premonitory dream	(Gen. 37.5-9, 19-20; 42.9; Judg. 7.13-14)
an allegorical dream	(Gen. 40–41 *passim;* Dan. 2; 4 *passim*)
a divine word heard	(Gen. 20.3-6; 28.13-18; 31.10-13; Num. 12.6-8; Joel 3.1; Job 33.14-16)
a dream theophany	(Gen. 28.12-13a; 1 Kgs 3.5; Job 4.12-16)

Finally, as said in the introduction, as well as denoting different aspects of dream experience, *ḥlm* can designate the more or less ritualized practices studied in Chapter 11. Here we are at the very limit of the semantic field, in so far as these practices are never explicitly referred to, but simply hinted at by *ḥlm*, by allusion or sous-entendu: practices such as the consultation of oracles (1 Sam. 28.6, 15), oneiromancy (Deut. 13.2-6; Jer. 27.9; 29.8), or incubation (1 Kgs 3.4-5), to mention only the passages where *ḥlm* actually appears.

2. *Historico-Critical Research*

Dreams in the Bible have been relatively little studied for their own sake, yet it is still not easy to give an account of the main lines of research, since the principal texts of the dossier have on the contrary been much studied in view of their individual literary context and the specific questions that each poses. The first monograph on the subject is the thesis of Ehrlich (1953), which aims to be a critical and methodical inventory of all the texts concerning dreams in the Old Testament. In view of the research undertaken in religious studies, there arose in him a desire to evaluate more precisely the theological role and significance of dreams in Israel and to make an exhaustive study on the subject. Two basic questions are tackled in the course of the six chapters of his thesis: incubation and the attitude towards dreams as a means of revelation.

Of all the texts reputed to give evidence of the practice of incubation in Israel (Gen. 15; 28.10-17; 46.1-4; 1 Sam. 3; 1 Kgs 3.4-15; Isa. 65.4; Ps. 3.6; 4.6; 17.5; 63), Ehrlich is of the opinion that only Solomon's dream at Gibeon (1 Kgs 3) is indisputable. His way of going about the problem and of arguing his case is characteristic of a certain way of tackling the question: starting with the classical definition of incubation (comprising sacrifices, purification, going to sleep in a sanctuary, the apparition of the divinity in a dream, sacrifices on awakening), he then proceeds to remark upon the absence of one or more elements in the schema in each of the texts examined, with the exception of 1 Kgs 3.4-15. Ehrlich's arguments have often been cited, and the question of incubation has scarcely been touched since.

Another important chapter is devoted to *symbolic dreams* (the dreams in the Joseph story: Gen. 37; 40–41; the Midianite's dream: Judg. 7.13-14; Nebuchadnezzar's dreams: Dan. 2; 4). These remain the closest to our common experience of dreams, and illustrate best the positive attitude of biblical authors towards them. In Gen. 41.25, the divine origin of this kind of dream is clearly affirmed, but if these authors allow for the possibility that such dreams are sent by God, they also underline the essential role of the interpreter, without whom the divine message would remain enigmatic. Ehrlich underlines how the author of the Joseph story contrasts the experience of Joseph with ordinary oneiromantic practices: it is God himself who grants the interpretation in so far as the dream comes from him. The biblical account therefore aims to highlight yet further the charism of the interpreter, through whom the superiority of the God of Israel over the wisdom of diviners is made manifest.

According to Ehrlich, *message-dream* narratives do not add a great deal to the subject, for they do not describe genuine oneiric experiences. Recounted for the most part in the patriarchal traditions of the Pentateuch, Ehrlich argues that the function of these accounts was above all to supply a framework that was both familiar and in which divine interventions were theologically acceptable. The main concern of these authors was to avoid any impression of physical proximity between God and man. Here, visibly, Ehrlich (1953: 128) is overtaken by theological concerns: 'Dreams are the form of revelation, in which God mixes least of all with the earthly things (Gunkel). Although God himself is involved in the incident, since it happens in a dream, he experiences it a one remove, from another dimension. He speaks "only from a certain distance created by the night and the dream… God does not speak with men as travellers with their fellow journeymen", agrees L. Köhler.'

The two last chapters of the work briefly review passages in which opposition to dreams as a means of hearing the word of God is clearly voiced, principally in Isaiah (29.7-8), Jeremiah (23.25-32; 27.9-10; 29.8-9), Deuteronomy (13.2-6), and *Ben Sira* (Sir. 34.1-8; 40.5-7). Ehrlich, however, does not attempt to explain these divergent attitudes to dreams, attitudes that appear as soon as the exile is over. The weakness of his analysis at this point stems from the fact that he pays insufficient attention to the diversity of the oneiric experiences and practices to which the texts refer.

In 1959, the collection 'Sources Orientales' published a volume (no. 2) devoted to dreams and their interpretation. This volume provided Caquot (1959) with the opportunity to situate the Canaanite and biblical texts in a historical perspective lacking up till then. He makes a short and remarkable synthesis of the dossier, and challenges Ehrlich's thesis as regards the question of incubation, vestiges of which he discerns in a few rare allusions in liturgical texts.

As regards *Formgeschichte*, an article written by Richter (1963) makes a precise analysis of the *Traumbericht* genre. Careful to retain only formal criteria in the definition of the genre, Richter takes as the starting point for his study symbolic dream narratives, that is, essentially the dreams in the Joseph story, the only ones, according to him, to display the characteristics of a complete literary form.

The form of these narratives is highly elaborate. It includes an introduction, a description of the dream, itself composed of several scenes (each with its narrative development), and an interpretation of the dream upon the dreamer's awakening. This interpretation is made by a third party, who picks different elements in the description. This structure, which is characterized by its own specific grammatical construction, is attested in each of the symbolic dream narratives. They are probably the complex literary elaboration of a simple, elementary form, composed of a single scene, followed by its interpretation: 'I dreamt (*ḥ^a^lôm ḥālamtî*): behold (*w^e^hinneh*)… (nominal clause: oneiric scene) and (*wyqṭl*) … (narrative clause). This is what it means (*zeh pitrônô*): the … (nominal clause), is … (nominal clause).'

From the constant recurrence of this *Grundform* in diverse literary traditions, Richter concludes that it was imposed by an institution that was recognized by all. The *Sitz im Leben* of this literary genre was therefore probably a commonplace and institutionalized practice of oneiromancy in Israel, as is attested by the interpretative part of each of the dream accounts, and several other allusions scattered throughout biblical texts.

The E document, however, to which Pentateuchal criticism attributed unanimously almost all the dream accounts, also contains message-dream narratives. They differ greatly from the above in form. For Richter, even more systematically than for Ehrlich before him, these message-dreams stray so far both from the *Traumbericht* model and from ordinary dream experience that they belong to the realm of literary device alone. Whilst recognizing the value of dreams as a means of communicating with God, Richter infers from the text that the Elohist was critical of dreams, prefering the clarity of the divine word to the confused ambiguity of images. By deliberately composing oneiric messages without images, the E redactor appeared to wilfully distance himself from the arbitrary science of diviners. The suspicion under which E puts an institution that Richter takes to be alive until the beginning of the monarchy would develop thereafter into the radical criticism of dreams characteristic of the prophets and Deuteronomy.

Richter's reconstitution does however have one awkward methodological weakness: if it is form alone that guarantees the objective definition of the genre, the latter will inevitably be determined by the texts selected for consideration. In according full typological status to the dreams in the Joseph story only, his choice is determined above all by the *contents* of the dream narratives and their proximity to our own experience of the dream world. Moreover, the literary form of message-dreams is fairly standard and is attested in all the literary traditions of the Near East, dating as far back as the lists in oneiromancritical collections. We cannot therefore simply speak of a literary device, and not consider either the value of the experience described or the eventual *Sitz im Leben* of the message-dream.

The theological function claimed for these message-dreams by Richter in the Elohistic document is typical of the numerous reconstitutions of biblical theology to which the documentary theory gave rise. Equally characteristic is the study of Jaroš (1982), undertaken just before the collapse of Wellhausen's system, and in which he devotes a chapter to the subject of dreams. He notes that E considers dreams to open up the real possibility of the intervention of the transcendant in the world: E, he suggests, had accepted and integrated this aspect of Canaanite piety, considering it to be compatible with Yahwistic faith on condition that certain precise boundaries be maintained. Jaroš emphasizes that E recounts dreams chiefly in the patriarchal traditions, thereby allowing him to make a qualitative distinction between the pre-Mosaic revelation and that at Horeb. For Jaroš, Num. 12.6-8 contains the key to the Elohist's attitude to oneiric revelations: in specifying that dreams and visions are the ordinary but enigmatic way in which God speaks to the prophets, he also makes it clear that the revelation received by Moses was of a superior order.

The authors above testify to what became of the historical schema fashionable among exegetes at the time of the documentary theory, in the attempt to account for the place dreams held in the traditions of Israel. It is recognized from Wellhausen onwards that, in the earliest strata of the Pentateuch, dream narratives are a concession, on the part of the Elohistic redactor, to the surrounding Canaanite culture, and the mark of his affinity with prophetic circles. In the context of the documentary theory, dreams would appear to decisively indicate material in a text belonging to E.

According to the theology attributed to the Elohist, dreams are a way of expressing a direct relationship between God and man without compromising the distance that separates them, and without having recourse to the over anthropomorphic theophanies characteristic of the Yahwist. If the Elohist dares to make a place for dreams in Yahwistic faith, it is because he simultaneously elicits an initially critical attitude as regards dreams: oneiric visions had no part in the revelation to Moses, who saw God face to face, and the prophetic circles that influenced the redactors of document E themselves appear to have already prefered—albeit in the form of a dream—the clarity of the spoken word to the ambiguity of images.

The way in which religion evolved, through the prophetic movement, Deuteronomistic reform and the wisdom tradition, meant that the process of desacrilization continued until dreams were reduced simply to natural phenomena belonging to the realm of deceptive illusion. Authors who favour this evolutionary approach quote Jeremiah's attitude towards those false prophets who claim to have had dreams (Jer. 23.25–32; 27.9; 29.8–9); the prescription in Deut. 13.1–6; the relative silence of Deuteronomistic historians on the subject, and the supposed scepticism of wisdom circles, for whom dreams are a symbol of evanescence and revelatory of the psychosomatic state of the sleeper (Isa. 29.7-8; Job 20.88; Eccl. 5.2, 6; Sir. 40.5-7). We will encounter, in our examination of the texts, the weaknesses and inconsistencies of this schema, a schema that is typical of certain theological reconstitutions, and which of course now feels the effects of currrent challenges to the documentary theory.

Though on the fringe of the historico-critical debate, Resch's essay (1964) in biblical theology attempts to evaluate the part played by divine intervention among the other various components of dreaming in dream narratives. From a rapid examination of modern dream theories and observation of the way in which the Old Testament is aware of the psychological dimension, he concludes that there is a certain convergence of the two, for the realism of biblical authors enabled them to recognize dreams as the product of psychological needs (Isa. 29.7-8), of psychic tensions (Eccl. 5.2, 6; Sir. 40.5-7) or of personal fantasies (Jer. 23.25-31; Zech. 10.2). Resch therefore argues that[2] 'In the Old

2. 'der Traum wird im A.T. immer nur als eine menschliche Potenz betrachtet, die von sich aus überhaupt keine Macht besitzt, sondern immer von aussen aktiviert werden muss' (1964: 38).

Testament, dreams are only ever considered as human potential, having no power in themselves. On the contrary, they must always be activated from without'. God, he argues, intervenes in dreams by playing upon psychic forces that act upon a capacity for extrasensorial perception inherent in oneiric activity. This capacity, he claims rather summarily, is attested by modern psychoanalysis.

Henceforth, Resch's procedure is a simple one: for each dream narrative, his analysis consists in distingushing what belongs to literary convention, to the historical or social conditioning of the dreamer, to his mental and psychological state, and to the natural precognitive function of the dream. What remains after this successive filtering is the specifically divine part of the oneiric contents, its prophetic dimension, which is always relevant. Indeed, the hypothesis rests from the very start upon a theological *a priori* that can never be proven, and the psychological analysis of the situations described in the texts is inevitably summary. The author's neglect of literary forms and of redactional problems means that the hypothesis depends on an implicitly historicizing reading of the texts.

Though this work has had little impact on research, Resch does draw attention to the need for an anthropological approach to the phenomenon. But at this point, though he himself does not identify it, he comes up against the major difficulty posed by his project: if the oneiric discourse functions essentially by means of semantic shifts, how then is it possible to reach the latent contents of the dream, given the mainly fictive nature of these accounts? This question is at the heart of the debate about the possibility of a psychoanalytical reading of biblical dream accounts.

3. *The Psychoanalytical Approach*

Strangely enough, attempts at a psychoanalytical reading of the Bible have up till now scarcely paid any attention to dreams. It is true that difficulties and pitfalls—which are not always avoided—abound, as do objections as to the pertinence of the enterprise itself. A Freudian analysis of dreams must take into account the different component parts of the work of the unconscious in dreams, in order to get at the latent discourse hidden behind the language of symbols. This work undertaken by dreams corresponds to a complex process of the psyche that results, by means of displacement, the elaboration of symbols and by condensation, in the disguised realization of a desire thus far unconscious owing to its incompatibility with the norms of the super-ego. That is to say, any genuine attempt to bring to light the latent contents of dreams, takes place first of all in the context of a therapeutic process, and develops in relation to factors set up by the psychoanalytical context.

It is clear that the biblical text cannot be considered to be the raw and therefore authentic relation of a real life dream experience: the majority, if not all the dream accounts are fictive; they are written up in a style using fixed literary forms and compositional conventions that remove any spontaneity from the narration. What can we really say about the dreaming subject or about the processes of his or her psyche when we have access to him or her only through the intermediary of stereotypical literary expressions?

Moreover, in contrast to modern literary works, traditional literature rarely gives any information about its real author. Critical examination of discrepancies and tensions in the written discourse can sometimes throw up evidence of a latent, often stratified discourse. This may be a rich source of memories as regards the redaction of the text, but instead of revealing something of the subjectivity of an author, it most often only ever reveals the complex interweaving of traditions, compilations and rereadings. The author of the text, as subject, appears to be as elusive as the dreamer of the dream recounted. It is impossible, therefore, to claim to have access to part of the unconscious psychological processes of the former by means of the latter.

It is not only the sometimes excessive prudence of exegetes that is responsible for the refusal to deal with the subject; authors who are better qualified in the subject have also shied away from biblical dreams. It is significant that Balmary (1986), in her psychoanalytical interpretation of 'the healing of Sarah' (Gen. 12; 16; 17; 20–21), does not devote a single paragraph to Abimelech's dream (Gen. 20). It is she herself, however, who points out that in the course of this very episode the symbolic order of things—father, daughter, husband—is restored and that Sarah is thus freed from the perverse possession that was the cause of her sterility. The only dream account that is rich enough in symbolic material to give rise to a few studies is Jacob's dream at Bethel.[3]

The episode at Bethel seems to Couffignal (1977) to deal with the initiation of a hero who is gifted with the revelation of that which is

3. See Niederland 1954; Couffignal 1977.

most mysteriously hidden within him. The dream is interpreted as a vision of sexual intercourse between parents; sky and earth symbolize father and mother, united by a staircase, the rhythmic movement up and down that is suggestive of coitus. The hero then erects and anoints a stela, and in so doing ritually frees himself of the desire for incest. Indeed, the entire Jacob cycle is thought to be the expression of the Oedipean tragedy:

> Jacob's fault—similar to Oedipus'—consisted first of all in turning against his father (Gen. 27), then at Bethel (Gen. 28), in consumating an incestous relationship symbolically (he erects a stone and pours a libation over it); finally, at the Jabbok, as a consequence of what has gone before, the hero is wounded in the hip, the equivalent of being castrated, by an unknown man who is clearly a paternal figure (Couffignal 1977: 359).

Psychoanalysis here supplies a number of symbolic correspondences, a cursory look at which enables the author to suggest a reconstitution of the latent contents of the text. There is no better example of reductionism as regards the use of psychoanalysis in interpreting an ancient text.

Gibert (1991) enquired further into the pertinence of Freudian psychoanalysis in interpreting ancient texts by attempting to overwhelm the supposedly nullifying distance between the written text and the psychological experience itself. He suggests that, in order to work, a dream account must be recognizable as such by the readers, who should be able to identify in the narrative the principal component parts of their own dream experience. Not only should wish fulfilment be what motivates the dream account or even the act of writing itself, but in the less 'artificial' accounts (like Joseph's dreams, for example), the condensing process (noticeable in the concision of the nominal clauses), displacement and the elaboration of symbols should also be present. Writing demands, as does every act of communication, a certain connivance between author and reader; the quality and credibility of the account therefore depend on the capacity of the author to recreate a likely oneiric narration, thanks to the presence of these elements in appropriate measure. Thus 'the redactor takes absolute and total responsibility for becoming almost entirely assimilated with the dreamer in the intimacy of his experiences' (Gibert 1990: 97) and reproduces, in his or her writing, the unconscious psychological processes that constitute the imaginative inventory of dreams.

The value of his hypothesis is proven when applied to the dreams interpreted by Joseph (Gen. 40–41): in these dream accounts, the contents of the dream greatly exceed their narration and literary function (the phenomenon of condensation); displacement is suggested by the discrepancy, noticeable in the writing, between the explicit desire of the dreamer (the butler's desire for freedom, for example) and his unconscious desire (his desire to deceive the Pharaoh). This is satisfied symbolically in the dream by means of the objective complicity of the birds who come and eat the Pharaoh's food.

A psychoanalytical interpretation of dream accounts seems henceforth to be possible, in so far as, behind all the literary conventions, the reader still discerns the functional pattern corresponding to his or her own dream experience. It is no longer the psychology of the imaginary dreamer that is revealed in the hidden contents of the account, nor even that of the deliberately depersonalized author, but the universal working of the human psyche, more or less well rendered by the author, and in which the readers recognize part of themselves.

Finally, we should note the existence of several essays that give a Jungian interpretation to dream reports, mainly in the Genesis narratives: the essays of Kühlewein (1980) and Hark (1982: 35-81) for Jacob (Gen. 28) and Joseph's (Gen. 37) dreams. Narratives describing an encounter with the divine are often dramatic and are understood to be a symbolic way of expressing the individual's confrontation with Self as he or she progresses towards psychological maturity (the process called individuation).[4]

4. *Different Types of Dreams*

Form criticism has contented itself up till now with the handy classification proposed by Oppenheim as applied to Mesopotamian literary texts. This classification distinguishes two basic types of dream accounts: *message-dreams* and *symbolic dreams*. As outlined above, this classification was first conceived by Artimedorus of Daldis. As regards form criticism, this typology seems on the whole to be well suited to the task of defining the various dream accounts we find in the Old Testament, characterized as they are by their own particular formulae and forms of expression. It does, however, prove to be very inadequate to the task of defining the psychological experience to which these different accounts refer.

4. See also Drewermann 1984.

Indeed, in his work devoted to the general classification of dreams, Artimedorus of Daldis was keenly aware of questions of oneiro-criticism, and distinguished dreams in which the relationship between signifier and signified is obvious (theorematic dreams) and those that on the other hand require interpretation (allegorical dreams). Oppenheim's classification differs from that of Artimidorus in so far as he proposes a typology based on exclusively literary criteria, without taking into account the psychological aspect of dreams. It is obvious, however, given what was said in the introduction regarding oneiric states, that the distinction between message-dreams and symbolic dreams also covers, at least in part, other very real categories of dream *experience*.

In fact, every dream recounted communicates a message, whether it be formulated in understandable language, or veiled in more or less enigmatic images. Indeed, this is an essential characteristic of the 'dream account' genre, which never consents to recounting an ordinary dream or one without significance. Consequently, it is their contents, primarily visual in some (symbolic dreams) and auditory in others (message-dreams) that determine their respective literary form and establish the distinction between dreams that are 'seen' and those that are 'heard'.

Furthermore, the dream accounts on which this distinction depends do not cover all the forms of dream experience referred to in the Old Testament, even though the references are sometimes veiled. Pertinent also are those allusions, be they ironic or polemical, that contribute to the diversity of oneiric experience to which the Old Testament bears witness. These experiences, pleasant or unpleasant, are never recounted as such but constitute the psychological and experiential backcloth out of which the dream accounts grow.

Oppenheim (1956: 331) suggested that the form of message-dreams was possibly the literary transcription of genuine oneiric experiences, occasioned by incubation rites, in the course of which the ritually solicited divinity suddenly appeared to the incubant to speak to him or her in their dream. For Richter (1963), the *Sitz im Leben* of symbolic dreams is the practice of oniromancy; the highly stereotypical forms of expresssion found there and the necessity of an interpretative phase strongly suggest this setting to him (see pp. 93-94). The original *Sitz im Leben* of these two basic types of dream accounts would therefore seem settled. It is noteworthy, however, that if, according to this schema, message-dreams schematize a particular type of *experience*, then symbolic dreams reproduce formulaic expressions and structures specific to a *practice*. Their points of reference are therefore not the same.

Moreover, to judge by the use made of them in the Old Testament, these accounts seem most often to be very far from their original *Sitz im Leben*. Set free from the institutional setting that first brought them about, they evolve as independent literary forms and are used to give expression to oneiric experiences different from those experienced during incubation or habitual oneiromantic practices. We will see, for example, that though it is possible to infer the practice of royal incubation from the account in 1 Kings 3, the account of Abimelech's dream in Genesis 20, which is similar in form, refers to a very different oneiric experience, that of a nightmare or the delirium of someone who is ill. Similarly, as much by reason of their form as of their content, the symbolic dream accounts of Genesis 40–41 or of Daniel 2 and 4 call to mind the practice of oneirocriticism, while Joseph's dreams (Gen. 37), which are symbolic in their own way, are immediately intelligible and relate more readily to ordinary dream experience.

We may conclude that if certain *practices* or institutions were responsible for bringing to birth these literary forms, the authors who use them do so in order to evoke a variety of oneiric *experiences*, experiences sometimes quite different from those that originally served as model. Henceforth, we will be even more attentive to their *Sitz in der Literatur* than to their *Sitz im Leben*.

Dream aetiology does not seem to have been the object of discussion in Israel, but it is possible, as in other domains of intellectual life, that it is simply the nature of the biblical texts that is responsible for our ignorance in this respect. Whatever the case, the general attitude towards and appreciation of the phenomenon rests upon a clear and simple notion of their origin, at least in the discourse of the dominant theology. Dream accounts only recount dreams of religious value: messages sent by God in symbolic form (Gen. 41.25; Dan. 2.28; 4.21), or visits from God 'in a dream'. The origin of these dreams is divine; whether it is the contents alone or the entire oneiric experience, the *ḥ^alôm*, which comes from God, is not clear.

What is certain is that the *ḥ^alôm* is never personified as a messenger, but is always felt as a state, or as a situation, experienced more or less passively by the dreamer. As in all the other neighbouring cultures of the ancient Near East, there is never any mention of a voyage undertaken by the dreamer to a land of dreams. If he or she is not simply the spectator of symbolic scenes and pictures, it is God himself who comes and appears in a dream.

The opposite of these religious dreams are ordinary dreams, for which we have no difficulty in establishing a relationship simply of cause and effect between their contents and the psychosomatic state of the dreamer: 'As when a hungry man dreams he is eating and awakes with his hunger not satisfied, or as when a thirsty man dreams he is drinking and awakes faint, with his thirst not quenched' (Isa. 29.8). Qohelet is equally realistic when he affirms, 'For a dream comes with much business' (Eccl. 5.2). Henceforth, dreams may be used as a metaphor for whatever is fleeting and lacking in consistency (Job 20.8; Isa. 29.5-7). Dreams belong to the world of darkness, and it is with the latter and the terrors that accompany them that they disappear in the morning, with the coming of the light of day (Ps. 73.20). In spite of the illusory character of dreams, and because they do not belong to the concrete reality of daytime, they also provide the opportunity for escape and for joys forbidden by the harshness of the world (Ps. 126.1).

Dreams therefore may have one of two possible origins, either natural or supernatural. The fact that there are two apparently contradictory conceptions should not be interpreted as evidence of a progressive desacralization of the phenomenon. Their ambivalence was recognized from early antiquity, as is evidenced by the practice of oneirocriticism at Mari, for example, and the distinction made in Homeric poems, and echoed in most Greek and Latin authors, between dreams issuing from the 'gate of horn' (real dreams) and those proceeding from the 'ivory gate' (false ones) (*Od.* 19.560-69).

Where there was certainly an evolution in Israel, at least in cultured circles, is in the appreciation of the intrinsic value of all kinds of dream experience other than those of divine origin, and in the development of criteria whereby one might discern the latter. This radical distinction between natural—and consequently deceiving—dreams (ἐνύπνια), and dreams of oracular value (ὀνεἱροι) came into force little by little under the influence of Hellenism, and seems to have been generally accepted in the second century BCE by intellectuals (see Sir. 34.6). This came about as the result of a rationalizing process, the advantage of which is obvious in the context of a strict form of monotheism, even though it meant that the variety of nuances between the two terms had to be ignored. We shall see, as regards nightmares, premonitory dreams and prophetic dreams, that the contours of dream aetiology were not always so clear-cut.

5. *The Literary Function of Dream Accounts*

Dreams also appear to be a compositional technique particularly well suited to the structuring of a narrative text. They do so in the following two ways:

1. Integrated into the situation described at the outset, the dream henceforth serves as the common thread, unifying the different elements in the narrative and bringing it to its conclusion. The plot is developed between the dream, which forecasts the outcome, and its realization, expected at the end of whatever perepeteia the author cares to imagine. In this context, the dream takes on the role of an *initial prophecy*.

The Joseph story is the best biblical example of a story in which dreams have this narrative function: the short story runs from a crisis towards its resolution, even though the latter is announced from the start in Joseph's dreams (Gen. 37), which also play a part in the origin of the crisis. As regards the epic genre, Jacob's dream at Bethel (Gen. 28), set as it is against his struggle by night at the ford across the Jabbok (Gen. 32), has a similar structuring function in the Jacob cycle. These two events parallel each other symmetrically at two significant points in the cycle, and make the patriarch's coming and going into a veritable initiatory journey, extending from a promise to its realization, from the initial conflict between the twins to the exchange of a blessing, hard won.

2. Another way in which dreams may structure a text is by permitting and indeed provoking the symmetrical organization of the text. Organized around an axis corresponding to the awakening of the dreamer, the narrative takes the form of a diptych, the panels of which often mirror each other word for word: the scene experienced in the dream will be lived out again in the wakeful world, for the dream acts as an inital prophetic element or instruction given to the hero of the story. Keret's dream, in the first episode of the Ugaritic epic, illustrates this procedure.

Similarly, though in a different way, the account of the abduction of Sarah by Abimelech (Gen. 20), takes the form of two symmetrical scenes, one in a dream, the other after the king has woken up. These scenes contain dialogues that are not identical in content, but which pursue the same argument by inversing the situations. Different again, but still operating according to the same principle, is Jacob's dream at Bethel (Gen. 28). It provokes the repetition of gestures accomplished the evening before (v. 11b) on awakening (v. 18), though with a significant reversal in the value of things and of place, a shift from the profane to the sacred.

In addition to having a structuring role, the dream account is a simple compositional technique whereby authors can introduce a dialogue between God and a human being. This oneiric dialogue may have some concrete end and be the opportunity for a direct intervention on the part of God in the evolution of the dreamer: it is thus that God comes to the aid of Keret (*KTU* 1.14) or of Jacob (Gen. 31), that he gives to Solomon (1 Kgs 3) or to Daniel (Dan. 2) the knowledge necessary for the accomplishment of their mission. But this dialogue may also be the form chosen in order to develop some aspect of teaching or for theological reflection. In this case, it provides the setting for a real debate, as in Genesis 20 between Abimelech and God, or the opportunity to underline certain theological principles at a key point in the story, as in Solomon's dream at Gibeon, for example.

6. *Selected Bibliography*

Bergmann, E., G. Botterweck and M. Ottosson, '*ḥālam* / *ḥ*ᵃ*lôm*', *TDOT*, VI, pp. 421-32.

Caquot, A., 'Les songes et leur interprétation selon Canaan et Israël', in *Les songes et leur interprétation* (Sources Orientales, 2; Paris: Le Seuil, 1959), pp. 101-24.

Cavalletti, S., 'Sogno e profezia nell'Antico Testamento', *RivB* 7 (1959), pp. 356-63.

—'L'incubazione nell'Antico Testamento', *RivB* 8 (1960), pp. 42-48.

Cooper, J.S., 'Sargon and Joseph: Dreams Come True', in A. Kort (ed.), *Biblical and Related Studies Presented to Samuel Iwry* (Winona Lake, IN: Eisenbrauns, 1985), pp. 33-39.

Couffignal, R., 'Le songe de Jacob. Approches nouvelles de Genèse 28, 10-22', *Bib* 58 (1977), pp. 342-60.

Ehrlich, E.L., *Der Traum im Alten Testament* (BZAW, 73; Berlin: Alfred Töpelmann, 1953).

Finkel, A., 'The Pesher of Dreams and Scriptures', *RevQ* 4 (1963–64), pp. 357-70.

Fishbane, M., 'The Mantological Exegesis of Dreams, Visions and Omens', in M. Fishbane, *Biblical Interpretation in Ancient Israel* (Oxford: Clarendon Press, 1985), pp. 447-57.

Gibert, P., *Le récit biblique de rêve: Essai de confrontation analytique* (Lyon: Profac, 1990).

Gnuse, R., *The Dream Theophany of Samuel: Its Structure in Relation to Ancient Near Eastern Dreams and its Significance* (Lanham, MD: University Press of America, 1984).

—'Dream Reports in the Writings of Flavius Josephus', *RB* 96 (1989), pp. 358-90.

—'Dreams in the Night—Scholarly Mirage or Theophanic Formula? The Dream Report as a Motif of the so-Called Elohist Tradition', *BZ* 39 (1995), pp. 28-58.

Guillaume, A., *Prophecy and Divination among the Hebrews and Other Semites* (London: Cassell, 1938).

Hark, H., *Der Traum als Gottes vergessene Sprache* (Olten: Walter-Verlag, 1982).

Husser, J.-M., 'Le songe comme procédé littéraire: à propos de Gn 20', *RevScRel* 65 (1991), pp. 157-72.

—'Les métamorphoses d'un songe', *RB* 28 (1991), pp. 321-42.

—*Le songe et la parole: Etude sur le rêve et sa fonction dans l'ancien Israël* (BZAW, 210, Berlin: W. de Gruyter, 1994).

Jaroš, K., *Die Stellung des Elohisten zur kanaanäischen Religion* (OBO, 4; Göttingen: Vandenhoeck & Ruprecht, 1982), pp. 31-50.

Jeffer, A., 'Divination by Dream in Ugaritic Literature and in the Old Testament', *IBS* 12 (1990), pp. 167-83.

Kühlewein, J., 'Gotteserfahrung und Reifungsgeschichte in der Jakob-Esau-Erzählung', in R. Albertz (ed.), *Werden und Wirken des Alten Testaments* (Festschrift C. Westermann; Neukirchen–Vluyn: Neukirchener Verlag, 1980), pp. 116-29.

McAlpine, T.H., *Sleep, Divine and Human, in the Old Testament* (JSOTSup, 38; Sheffield: Sheffield Academic Press, 1987).

Miller, J.E., 'Dreams and Prophetic Visions', *Bib* 71 (1990), pp. 401-404.

Oepke, A., 'Ovαρ', *TDNT*, V, pp. 220-38.

Pedersen, J., *Israel, its Life and Culture*, I, II (London: Cumberledge; Copenhagen: Bramer, 1926), pp. 133-45.

Priest, J.F., 'Myth and Dream in Hebrew Scripture', in J. Campbell (ed.), *Myths, Dreams and Religion* (New York: Dutton, 1970), pp. 48-67.

Resch, A., *Der Traum im Heilsplan Gottes* (Freiburg: Herder, 1964).

Richter, W., 'Traum und Traumdeutung im Alten Testament', *BZ* 7 (1963), pp. 202-20.

Schmidtke, F., 'Träume, Orakel und Totengeister als Künder der Zukunft in Israel und Babylon', *BZ* 11 (1967), pp. 240-46.

Silva, A. da, *La symbolique des rêves et des vêtements dans l'histoire de Joseph et de ses frères* (Héritage et Projet, 52; Montreal: Fides, 1994).

Thomson, J.G., 'Sleep: An Aspect of Jewish Anthropology', *VT* 5 (1955), pp. 421-33.

Vergote, J., *Joseph en Egypte* (OBL, 3; Louvain: Publications Universitaires, 1959), pp. 46-86.

Westermann, C., 'Der Traum im Alten Testament', in C. Westermann (ed.), *Traüme verstehen—Verstehen durch Traüme* (Munich: Schnell & Steiner, 1986), pp. 8-23.

Wikenhauser, A., 'Doppeltraüme', *Bib* 29 (1948), pp. 100-11.

Zeitlin, S., 'Dreams and their Interpretation from the Biblical Period to the Tanaanite Time: An Historical Study', *JQR* 66 (1975-76), pp. 1-18.

Chapter 7

SYMBOLIC DREAMS

1. *The Egyptians' Dreams: Genesis 40–41*

Symbolic dreams in the Old Testament are almost all to be found in the Joseph story (Gen. 37; 40-41) and in the Aramaic chapters of Daniel (Dan. 2; 4; 7). Only one is recounted elsewhere: the dream of the Midianite soldier, heard by Gideon in Judges 7. It is clear, therefore, that the narrative and highly literary context of these accounts must be amply taken into consideration. The dreams of the Egyptian officers, Joseph's companions in misfortune (Gen. 40), followed by the Pharaoh's double dream (Gen. 41) are those that display the most rigorous syntactical structure and that, from Richter's study (1963) onwards, commonly serve as the reference for this literary form. They remain so for us, though we should avoid treating variants as deviants. A complete account consists of three or sometimes four elements: (1) introduction, (2) description of the dream, (3) interpretation, (4) realization.

In the introduction, different forms of the root *ḥlm* (see p. 88) are used depending on whether the dream is recounted in the first or third person. In the case of the latter, only the verb is used (Gen. 41.1: *ḥolēm*; 41.5: *wayyaḥ*^{a}*lom*). When the dreamer himself recounts his dream, he introduces it simply by *baḥ*^{a}*lômî* (Gen. 40.9, 16; 41.17, 22). The paronomastic expression *ḥ*^{a}*lôm ḥālamtî* alerts the reader to the presence of a symbolic dream but does not directly introduce a description of it (see Gen. 37.9; Judg. 7.13). Noteworthy is the fact that the verb 'to see' in 41.22 (*wā'ēre' baḥ*^{a}*lōmî*) is a hapax in this context.

Descriptions of dreams tend to be stereotypical and take the form of a series of pictures: each picture (itself possibly developed in diverse ways) is introduced by *hinnēh* followed by a nominal clause that describes the principal scene. If other pictures are added to the description of this scene, the nominal clauses respective to each are simply coordinated with the first (see 40.16a-17). If the picture also contains an action that allows the situation to develop, then the nominal clause is continued by one or more verbal clauses in the complete tense (see 40.9b-10). If, on the other hand, the action develops from the very first picture, the nominal clause is followed by verbal forms in the incomplete tense using the *wav* consecutive (see 41.2, 3-4). The dream can then continue with a new picture, introduced by *hinnēh*, followed by a further nominal clause, and its eventual developments (see 41.1-4).

Such is the subtle and precise nature of the syntax elucidated by Richter (1963) with reference to the dreams of Genesis 40–41; it is not applied with the same rigour in Genesis 37 and Judges 7, but what does always remain is a nominal clause describing the principal or initial scene in the dream, preceded by *hinnēh*. It is remarkable how successful this compositional procedure is in actualizing the oneiric scene for the reader or listener. The dream is described as a living picture whose movement is tempered by the succession of nominal clauses.

Each of the dreams in these two chapters is followed by its interpretation by Joseph. In ch. 40, this third element is introduced by the expression *zeh pitrōnô*, 'this is its interpretation' (40.12, 18). Use of the formula is not systematic, however, for it is not present in 41.25-26. For each of the dreams, the first part of the interpretation translates numerical data, understood to refer to periods of time (three days: 40.12, 18; seven years: 41.26-27a), using nominal clauses that juxtapose the oneiric image and its meaning. Verbal clauses in the future tense (*yiqṭol* and *wᵉqāṭal* forms) are then used for the interpretation of additional elements. The syntactic form of the interpretation therefore mirrors in simpler form the style and compositional techniques of the dream description itself.

The realization of the dream is not necessarily to be found in what immediately follows, for it is precisely through it that the dream account is integrated into the rest of the story. It is not characterized by any specific stylistic form, since it is entirely one with the narration. From a strictly formal point of view, the realization of predicted events does not belong to the dream account itself but constitutes an echo of the dream in the story that follows, giving it purpose. Consequently, this part of the narration is fashioned more by different narrative techniques than by a specific literary form: the realization of the dream and the imminent or distant consequences that they involve allow the narration to continue.

In counterpoint to source criticism, form criticism brings to light several components in the Joseph story, namely two different types of narrative, one slotting into the other: a family saga concerning Joseph and his brothers, and within it a story with political connotations concerning Joseph's rise to the highest level in the state (chs. 39–41). This story corresponds to a type of popular tale in which a young slave, endowed with the utmost discretion and great wisdom, and unjustly punished, reaches the summit of power. One of the characteristics of this kind of tale is that the hero undergoes a test, constituted here by the enigma set forth by the king (ch. 41), and that the young man of humble origins is exalted in reward for the solution he manages to find.

In spite of the complex redactional history of the Joseph story, it is unlikely that chs. 39–41 ever constituted an autonomous narration. Indeed, numerous indices suggest that ch. 39 is a rather late addition. On the other hand, chs. 40–41 appear to be a narrative unity in which the dreams and their interpretation have a key role, that of providing the test that permits Joseph to pass from an initial humble to a final, elevated situation. Full use is made here of a narrative motif belonging to the literature of folktales. The function of these chapters, however, goes well beyond this.

Several features draw attention to the realism with which this interpretative situation is evoked, as well as to its theological value. Of the two Egyptian officers on the morning after their dreams, it is said that Joseph found them 'downcast' (Gen. 40.6: *zo'ᵃpîm*); so downcast that their desolation finds expression on their faces, the explanation being their inability to find anyone to interpret their dreams (40.8). Similarly, after his two successive dreams, Pharaoh wakes up in the morning 'and his spirit was troubled' (41.8: *wattippā'em rûḥô*). Nebuchadnezzar is said to suffer from a similar state of anxiety after his dream; the same root *p'm* is used (Dan. 2.1, 3). The only possible explanation for this anxiety on awakening lies in contemporary interpretative practices, such as those evident in Mesopotamia. There, whatever the contents of the dream, its interpretation takes on the characteristics of a genuine exorcism, freeing the dreamer from the power that his dreams have upon him so long as they have not been recounted and explained. The texts refer to this precise psychological situation.

Moreover, the reduplication of Pharaoh's dream (ch. 41) is not simply a narrative motif or a rhetorical technique, but has its origin in the traditional experience of oneirocriticism. Indeed the text states this clearly, using Joseph as mouthpiece: the two dreams are actually only one (Gen. 41.25), and their repetition is proof of their undoubted oracular value (41.32). To use reduplication as the criteria for authentificating the truth of a dream is attested, parsimoniously, but consistently, from the Mari letters onwards up until the Roman period (Wikenhauser 1948). As regards Gen. 41.32, the Talmud cites the commentary of R. Johanan (*Ber.* 55b): 'Three (kinds of) dreams are realised: a morning dream, a dream a man had about his friend, and a dream which was interpreted within a dream. Some say also a dream which came for a second time, as they say... (Gen. 41.32).' The situations evoked in Genesis 40–41 therefore refer to a well-known reality, to which we will return when we consider interpretative practices.

Finally, by means of their narrative function and thanks to reference to an oneirocritical practice thought to be known to the reader, certain theological considerations relative to dreams in general are developed. As has often been noted, one of the characteristics of allegorical dream accounts in the Bible is the emphasis upon the role of the interpreter. Corresponding to this emphasis is the abundant use—unique in the Old Testament—of the root *ptr* in these chapters. It appears in verbal or nominal form seven times in ch. 40 and again seven times in ch. 41, a detail that underlines the importance accorded to the role of the *potēr* in these accounts. The latter, here Joseph, takes his theological significance from his relationship, both with the official diviners whom he surpasses on the one hand and with the message contained in the dreams on the other.

In Gen. 41.8, the list of specialists consulted by Pharaoh to interpret his dreams is summarized by the expression *kol ḥarṭummê miṣrayim w*^{e}*'et kol ḥ*^{a}*kāmêāh*. In v. 24, *ḥarṭummîm* alone is enough to denote all the dream specialists. Apart from a few passages in the book of Daniel, which we will look at later, the term is to be found only in the priestly account of the plagues of Egypt (Exod. 7.11, 22; 8.3, 14, 15; 9.11). The word *ḥarṭom* is thought to be a transcription of the second element of the Egyptian title *ḫerî-ḥeb ḫerî-tep*, 'chief reader priest'; designating a specialist in liturgical books and ancient mumbo jumbo, he became synonymous with 'magician 'or 'diviner' (see p. 65 above). Noteworthy throughout this chapter, in contrast to the priestly account of the plagues of Egypt, is the discretion of the Egyptian diviners; mentioned on two brief occasions as incapable of interpreting dreams (41.8, 24), they fade away without resistance or trace before the young Hebrew who is rescued from his jail.

God grants the interpretation (Gen. 40.8; 41.16, 38), for he is also and most importantly the source of the coded message: 'God has revealed to Pharaoh what he is about to do' (41.25b: *'ᵃšer ha'ᵉlohîm 'ōśeh higgîd lᵉpar'ōh*). The same expression is to be found in v. 28b where the verb *ngd* (hiphil) is replaced by *r'h* (hiphil). This insistence on the fact that God alone is capable of announcing (*ngd* hiphil) future events is characteristic of Deutero–Isaiah;[1] it implies that he alone guides these events, and those well beyond the history of Israel, as is the case in the story of Joseph. The oneiric message (dream + interpretation) is therefore here accorded the same value as that of prophecy as it is understood from the end of the exile onwards. It is at this period that the composition of Genesis 40–41 should be situated.

In the three dreams interpreted by Joseph, numerical references are characteristically interpreted in terms of time: three days, seven years. Why the number should in one case refer to days and in another to years, depends, it seems, solely on the decision of the author. It has been argued that Pharaoh's dream possibly refers to an Egyptian written form from the Ptolemaic period in which the word 'year' is represented by a cow. The association of a cow with a year is not attested any earlier, however, and remains very rare. The interpretation of numbers is the only element that gives the illusion of an even slightly rational approach to the elucidation of the dream. Undoubtedly, the reference here is to oneirocritical practices.

As for the significance of the images, once the numbers are translated, the allegory is fairly obvious, at least in its general lines. The interpretation of the officers' dreams (ch. 40) depends in part upon the opposition between the responsibilities that their respective functions impose on them and the manner in which they are carried out in the dream. As regards Pharaoh's dreams, scholars have looked to Egyptian figurative representations, and in particular to the seven cows in procession, which, according to ch. 148 in the *Book of the Dead*, are the celestial providers for the deceased. Vergote (1959: 52-65) has pointed out the fragility of this connection and prefers the hypothesis of Heyes who claims that the image of the cow is an allusion to the fertilizing power of the floodwaters of the Nile. According to him, a cow called

1. See Isa. 41.21-26; 43.9-12; 44.7-8; 45.21; 46.10; 48.5.

mehet uret, 'the great flood', the personification of the primordial deep in which the Nile has its source and identified with Hathor the celestial cow, was the object of veneration.

This erudite hypothesis seems a little far-fetched, and it may well be that the author, assuming a general knowledge of Egyptian culture on the part of his readers, simply intended a play on words based on the homophonic possibilities of the root *parah,* evoking both 'cow' and 'to be fertile'. There are numerous examples of this procedure in *dream books*. As for the general theme of seven years of famine, it has been associated with the *Famine stela* found near the first cataract (see p. 63). In it, the god Khnum appears in a dream to the Pharaoh (Djoser, 3rd Dynasty) to announce the return of the Nile floodwaters after seven years of drought. But the inscription is apocryphal and in reality dates from the second century BCE. The figure seven is widely used in the Near East of the cycles that characterize agricultural fertility: sabbatical years, the cycle of seven years in which Baal and Mot struggle with each other at Ugarit (*KTU* 1.6 v), for example (Gordon 1953).

2. *Joseph's Dreams: Genesis 37*

If one considers biblical accounts of allegorical dreams as a whole, those recounted in Genesis 37, 40–41 and Judges 7 display a genuine similarity as regards syntactical and literary form but also significant differences. The literary form of these accounts, such as we have seen in Genesis 40–4l, includes a report of the interpretation of the dream, the latter lying symmetrical to the description of the dream itself. But while the interpretation of the dreams is minutely recorded in the narratives of Genesis 40–41, according to the schema outlined above and with a precise theological goal in mind, this schema is only loosely adhered to in Judg. 7.13-15 and is entirely absent from the accounts of Genesis 37. The syntax, too, in Joseph's dreams is freer than in the dreams of Genesis 40–41 where the style is fairly rigorous. This is particularly true of the first of Joseph's dreams (37.5-8) which is more developed than the second (37.9-11). The dream account (v. 7) does indeed begin with a nominal clause introduced by *hinnōh*, describing the principal picture in the dream. The two subsequent actions, however, are described using verbal clauses, also introduced by *hinnēh*: the first (v. 7aβ) with two *qatal* forms, the second (v. 7bα) with a *yiqtol* form, expressing duration in the past.

There are also some significant variants in the introductory formula of these allegorical dreams recounted in the first person. Whereas in the Egyptians' dreams (Gen. 40–41) the construction is always of the type *wayyō'mer lô baḥ^a^lmî w^e^hinnēh* (40.9b, 16b; 41.17a), the exposition of Joseph's dreams always begins with the verbal form *ḥālamtî* followed by *w^e^hinnēh* (37.6b, 7aα, 9b), as in that of the Midianite soldier in Judg. 7.13b. There is indeed a remarkable similarity of expression between Gen. 37.9b (*wayyō'mer hinnēh ḥālamtî ḥ^a^lôm 'ôd w^e^hinneh…*) and Judg. 7.13b (*wayyō'mer hinnēh ḥ^a^lôm ḥālamtî w^e^hinnēh…*).

Joseph's dreams (Gen. 37) thus appear much closer to the Judges 7 narrative than to those of Genesis 40–41, as much on account of the style as by reason of the absence of any mention of the practice of dream interpretation. This allows us to envisage the possibility that, contrary to the long-held presuppositions of the documentary theory, the dream narratives of the Joseph story do not necessarily all belong to the same redactional source. When we come to look at dreams in wisdom circles, we will discover indications that perhaps suggest that Genesis 40–41 should be attributed to a fairly late rereading. By contrast, Joseph's dreams in Genesis 37 cannot be dissociated from the weft of the original narrative.

If the Egyptians' dreams in Genesis 40–41 serve to illustrate a theological point, namely the divine origin of certain oneiric revelations, in so far as the dreams are associated directly with the inspired interpretation given them, their narrative function in the story of the ascension of Joseph is rather different from that of Joseph's dreams in Genesis 37. Following Gunkel, commentators have all remarked upon the two folk motifs that give the story its basic movement: the youngest brother, who is naïve but shrewd, who ends up overtaking his elder brothers; the initial prophecy that indicates more or less clearly from the beginning what the result of the story will be. In both of Joseph's dreams, it is the general outline of the plot that is set forth: the dreams not only contribute to the animosity of the brothers towards their youngest member, but above all announce the resolution of the crisis. They thus play a central functional role in the narrative.

This structuring function of the dreams is confirmed by the recurrent use of the verbal form *hištaḥ^a^weh*, 'to bow down'. We meet it six times in all: three at the beginning of the dream accounts (37.7b, 9b) and in Jacob's retort (37.10b); and three times once the dreams are fulfilled, at each of Joseph's two interviews with his brothers (42.6b; 43.26b, 28b).

The inclusion is obvious. It is underlined further by the precision made in 42.9a, 'and Joseph remembered the dreams which he had dreamed'. The reduplication of elements in the narrative is now recognized to be a compositional technique characteristic of the work, rather than to be the sign of different literary sources. If we continue along these lines, the contents of the two dreams may offer another way of anticipating future events. It is possible to see in the dream of sheaves the foreshadowing of the reason for the journeys undertaken by Jacob's sons in Egypt, and in the motifs of the stars, of the sun and moon paying homage to the dreamer, an even more explicit prediction of Joseph's future political authority over his entire family.

Although these dreams are usually classified as symbolic dreams, the fact that they are not followed by an account of their interpretation distinguishes them from other dreams of this type. Indeed, when compared with the dreams of Genesis 40–41, the difference is even more subtle and perhaps also more radical. The text does actually offer us a clear explanation of the oneiric images, first in the form of the reaction of the brothers (37.8a) and secondly in the reaction of Jacob (37.10b). However, the ease with which the narrative includes the interpretation, which is not announced as such, suggests that the meaning of the dreams was obvious to those to whom Joseph recounted them. Was it so obvious to him, one might ask? It seems not, for the naivety with which he recounts them to his entourage suggests that he did not grasp their significance. The phrase we quoted above, 'and Joseph remembered the dreams which he had dreamed' (Gen. 42.9a), would suggest that he only understood them at this point of the story.

The absence of an interpretative phase in the economy of the dream account fulfils a precise narrative function here: to underline the naivety of the youngest brother as he confronts his kin. Scandalized, they understand only too well what his dreams announce. Similarly and inversely, the emphasis placed on the interpretative phase in the narratives of Genesis 40–41 has an equally precise function: to highlight the fact that dream interpretation is a special charism, a prophetic act inspired by God, by contrast with the methods of diviners. The presence or absence of interpretation, therefore, is not just a question of literary form, a form that may be more or less complete, but relates directly, in these precise cases, to the significance and function of the dream narratives.

To take the comparison a stage further, it is noteworthy that, contrary to the narratives of Genesis 40–41, in which the divine origin both of the dream and its interpretation is affirmed, in Genesis 37 there is no allusion to any kind of divine intervention in Joseph's dreams. This is simply further evidence of the existence of different narrative perspectives, perhaps of distinct redactional layers, but also, as regards Genesis 37, of a greater proximity to the original folk motif. Nothing tells us where Joseph's dreams come from. Indeed the narrator does not seem to be interested in the question.

Here we touch upon a point that obliges us to nuance the rather simplistic dream aetiology elaborated in the Hellenistic period (see p. 102). Between dreams of natural origin, assimilated with lies and illusion, and grandiose dreams sent by God, there are others whose origin tradition has never bothered to define yet which are 'real' in so far as they predict the future. Here, we are in the realm of tale and legend, where it is not appropriate to seek to define with any precision the frontier between the human and divine. Whilst they fulfil the role of an 'initial prophecy', these dreams remain very close to ordinary dream experience, and they are more readily classified as *premonitory* than as allegorical dreams.

However, over and above its narrative function, the prophecy concerning Joseph's domination of his brothers, brings us to the political dimension of the tale as a whole. There is no doubt that by means of this tale—whatever wisdom or theological themes might also be noted—certain political questions are addressed, even though it is difficult for us to define what the aim might be: defence or criticism of the Davidico-Solomonian monarchy? an apology for the monarchy of Jeroboam I? a model for the Jews involved in functions of state in the diaspora? Theories vary according to the dates and origin attributed to the different redactional layers.

Even more so than with the dreams of Genesis 40–41, the rare commentaries concerned with the oneiric images of Genesis 37 and their symbolism do not go beyond very general considerations. Typical, is the opinion of von Rad (1985: 331), according to whom the dreams, which always appear in pairs in the Joseph story, contain no profound, possibly mythological symbolism or anything of the sort. They must be considered just as they are, and they say neither more or less than what is openly expressed in them; they are quite simple, pictorial prefigurations of coming events and conditions. Scholars content themselves with noting references to the patriarchal structure of society or to an agro-pastoral economy in the contents of the dreams, principally in the first. In so far as their significance is apparently obvious and easily grasped, more time is spent on the terms of interpretation than on the symbolism of the images.

It has been suggested that the eleven stars in Joseph's second dream—Joseph being implicitly the twelfth—allude to the signs of the zodiac, attested since about 700 BCE in Babylon (see van der Waerden 1953). But in spite of several attempts in this direction, it is actually doubtful that this dream draws on a kind of *koinè* of astral mythological language current among Semitic peoples. Rather than look for any such mythological correspondences, more relevant here is Ps. 148.1-3, where the same circle of heavenly bodies celebrates the king of heaven. It is not without significance that we find the same sequence of sun–moon–stars here, for the usual order of precedence in Mesopotamian mythology is Sin–Šamaš–Ištar–the other stars, in accordance with a model of kinship that makes the Sun and Venus the children of the moon god. The idea that the sun and moon might be father and mother of the stars, as the interpretation of the dream proposes, is foreign to all the old mythological systems of the Near East, and all the more so to the western Semites for whom Šamaš is a feminine divinity and Yariḫ, the moon, a masculine divinity.

Independent of the political question and the search for mythological references, Gibert (1990: 43-47) has shown that the symbolism of these dreams is rich enough to ably reflect the principal components at work in dreams according to Freudian analysis. 'The dream is not exclusively the invention of the narrative, but is well respected as such. It is simply underexploited on account of the fact that the final source of interest of the story lies elsewhere. This means that it can neither be totally artificial nor a literary genre specially designed to suit the needs of the narrative' (Gibert 1990: 62).

As for the dream about the sheaves, 'one can easily detect a complex implying the very strong desire, not only to be recognised by his numerous older brothers, but also to dominate them. Consequently, "the dream" is really "the (disguised) fulfillment of a (supressed or frustrated) wish" (Freud)' (Gibert 1990: 44).

Gibert clarifies the symbolic dimension of the sheaves, and above all of the gesture of binding them, which, from a Freudian perspective, signifies the mastery of an element of food and of fertility. As for Joseph's sheaf, which rises in such a way as to suggest male erection, 'the reference is to Joseph's power, symbolised by his virility which is open to challenge both by virtue of his position among his siblings, and by his age. On the other hand, the other sheaves are "prostrate" and so appear "impotent"... His brothers are thus deprived of their virility. The latter are not duped, for they interpret the dream in terms of sovereignty and power' (Gibert 1990: 45).

As stated above, this psychoanalytical reading is legitimate only in so far as we recognize that the author has talent enough to recreate in his writing, by means of style, images, and what is left unsaid, a dream account in which *the reader* recognizes intuitively all that makes up the work of the unconscious in dreams, a process that includes condensation and symbolic deplacement. On this condition, the attempt at interpretation summarized here, far from being reductionist, contributes towards our appreciation of the techniques of literary composition.

3. *The Dream of the Midianite Soldier: Judges 7.13-15*

As pointed out above, the formula introducing the dream of the Midianite soldier (Judg. 7.13b) resembles the formula used to introduce Joseph's dreams in Genesis 37, particularly the second (Gen. 37.9b): *wayyō'mer hinnēh ḥ*[a]*lôm ḥālamtî w*[e]*hinnēh...* Over and above this stylistic detail, several analogies make this dream and those of Joseph comparable: the lack of any reference to an institutionalized practice of dream interpretation, a dream account using symbolic language that is immediately intelligible to the listener and above all the absence of any explicit mention of divine intervention, both as regards the dream itself and its interpretation. Like Joseph's dreams, the dream of the Midianite soldier is more readily termed a *premonitory dream* than an allegorical dream, by reason of the lack of any supernatural aspect to the dream, and on account of its interpretation, which is neither particularly learned nor inspired.

These dream accounts are therefore different from those of Genesis 40–41 in all these respects. Dream interpretation is, however, not absent from this chapter of Judges, but it differs markedly from the form and contents of the schema defined in Genesis 40–41. The essential element in the dream is indeed rendered by a nominal clause (v. 14a). The latter does not re-employ the terms used to describe the oneiric images, however, but rather simply summarizes them using the pronoun *zôt*. Moreover, if the repetitive use of the root *ptr* as regards the interpretation of Joseph's dreams underlines the significance of the term, it is totally absent here. On the contrary, an entirely unexpected term appears in v. 15: 'When Gideon heard the telling of the dream and its interpretation [*'et mispar haḥ^{a}lôm w^{e}'et šibrô*], he worshipped.' The word *šeber*, 'fracture, break, breakdown', appears only in this passage in the derived sense of 'solution, explanation', and does not seem to belong to the specific terminology of the science of dream interpretation.

There is absolutely no question of such a science here: Gideon overhears a conversation between two soldiers belonging to the Midianite camp, neither of which is presented as a specialist in oneiromancy. The narrator gives no indication whatsoever as to what motivates the soldier who recounts his dream; we do not know if he himself understood it—a possibility that does not detract in any way from the logic of the account—or if he recounts it in the hope that his companion will be able to explain it to him. The dialogue is composed in such a way as to give the impression of a very natural conversation between interlocutors who are unaware of the oracular value that the dialogue holds for Gideon, who overhears them. The meaning of the dream is immediately clear to his companion, in the same way that Joseph's brothers and father understand his dreams.

The literary function of this dream account appears to be as complex as the redactional history of the entire Gideon cycle. The text in its final state should be read in the context of vv. 9-11a, which makes it into an implicit war oracle. Indeed, its role is to authenticate the word of Yahweh previously received directly by Gideon (v. 9) by reiterating the same message in the form of an allegory. The narrative context implies that the dream was effectively sent by Yahweh, and on this account it may be described as a *prophetic dream*. Moreover, the two Midianites each contribute to the expression of the oracle, and the one who interprets the message contained in the images is also supposed, to some degree, to be inspired.

The above, however, is a 'Yahwization' of a narrative that originally only mentioned Gideon's spying expedition in preparation for an attack on the Midian camp. In vv. 9-11a, there are traces of a rereading designed to transform the old traditions transmitted by the *Saviours' Book* into narratives about a holy war (Richter 1966). In the original text, however, the *premonitory dream*, provoked by the anxiety of a soldier before battle, was received as a favourable presage by Gideon and his companion Poura. As already stated, the early narrative does not seek to emphasize the supernatural character of the event, nor does it explain the origin of the dream, which is viewed from a popular, non theological perspective, close to that of Egyptian or Mesopotamian dreams books.

As for the explicatory principle that permits the interpretation of the dream, it seems fairly straightforward for, of all the images mentioned, only that of the tumbling cake of barley bread is treated as an allegory. The barley bread has been interpreted as a symbol of the sedentary lifestyle of the Israelites by contrast with the Midianites, whose nomadic way of life is represented by a tent; this reading, however, does not take into account the fact that according to the interpretation offered by the text, the camp, the tent and its destruction are not symbols but are understood literally.

It is more likely that the interpretation of the dream depends on a play on words using the root *lḥm*, which gives *leḥem*, 'solid food, bread', *nilḥam*, 'to fight', *milḥamāh*, 'battle, war', and derivatives of the qal: *loḥēm*, 'fighter, warrior'. Thus a tumbling barley bread may readily evoke a fight or a combatant turning like a sword (cf. Gen. 3.24) in the camp. This principle of interpretation was widespread, as is attested in a good number of dream books. Here is an example from the Chester Beatty III papyrus (18th–19th Dynasty): 'If, in a dream, a man sees himself looking into a well of deep water,—bad: he will be put in prison' (recto 8.5). The protasis puts forward the idea of drawing water (*'itḥ*), which in turn calls up the image of a prison (*'ith*) by virtue of homonymy.

4. *Nebuchadnezzar's Dreams: Daniel 2 and 4*

It has long been usual to see in these narratives, and especially in Daniel 2, haggadic developments of Genesis 41. In fact, if one cannot exactly define them as *midrašîm*, everyone agrees that there are numerous parallels between these narratives and the Joseph story. They are well known and concern just as much the general layout as a number of details: the dreamer's disarray on account of the dream (we find the verb *p'm* both in Gen. 41.8 and Dan. 2.1), the affirmation that it is God who reveals to the king what will happen (Gen. 41.16; Dan. 2.28), the king's acknowledgment that the interpreter is inspired by God (Gen. 41.38; Dan. 2.47), the exaltation of the interpreter at the end of the narrative (Gen. 41.40-45; Dan. 2.48-49). Moreover, they have in common the title *ḥarṭummîm*, of Egyptian origin, denoting a group of specialists at the court of Nebuchadnezzar (Dan. 2.2). Also, the root *ptr*, used exclusively in Genesis 40–41 to denote dream interpretation, reappears in the Aramaic narratives of Daniel 2; 4; 5; 7 under the guise of *pšr*. There are no less than twelve occurrences of the noun in ch. 2. In each case they are the complimentary object of the verbs *yd'* (haph.): vv. 5, 25, 26, 30, or *ḥwh* (poel or haph.) : vv. 4, 6, 7, 9, 16, 24, 26).

Daniel 2 is not just a carbon copy of Genesis 41, however; once the parallels have been acknowledged and the dependence of Daniel 2 upon Genesis 41 recognized, the differences appear all the more significant. These all tend towards an emphatic overstatement and dramatization of elements in the narrative in the manner of a popular tale, but they are also the result of an apocalyptic rereading of haggadic tales: the febrile impatience of the king (vv. 1b-3), his exorbitant demand to be told the contents of his dreams before their interpretation (vv. 5-6, 9-10, 26), the death threat with which he threatens all the wise men of Babylon (vv. 55b, 12-13), the dramatic confrontation between the king and the wise men (vv. 2-12), the prayer of Daniel and his companions that they might learn the solution to the enigma from God (vv. 17-23) the insistence upon the incapacity of human knowledge to fathom the mysteries of God (19.21b–22.28).

Returning to the analogies between the two texts, it is interesting to try to discover what in the narrative of Genesis 41 could have led to these developments. Nebuchadnezzar's dream is indeed a royal dream comparable to that of Pharaoh. Where it differs is in the significance of the dream that, in Daniel 2, extends far beyond the fate of the kingdom. Essentially, what the reader retains is a revelation about the course of history in general and about God's intervention in the near future. This is a characteristic of apocalyptic literature still foreign to the text of Genesis 41 and no doubt also to the first redaction of the Aramaic narratives. The idea that God, by means of a dream, informs the king 'as to what he is going to do' (Gen. 41.25, 28), is nevertheless the very same idea that we find once more in Dan. 2.29, 45b. Here, it contributes to the composition of a narrative in which the theological dimension is henceforth preponderant. The oracular dimension of the dream, which had above all a literary function in Genesis 41, fulfils an indispensable theological role here: it is upon it that will depend the prophecy that now constitutes the essential motif in the narrative. Several rereadings, to which we are alerted by the addition of a number of verses (vv. 14-23, 28b, 41-43), give the text its present eschatological and apocalyptic dimension. In it, the function of both the dream and of the night vision is even more decisive.

By means of transposition (Nebuchadnezzar being identified with Nabonidus), Daniel 4 refers back to the apocryphal legends concerning Nabonidus, the last sovereign of Babylon, who precisely got a name for himself thanks to his dreams. In this narrative, the dream does not have the eschatological character of the precedent, but transmits a prophecy that far exceeds the personal destiny of the king. In spite of its importance, neither does it have a central role in the story as a whole, whose thread keeps faith with the legend about the mad king. Its function seems several fold; it once more creates the opportunity to oppose Daniel's inspired wisdom with that of 'all the wise men of Babylon'; it allows the author to proclaim no less than five times an oracle that contains the central idea in the narrative, namely God's mastery over the destiny of kings; finally, it permits the introduction of metaphorical and symbolic language that amplifies considerably the discursive possibilities of the narrative.

In Daniel 2 and 4, it is the contents of the dreams that undergo a development entirely new in Israel. The literary composition seems no longer to be concerned with recreating in any way the ordinary experience of dreams; the rich, highly elaborate symbolism, with mythological and quasi-universal overtones makes the reader forget the dreamer and his situation and instead highlights a message that one expects to be all the more true for the mysteriousness of its language. It is not worth reproducing here the abundantly documented commentaries concerning the origin of the representations and symbols present in these two dreams. The diversity of these references, drawing on Greek, Persian, Mesopotamian and biblical mythology and historiography and the subtlety with which they blend and combine, speaks eloquently of the art and erudition of their authors. What holds our attention is the consistency with which dreams serve as the literary context for scenes that evoke a mythical narrative, a prophetic vision, or a wakeful dream rather than a hypnic dream strictly speaking.

This apparent confusion between dreams and visions is characteristic of apocalyptic literature. The book of Daniel, due to the particularity of its compostion, is no doubt the best example of the progressive assimilation of dreams with prophetic visions. For if, in the tales (chs. 2 and

4), the dream fiction is still relatively faithful to the conventions of the genre by virtue of the distinction that is maintained between the oneiric experience and the interpretative discourse on the following day, the situation changes as soon as the Aramaic book is constituted. In Dan. 7.1, the 'night vision' is indeed presented as a dream that Daniel had actually had. Its interpretation, however, is integrated into a visionary experience corresponding to classical accounts of visions of this kind. Henceforth no further mention is made of dreams.

A clue in the vocabulary demonstrates clearly that, in spite of the dream fiction maintained in Daniel 2 and 4, it is to the visionary experience of the prophets that the author refers in his writing. Each of these dreams is composed of two parts: (1) a description of the main picture (the statue/the great tree), (2) external intervention that transforms the object of the vision (the stone which shatters the statue/the Watcher who delivers his sentence). Each part is introduced by the formula, 'You/I looked, and behold...' (*ḥāzēh h*^{a}*way*^{e}*tā wa'*^{a}*lû*, 2.31; 4.7, 10). The second part of the first dream has a slight variant: 'As you looked...' (*ḥāzeh h*^{a}*way*^{e}*tā 'ad dî*, 2, 34). The expression is henceforth very common, with variants, in the visions of ch. 7; 8; 10–12; it is the equivalent of the formula introducing the visions of Proto-Zechariah: *rā'îtî/wā'ēre' w*^{e}*hinnēh* (Zach: 1.8a; 2.1, 5; 4.2b; 5.1, 9; 6.1). But if the verb 'to see' (*r'h* or *ḥzh*) is frequently used in the accounts of visions, it is not normally used in dream accounts. There are two exceptions: Gen. 41.22 (*wā'ēre' baḥ*^{a}*lôm w*^{e}*hinnēh*), Pharaoh's second dream, and Gen. 31.10 (*wā'ēre' baḥ*^{a}*lôm w*^{e}*hinnēh*), which can only be explained in terms of the influence the language of prophetic visions must have had upon the redactors. This seems certain as regards Gen. 31.10 (see pp. 135-38).

Even if these dreams are composed according to the pattern of visions, one detail shows that, conceptually, dreams and visions are nevertheless still distinguishable. It seems certain that, in ch. 2, vv. 14-23 are a redactional addition, probably attributable to the author of ch. 7. Though these verses accord well with the narrative, they accentuate its apocalyptic dimension, with the reminder that it is God who is the master of history (v. 21a), who grants wisdom (vv. 21b-23), who reveals what is hidden (v. 22). According to the logic of the author of this text, however, the mystery can only be revealed 'in a night vision' (v. 19, *b*^{e}*ḥezwā' dî lêlyā' rāzāh g*^{a}*lî*). Here we have, therefore, not a *dream,* but a '*vision* in the night'; the author seems deliberately to underline the difference between these two modes of revelation: the first requires interpretation, the second is the place where the key to the mystery is given (even if an angel must intervene to interpret).

The persistence of the literary dream fiction in the Aramaic narratives of Daniel, in spite of an orientation in thinking that differs henceforth, may be explained in two ways: (1) a conservative adherence to the models that served as a starting point for the tales; (2) the advantage to be gained from retaining the interpretative phase and general divinatory context, in order to underline the difference between the king's dream and Daniel's inspired knowledge, and in order to discredit the pagan knowledge of diviners. Echoes of a long-standing polemic…

The fact that the vision of Daniel 7 was presented as a dream is characteristic of the pivotal position of this chapter between the tales and the apocalyptic part. Mention is made of a dream only as a means of transition, since the text henceforth has all the stylistic traits and layout of a vision. However, this way of going about things is not just a redactional device, for the assimilation of dreams with visions reappears entirely systematically in the fourth section of *1 Enoch* (cf. 83.1-7; 85.1–90.40). It seems that, in the apocalyptic writings, the apologetic concern to distinguish the pagans' dreams from the inspired visions of loyal Jews was no longer relevant.

Chapter 8

MESSAGE-DREAMS

1. *Dream and Theophany*

As explained in the introduction, the primary characteristic of message-dreams is that they are above all auditory: the message they transmit is expressed in words rather than in images and these words are clear, intelligible from the outset and require no interpretation. Dreams of this type, however, may occasionally include a visual element, which is not explicitly symbolic, as in Gen. 31.10-13, or indeed a veritable theophany, as in Gen. 28.12-13a. Literary criticism must establish in each case whether this formal 'anomaly' results from the redactional process or not. As for the auditory element, it appears in diverse forms: as an oracle (Gen. 31.12b-13), a promise (Gen. 28.13-15) or a dialogue (Gen. 20.3-7; 1 Kgs 3.4-15).

Consequently, in this type of dream, *ḥ^{a}lôm* designates less a form of perception than a state, a 'place' in which God or an angel intervenes. Thus, 'in a dream', *baḥ^{a}lôm*, Yahweh/Elohim/the angel of God…

'comes' *(bw')*:	Gen. 20.3; 31.24; [Num. 22.9, 20; 1 Sam. 3.10],
'appears' *(nr'h)*:	1 Kgs 3.4; 9.2,
'stands' *(nṣb)*:	Gen. 28.13; 1 Sam. 3.10 *(htytṣb)*,
'terrifies' *(ḥtt)*:	Job 7.14; 33.16,
'speaks' *(dbr)*:	Num. 12.6,
'says' *('mr)*:	Gen. 20.6; 31.11; 28.13,
'reveals' *(glh)*:	Job 33.16,
'replies' *('nh)*:	1 Sam. 28.6.

An introductory formula is to be found no less than four times in the Pentateuch alone: 'And God came to N. in a dream by night' *(wayyābo' '^{e}lohîm 'el xx baḥ^{a}lôm hallāy^{e}lāh)*: Gen. 20.3; 31.24; Num. 22.9, 20 (*baḥ^{a}lôm* is missing in the two references in Numbers). This is a widespread literary commonplace, for the formula is found, word for word, in the Deïr 'Alla plaster inscription (see pp. 83-84).

We noted in the preceding paragraph the extent to which use of the verb 'see' is exceptional in symbolic dream accounts (it is attested only once, in Gen. 41). The same is true of hearing the divinity in a dream: use of the verb *šm'* is not attested even once. The sobriety of these oneiric meetings with the divinity brings the biblical accounts closer to the archaic Greek model than to the Mesopotamian one, in which there are often impressive descriptions of the apparition of gods in dreams. In general, 'the coming' of God in a dream is not accompanied by any particular manifestation; neither is it the occasion for any description of God or of any of his attributes. Here, we are far from the spectacular aspect of ordinary theophanies, for God comes in dreams most discretely. Jacob's dream (Genesis 28) appears to be an exception to this rule, but the vision that characterizes it is perhaps a late addition.

This being so, we should be careful about using the term *theophany*, for, contrary to the standard definition of the phenomenon, oneiric manifestations of God are in this context not accompanied by visual images. The recurrent use of verbs like 'to come' *(bw')*, 'to stand beside' *(nṣb, htyṣb)*, 'to appear' *(nr'h)*, seems to describe not so much a visual perception as the sensation of a presence, or a sense of the nearness of the divinity. An oneiric theophany, in the Old Testament, is a *theophany without vision* of God.

2. *Solomon's Dream: 1 Kings 3*

In all the Bible, Solomon's dream at Gibeon (1 Kgs 3.4-15) is the one that resembles most closely other message-dreams recounted in the various literary traditions of the ancient Near East. It does so by virtue of the circumstances described, the contents of the dream and the involvement of the king. On the other hand, as we have just said, and in accordance with the absence of any anthropomorphic representation of the divinity, the oneiric 'theophany' is alluded to only rapidly in an introductory formula in which there is no descriptive detail whatsoever: 'At Gibeon the Lord *appeared* to Solomon in a dream by night' (v. 5: *b^{e}gib^{e}'ôn nir'āh yhwh 'el š^{e}lōmoh baḥ^{a}lôm hallāy^{e}lāh*).

Some scholars[1] argue that this introductory narrative to the story of Solomon imitates the Egyptian *Königsnovelle*, a literary genre identified in 20 or so royal inscriptions as early as the Middle Empire (Hermann

1. The first to propose this definition of the literary genre was Hermann 1953–54.

1938). This genre, in its varied forms, is generally composed of a narrative in which the Pharaoh or his officers are presented in circumstances favourable to the celebration of a memorable deed, of which he or they are the instigators: a military campaign, a cultic foundation, etc. The parallel with 1 Kings 3 rests, in particular, upon a comparison between Solomon's dream and that of Thutmosis IV, asleep in the shade of the Sphinx at Gizeh. Apart from the fact that in each case it is a royal dream, the comparison does not in fact appear to be pertinent as regards the details of the constituent elements of the two narratives. The respective function and significance of these two texts are too different: the youth of the king (at the beginning of his reign), or of the prince (before his reign), the reason and circumstances concerning sleep in a sacred place and the nature of the message received.

The parallelism with the Sphinx inscription has also been used by exponents of the cultic *hieros logos* theory to identify the literary genre of 1 Kgs 3.4-15. In Thutmosis IV's dream, the god enjoins the young prince to disengage the Sphinx from the sands that cover him, just as Gudea at Lagash (cylinders A and B) and Nabonidus at Harran were ordered, also in a dream, to build or to restore a sanctuary. The revelation, mediated by means of oracles or visions, of the plan of a sanctuary at its foundation is a commonly found literary *topos*. Supposing, therefore, the existence of an early text now lost to us, Solomon would have received in a dream at Gibeon, in the same manner as Gudea, the instructions necessary for the construction of the temple in Jerusalem.

Apart from the thorny question of trying to define the literary genre of a text on the basis of contents different from those that exist in the present text, this hypothesis fails to notice what is particular about this text. From the very beginning (v. 5b), the divine word determines the structure of the dialogue that follows: 'Ask what I shall give you!' The body of the dream is thereafter divided into two equal parts, corresponding to the two parts of the dialogue already begun: the king's request (vv. 6-9) and God's gift (vv. 11-14). The text here uses a motif well known in folk tales, that of the wish, by means of which a divine being, a witch or fairy, offers to grant a human whatever he or she wants. We have already met this motif at Ugarit, in Keret's dream. There, El, anticipating the king's request, offers him divine kingship, gold, chariots and horses, while Keret in fact only wants a wife (*KTU* 1.14: i 38–ii 5). In each of these two cases, the folk tale motif is adapted to the specific context of the monarchy in the ancient Near East; in both, the tutelary divinity is willing not only to offer much more than that which the king asks, but things of a different order. This reveals the king's wisdom or his purity of heart, for which he will be rewarded.

Against this background, 1 Kings 3 in its present form develops a rhetoric whose style and contents have nothing folkloric about them, but which express a precise theological aim. It is not difficult to show the Deuteronomistic origin, if not of the entirety of the subjects dealt with (Yahweh's faithfulness to the Davidic dynasty, the king's relationship to the Torah, the general outline of a covenantal treaty), at least of their definitive formulation.[2] In spite of the attempts of many scholars to do so, it appears impossible to cut up the text in such a way as to distinguish elements belonging to a *Grundlage* from redactional additions attributed to the Deuteronomist. The well-balanced nature of the text as a whole, and the ease with which it runs, preclude this possibility: Deuteronomistic historians have entirely rewritten the text and it is to them that we owe its present formulation. The existence of a pre-Deuteronomistic document which served as the basis for the present text is, however, probable; a number of indications in the text point us in this direction:

1. The very presence of a dream, experienced outside Jerusalem in a 'high place' where the king probably used to go to make burned offerings. Not only does the interpolated clause in v. 2 show the degree to which this tradition was embarrassing for Deuteronomistic Temple theology, but, if the Deuteronomistic redactors had themselves composed this narrative, other sanctuaries more traditionally associated with Yahweh might have been chosen. Furthermore, Gibeon appears to have benefited from a political and cultic particularity in pre-monarchic traditions sufficient to make it suspect as a 'high place'.

2. The *Acts of Solomon* are mentioned in 1 Kgs 11.41 as a source of Deuteronomistic history. This is the same document that is reputed to have extolled the wisdom of the king. It seems fairly unlikely that the Deuteronomistic historian would have so explicitly associated the divine gift of wisdom with dreams, at a time when observance of the Torah had become the reference for wisdom (cf. Deut. 4.6). Moreover, for the Deuteronomist, Solomon could not be the wise king *par excellence*; by introducing into the dream, fidelity to the Torah as the condition upon which one might receive the fulness of wisdom, the Deuteronomistic

2. See among others Brekelmans (1982) and Kenik (1983).

redactor anticipates the negative judgment laid upon the king *in fine* (1 Kgs 11.9-13).

3. The basic structure of the oneiric dialogue reproduces an important element in royal Syro-Palestinian ideology: the king's freedom to have recourse to the monarchy's tutelary divinity/divinities, a specific adaptation of the popular motif of the free wish. This theme is attested in Ugarit in the above-mentioned passage of the *Keret Epic*. It is also found in the Panamu inscription at Zenjirli (*KAI* 214: 4), in which the binomial *š'l–ytn* recurs insistently. Von Rad (1958) has underlined its frequent appearance in coronation psalms (Ps. 2.8; 21.35; 20.5, 6) and it is generally agreed that it is an element of the enthronement liturgy.

If the request for gifts from the divinity did indeed belong to the royal liturgy, then the repeated affirmation of the effective granting of these gifts and their enumeration in written documents fulfil the obvious function of legitimation. This is particularly pertinent in the case of the Zinjirli inscription. There is no doubt at all that the *Acts of Solomon* served the needs of propaganda in just such a way, and that the dream report made its own contribution in a quite particular way. Situated at the beginning of the history of Solomon's reign, it confirms his legitimacy. In the present text, the king's legitimacy is defended from two different perspectives:

1. By referring, as we have just done, to the rite of enthronement and to the royal privilege of free recourse to the titulary god, reference to which is inscribed in the structure of the text itself.

2. By reminding the reader (v.6) of Yahweh's faithfulness to David (echoing the dynastic promise of 2 Samuel 7), and of the outcome of the succession crisis as it is presented by the Deuteronomistic redactor of 1 Kings 1–2. The theology and phraseology are clearly Deuteronomistic: it is the promise made to David, who 'walked before thee in faithfulness, in righteousness, and in uprightness of heart' (v. 6aβ) that assures Solomon's royalty, and no longer the direct and privileged relationship that the king enjoys with the divinity of the dynasty.

We can discern two distinct strata here, and might add that if the Deuteronomistic historian entirely rewrote the contents of the oneiric dialogue, he nevertheless respected its basic structure, articulated around the binomial expression *š'l–ntn*, a structure that retains the marks of another way of legitimating the reign of a king, namely that proposed by Syro-Canaanite ideology. It is therefore likely that it is to the pre-Deuteronomistic version of the dream that the concern with legitimacy goes back, for it is no longer the legitimacy of Solomon's reign as such that poses problems to the Deuteronomist. Rather, his concern is to rectify the theological argument upon which it is founded. Studies on the subject of the succession narrative show that opposition to Solomon's accession upon the throne of David was stronger and better organized than 1 Kings 1–2 would have us believe. Given that his kingship was likely to be contested, it was at the beginning of his reign that Solomon most needed to authenticate his right to rule. Indeed it is certain that a tradition such as that of the dream at Gibeon contributed greatly to the effort of spreading the necessary propaganda.

What we have here then, at this stage in Gibeonite tradition and in the redaction of the *Acts of Solomon*, is a piece of written propaganda that is not only characterized by themes specific to royal ideology but has recourse to a situation that of itself has power to legitimate: the royal dream. It is in his dream that the king enjoys the exceptional favour of being able to converse with the god who protects the dynasty. That a dream should be considered apt to authenticate the right to rule is all the more remarkable given that no one other than the dreamer can testify to it. For the modern mind, quick to spot any trace of fraud, this amounts to a surprising form of self-legitimation. But if this instrument of propaganda works well, the incongruity of the procedure being apparent only to the modern critic, it is because the facts related are normally and habitually associated with the monarchy.

The legitimizing function of royal dream accounts is well-documented in the Ancient Near East: we have seen how they function at Ugarit in the *Keret Epic*, among the Hittites, where the autobiographical inscriptions of King Hattusili III relate a quite exceptional number of dreams, and finally in Mesopotamia, where the only dream reports that exist in the royal neo-Babylonian inscriptions date from the time of the usurper Nabonidus, whose reign was also contested. We will come back later (Chapter 11) to the much-debated question of incubation as regards this text.

3. *Jacob's Dream at Bethel: Genesis 28*

In terms of the accepted classification of dream reports, that of Gen. 28.10-22 appears entirely atypical, displaying elements from one category and then the other without really belonging to either of them. Verses 13-15 correspond in every respect to the typology of message-dreams, but the vision described in v. 12 does not correspond to that of ordinary symbolic dreams, except in its formulation where it picks up the construction *hinnēh* + nominal clause. Source criticism has long sought to disengage two distinct narrative lines from the present text, narrative lines corresponding to the J and E documents of the Pentateuch. According to this perspective, the vision (vv. 11-12), Jacob's fear upon awakening (v. 17), the erection of the stela (v. 18) and the vow (vv. 20-22) were generally attributed to E, while the theophany (v. 13), the promise (vv. 14-15) and Jacob's awakening (v. 16) were associated with J. The analysis of documentary critics seems to solve the problem by discerning a visual dream in the Elohistic account and a typical message-dream in the Yahwistic version. However, most commentators have felt the need to add a word from the divinity to the original E document, the result of which is to render the dream atypical once more.

It is my opinion that the solution to the different questions posed by the text should be envisaged without reference to the documentary theory, given that the structure of the account seems to exclude the combination of two parallel sources. The latter appears to have been constructed with great care; it is made up of three concentric frames, each one fitting neatly into the other so as to form a structure organized around a central axis, the latter dividing the account into two symmetrical parts, ABCC'B'A'. The outer frame (AA': vv. 11aα + 19a) defines the scope of the narrative by focusing attention from the outset on one of the key words of the passage, *maqôm*. The latter appears no less than six times between vv. 11 and 19; indeterminate at the beginning, this *place* finds its meaning and identity as the narration advances, and finally receives its name in v. 19a.

The intermediary frame (BB': vv. 11* + 18) comprises the chronological indications of the narrative and the actions pertaining to each of the two moments indicated: 'at sunset' (*kî bā' haššemeš*), the arrangements made in order to spend the night; 'in the morning' *(babboqer)*, waking up and the ritual gestures accomplished. Noteworthy is the parallelism evident in the expressions set out in the form of three propositions describing the activity of Jacob at these precise moments: the three profane evening activities (*wayyiqaḥ—wayyāśem—wayyiškab*) are matched by three ritual gestures accomplished in the morning (*wayyiqaḥ—wayyāśem—wayyiṣoq*).

The inner frame (CC': vv. 12-13aα + 16-17) describes the central event in the narration, the dream itself and the newly awoken dreamer's realization as to what has happened. The message pronounced by

Yahweh (vv. 13b-15) is fitted in between the two elements in this frame, between the theophany and the dreamer's awakening. The oneiric pictures are presented according to the classical model described above, that is, three nominal clauses introduced by *hinnēh*, arranged in a growing progression: the staircase, the messenger and finally Yahweh himself. Jacob's words (vv. 16-17) recall the same process of graduation but this time in reverse order, proceeding from elements of greater to lesser importance. The propositions themselves also progressively decrease in length, as if to echo the depth of emotion provoked by each image: Yahweh, the 'house of God', the 'gate of heaven'.

The text situated between vv. 11 and 19 thus appears to be well-defined; it could originally have been a narrative independent of the Jacob cycle, and its aetiological function is obvious. This aetiological character is not only evident in the name given to the place in conclusion, but in the structure of the narrative as a whole. The three concentric frames are arranged around a symmetrical axis, which runs though Jacob's awakening (v. 16aα), and which uses chiasmus to oppose, by means of a subtle game involving the reuse of the same terms,[3] events that occurred after sunset with those that take place the following morning. The gestures, the objects and the place thus seem to acquire the degree of symbolization necessary to make them pass over from one side to the other of this axis, from the profane world to that of the sacred. The name given to the place simply makes explicit the sacredness of a place whose sacrality is disclosed in the course of the entire narration, and which henceforth extends to the things and gestures within its walls: there is no more typical example of a cultic legend.

The stylistic elegance of this literary structure does not efface all trace of its complex redactional history, however, and in particular the imbalance introduced into its symmetry by vv. 16-17, which are superfluous. There is also the problem of why the name *Yahweh* is used in a narrative that seeks to explain the origin of Beth-*El*. Whatever may have been the relationship between this dream account and the cultic tradition at Bethel, it takes on its definitive character on its integration into the epic Jacob cycle, thanks to the addition of Jacob's vow (vv. 20-22). It not only integrates the episode into the general movement of the hero who moves away and comes back again, but also transforms the

3. *wayyiqaḥ*; *'eben*; *wayyāśem*; *m^{e}ra'^{a}šotāyw/ro'šāh*; *niṣṣāb/maṣṣēbāh*; *mal'akê '^{e}lohîm/bêt'^{e}lohîm*.

aetiological value of the incident. Henceforth, it is no longer an unexpected oneiric theophany, but rather a pious action on the part of the patriarch that is at the origin of the sanctuary.

Other changes are made in the text in the course of successive readings, in particular the contents of the message itself (vv. 13aβ-15); the introduction of the divine name Yahweh, the development of Jacob's words on his awakening, and probably also the *vision* of the staircase and of the angels of God. The latter (v. 12) should be distinguished from the *theophany*, strictly speaking (v. 13aα: *w*^{e}*hinnēh yhwh niṣṣāb ʿālāyw*), which, on the other hand, is entirely characteristic of *message-dreams* or of *oneiric oracles*. The incongruity of finding a vision in a dream account of this kind is very likely due to its being a late addition to the text, an addition tending to transform the *dream* into a *vision* comparable to those that apocalyptic writers later describe (Husser 1991b). The motifs of 'the heavens opening' and of the coming and going of angels through 'heaven's gate', are frequently found in the introductory parts of accounts of visions from Ezekiel onwards (Ezek. 1.1b), and become popular in apocalyptic style writings (cf. *T. Levi* 2.5-7; 5.1; *3 Macc.* 6.18; Rev. 4.1; Jn 1.51).

Even without the grandiose vision (v. 12) and Jacob's reaction that refers directly to it (v. 17bβ: *w*^{e}*zeh šaʿar haššāmāyim*), the original dream account, a message-dream by nature, does nothing to upset the balance of the structure described above: only the inner frame (CC': vv. 12-13aα + 16-17) is slightly modified (probably reduced to vv. 13aα + 16aα-17aα, bα). This typical message-dream was simply introduced by the formula *wayyaḥ*^{a}*lom w*^{e}*hinnēh ʾel niṣṣāb ʿālāyw wayyōʾmer*, replacing Yahweh by El (or Elohim) in accordance with the aetiological function of the narrative. As in Solomon's dream, the theophanic element is expressed in the simplest way possible: 'And behold, the Lord stood above (or beside) him.' There is no description, no strictly visual detail mentioned; a divine presence simply makes itself known in advance of the words that are heard.

In spite of its discretion, we are surprised by the nevertheless central role occupied by the 'theophany' in the aetiological designs of the narrative, while the text containing the message, of whatever it may have consisted originally, does not seem to have been taken into consideration at all. Jacob apparently does not take account of the words spoken by the divinity in his reaction: in transposing the sequence of gestures accomplished the evening before into something of the order of a rite, he sacralizes the place by means of a pillar *(maṣṣēbāh)* that signifies the presence of God as revealed in the theophany, and no more. The contents of the message therefore do not appear to be implicated in the aetiological function of the narrative; it is *the experience* of the presence of God in the dream that alone founds the holy place. It is, of course, impossible to try to reconstruct the original text of the message transmitted in the dream. There are, however, two possibilities: either there was no word from the divinity imparted in this *hieros logos* at Bethel, or it may be that the narrative, ever since it was put in writing, was joined to the Jacob cycle, by reason of the contents of the message.

The remarkable symmetrical construction of the text helps to highlight God's words, enclosed as they are within a triple narrative frame, words that, given the present state of the text, rather eclipse the cultic legend. At some point in the redactional development of the text, the message became more important than the dream itself. It survives simply as the literary framework for words whose theological content henceforth captures all the attention. On a superficial reading, the intrinsic value and initially religious function of the oneiric experience is overshadowed little by little by its literary function. Whether it be the legitimation narrative in 1 Kings 3, or the cultic legend in Genesis 28, the original function of these narratives in fact depends more on the *oneiric experience* for its own sake—meeting God in a dream—than on the contents of the message heard.

Paradoxically however, and no doubt by reason of the theological importance of the promise and of the words of salvation expressed in the message (vv. 13-15), the dream regained some of its prestige at a later period with the addition of the *vision* of the staircase and of the angels in v. 12. The aim apparently was to touch up a divine manifestation that no doubt was considered too bland for the taste of the day, and to place the words that follow in a context of greater solemnity. The same tendency is evident in the narratives of Daniel 1–7, where, little by little, dreams are absorbed into the apocalyptic vision.

4. *Abimelech's Dream: Genesis 20.3-7*

This dream is the essential element in a pericope that presents a second version of the account of the abduction of the patriarch's wife. The text has long been unanimously attributed to the E document, precisely by reason of the dream, in addition to other elements, such as the literary form of the dialogue, the exclusive use of the name Elohim, the reference to Abraham as *nabi'* and the theme of the fear of God. Several recent studies, however, assert that Genesis 20 cannot be considered to be an independent, parallel version of the saga related in Gen. 12.10-20, but that it is rather a theological rereading of the latter.

In fact, given the way in which the text is composed, we are forced to admit that the argumentation of Genesis 20 is scarcely comprehensible without foreknowledge of Genesis 12. The strictly narrative element is indeed extremely scanty throughout the text concerned: no reason is given for the presence of Abraham at Gerar (v. 1b), the ruse and its execution only take up half a verse (v. 2a) and the reason for this strategy is only given in v. 11. Three half verses (1b, 2ab) summarize the story that Genesis 12 sets out in the course of eight verses (10-17). It is therefore a well-known story that is used here; the redactor contents himself with recalling the main elements before going on to develop new thoughts on the subject. The highly theological character of the account of Genesis 20 is, moreover, not a recent discovery.

The story of the abduction of Sarah has become the literary framework and pretext for a scholastic discussion, permitting a debate on the delicate moral question of crimes committed inadvertently. Abimelech is objectively guilty of taking a married woman into his harem, but he is subjectively innocent, owing to the fact that he was unaware of her real situation. Can a man found guilty in all innocence be punished by God (vv. 5b-6)? Is it possible for an inadvertently guilty king to implicate a just people in his difficulties (v. 4b)? Such are the questions that arise from this traditional narrative.

In comparison with the narrative line of Gen. 12.10-20, and apart from the change in place, the new element in the pericope of Genesis 20 is none other than the dream. From the start, this difference suggests that it is a literary device. The aim of the dream is not only to reply to the question as to how the king learned that Sarah was in fact married, for primarily it is a structuring device essential to the composition of the text. As for the substance of the text, it also provides an answer to the theological problem in question. At a formal level, therefore, the dream operates in two distinct ways:

1. It not only allows for but creates the possibility of a pericope with a symmetrical construction at its core: the latter works like a diptych in which two dialogues are set against each other, one belonging to a dream and the other to a state of wakefulness. These two dialogues are

of exactly the same length (vv. 3-7, 86 words [discounting the gloss in v. 4a]; vv. 9-13, 86 words), and converge upon v. 8, which relates what happens when Abimelech awakes. The first puts God and Abimelech in each other's presence behind closed door's, that is, in the context of the complete confidentiality assured by the dream, the second puts Abraham and Abimelech together in the concrete world of wakefulness. The situations in the two wings of this diptych are analogous and symmetrical, but the passage from dream to reality provokes a reversal in the situation of the dreamer (Abimelech): he who is initially accused becomes the accuser.

2. It is the dream as a literary device that allows the redactor to introduce a dialogue between God and man, a dialogue that here takes the form of a tribunal scene. The latter begins with a speech for the prosecution, threatening the accused with death (v. 3). Thereafter comes the accused's defence (vv. 4b-5). In a second part of the dialogue, opened in v. 6a with a new introductory formula (*wayyō'mer 'ēlāyw ha'ᵉlohîm baḥᵃlôm*) that recalls v. 3, God speaks as if he were a real judge, taking into account the requirements of the law and the arguments proposed by the defence (vv. 6b-7).

If the dream narrative appears to be a handy literary device for the reasons we have just enumerated, it also appeals to different types of oneiric experience, the identification of which is not without importance for the evaluation of its operative role in the text. Over and above its structuring and narrative function, the dream is the bearer of real demonstrative significance. The dialogues, which occupy such a large place in the pericope, are, it has been said, the literary expression of reflection upon a theological theme. But all the while that the judiciary metaphor is used in the oneiric dialogue, there is never any reply to the theoretical question of how God might judge inadvertent guilt. All we hear is a sentence expressing the clemency of the divine judge. The solution to the problem posed is not found in the arguments exchanged in the course of the discussion, but in the circumstances of the latter, the oneiric meeting. In the event of a grave sin committed in all innocence, God can 'come' in a dream to instruct man and turn him away from his fault.

Thus the literary form of the oneiric dialogue has itself demonstrative value, in so far as it evokes the circumstances by means of which God enlightens man as to the moral import of his acts. Underlying is the idea that dreams might be a possible place of divine instruction, an idea developed in Job 33, as we shall see. To introduce a dream into this context is therefore not only a literary device, for the dream seems to be an essential element in the way in which the text is argued (Husser 1991a).

The value of this arguement depends on the theological interpretation of a particular oneiric experience, the *nightmare*. Abimelech's reaction, as much during the dream as upon his awakening, is fear in the face of the death threat with which he is confronted. The terror and dread that may be experienced in dreams are only mentioned in wisdom texts in the context of the torments experienced by the reprobate. This is a theme to which we will return. But the recognized moral dimension to certain oneiric experiences, normally experienced as nightmares, is characteristic of a development in wisdom thinking after the fifth century BCE.

Though the literary form is similar, the narrative of Genesis 20 does most certainly not refer to the same type of oneiric experience as that refered to in Solomon's dream at Gibeon. The latter is a straightforward message-dream: an oneiric theophany accompanied by an oracle in the form of a promise, perhaps in the context of incubation. The dialogue between God and Abimelech in a terrifying dream is perceived as the expression of divine judgment. From this we see that the typology of literary forms matches psychological reality only accidentally and that this psychological reality, though still identifiable by the reader, is for the most part obscured by literary convention.

5. *Jacob's Dream on Leaving Laban: Genesis 31.10–13*

Jacob happens to be the beneficiary of a second dream, which is rather strange and difficult to classify from a literary point of view. Once more we notice a mixture of visual and auditory elements, and, something that is exceptional in biblical dream accounts, it is related in the first person. In fact it is probable, as we shall see, that we have here another *message-dream*, on to which an oneiric *vision* has been superimposed.

Numerous recent critics have given up looking for two parallel sources in ch. 31—the distinction between which becomes very problematic from v. 26 onwards—and opt for a single narrative, completed and enlarged by various additions. Verses 4-16 are part of these secondary developments, the aim of which is to make corrections to the narrative in order to make its contents more theological. For example, when the events of ch. 30 are reiterated in a dialogue between Jacob and his wives, vv. 4-16 cited above attribute Jacob's enrichment to the intervention of God rather than to the artfulness of the shepherd. Throughout this passage (31.4-16), Jacob's dream occupies a central position, since it is thanks to it that God's intervention, which reorients the narrative theologically, is revealed (*a posteriori*, since it is a retrospective narrative).

The text containing the dream presents real difficulties, and in line with Wellhausen, scholars are agreed that vv. 10 and 12 are redactional additions. Verse 12 is an intrusion into the the narrative between 11 and 13 and delays God's self-introduction until the end of the dream. Moreover, with vv. 10 and 12 situated where they are, the means by which Jacob is able to increase his flock is revealed to him at the very moment he receives the order to leave. We can correct this up to a point by taking into account Westermann's hypothesis (1985: II, 491). He retains v. 12b and reconstitutes the following sequence, vv. 11, 13a, 12b, 13b. As such it contains a typical message-dream:

11 The angel of god said to me in a dream 'Jacob!' and I replied: 'Here I am!'

13a He said to me: 'I am the God of Bethel where you anointed a stone and where you made a vow.

12b I have seen everything that Laban has done to you. Now, get up, leave this country,

13b and return to your family's country!'

In this restrospective narrative (vv. 6-13), which is no more than a redactional device, the dream account seems like a veritable *midrash* upon v. 31.3. What is the intention of a rereading such as this? It so happens that the dream reconstructed thus reproduces exactly the pattern of the theophany in Exod. 3.2-10, and we recognize the same component parts in the two texts: the manifestation of the angel of God in a dream (Gen. 31.11a)/in a flame (Exod. 3.2a); he calls the man by name (Gen. 31.11b/Exod. 3.4b); he refers to himself as the God of Bethel (Gen. 31.13a)/of the Fathers (Exod. 3.6a); he declares that he has seen Jacob's distress (Gen. 31.12b)/that of his people (Exod. 3.7a); he orders him to leave the land where he is (in Gen. 31.13b)/to take his people out of the land (Exod. 3.10).

The parallelism noted above suggests that the redactor of Gen. 31.11-13 copied the Deuteronomistic narrative of Exodus 3. This in turn helps to explain our *midrash*: in establishing a parallel between Jacob and

Moses by means of a theophany that makes explicit the order received in 31.3, the reader is encouraged to read the events that follow according to the pattern of the Exodus and to see in Jacob's return a prefiguration not only of the flight from Egypt but above all of the second Exodus. It is therefore very probable that if not vv. 4-16 as a whole, at least the dream account (vv. 11, 12b, 13) is a late exilic composition. The words of the message, 'leave this country and return to the country of your family', heard beyond the Euphrates by the people's ancestor, were a fitting way to keep the exiles' hopes up. The choice of a dream as the context for this theophany is easily understood given the explicit reference to the Beth-El tradition in v. 13. We should also note that it once more has the effect of highlighting God's word.

The redactional addition of vv. 10, 12a transforms this message-dream into a sort of oneiric *vision*. If the succession of phrases that results lacks order and unity, the aim envisaged by this development seems clear: to attribute the means by which Jacob gains his riches to divine revelation. We should note that the list of three adjectives describing the coats of the animals in the flock is different in one respect from that of 30.39, in so far as *ṭ*^{e}*lu'îm*, 'speckled' (30.39b), is replaced by *b*^{e}*rudîm*, 'spotted' (31.10b). The only other place in which this last term is used is in Zech. 6.3, 6 where it describes the colour of the horses of the last chariot in the vision. Other indications allow us to fill out this unexpected comparison with the visions of Proto-Zechariah.

The introductory formula characteristic of the *visions* of Zechariah 1–3, *wā'eśā' ('et) 'ênay wā're' w*^{e}*hinnēh* (Zech. 2.1, 5; 5.1, 9; 6.1), does not occur in any previous prophetic vision, but twice in Daniel (8.3; 10.5) and precisely in this *dream* account of Jacob's (31.10a: *wā'eśā' 'ênay wā're' w*^{e}*hinnēh*). In Jacob's vision, the words of the angel in 31.12 *(śā' nā' 'ênêka ûr*^{e}*'ēh)* are found word for word in Zech. 5.5b. Moreover, owing to the addition of vv. 10, 12a, we observe in the present text of the dream a schema analogous to those of Zechariah's visions: the information given by the angel (v. 12a, cf. Zech. 5.2b), the reference back to the vision (v. 12a, cf. Zech. 5.2b), the interpretation of the vision in the form of an oracle (vv. 12b-13, cf. Zech. 5.3-4). We may conclude that the insertion of vv. 10 and 12a in the original dream account had the effect of reformulating the latter in terms of a *prophetic vision* according to the model of visions of Proto-Zechariah. This also explains the unhabitual use of the verb *rā'āh* (vv. 10a, 12a) in a dream account, a verb that is commonly used in the accounts of prophetic visions.

This rereading has therefore given an ordinary dream account the general appearance of an oracle preceded by a vision. The dream fiction is partly maintained on account of the weight of tradition, which makes Jacob into a specialist of this kind of divine revelation, but also, it appears because reference to Zechariah's visions made possible the assimilation of dreams to this kind of experience. This observation leads us directly to the question of the place of dreams in prophetic practices.

Chapter 9

Dreams and the Prophetic Vision

The rare occasions on which the word *ḥ*^{a}*lôm* is mentioned in prophetic literature is in the context of the polemic against false prophets (Jer. 23.25-32; 27.9; 29.8; Zech. 10.2) or in a negative sense (Isa. 29.7-8). Did the prophets altogether reject dreams as a means of communicating with the divine, or did they simply object to their manifestations and the use made of them, which they considered too extravagant? Is there really very much difference on this point between the 'orthodox' prophets and those whom they so violently opposed? The hypothesis presented here is that the prophets—or at least some of them—cultivated a particular and specific kind of oneiric experience, which was not the same as the dream experience denoted by *ḥ*^{a}*lôm,* and which in some cases was called *ḥāzôn*.

The redactional history of Jacob's dreams at Bethel (Gen. 28) or on leaving Laban (Gen. 31) shows the tardy superposition of a visionary element characteristic of prophecy upon ancient message-dream accounts. This observation suggests that, at least at a late period, dreams and visions were thought to have a similar origin. That these dream accounts could be so easily transformed into the accounts of visions thus constitutes one of the clues as to the identification of the prophet's dream experiences. To go back yet further, to the still vague origins of prophecy in Israel, it should be remembered that dreams are well-attested in Mari as mediators of spontaneous divine oracles (see p. 44). In the less distant past, the Deïr 'Alla plaster text, which is contemporary with the classical prophets and close to Israel, speaks of a prophet receiving a visit from the gods by night.

1. *Dreams in Polemic*

Even if, on the few occasions on which *ḥ*^{a}*lôm* is used in prophetic literature, it is almost exclusively in the context of the polemic that confronts Jeremiah with other prophets, the question of dreams is nevertheless a minor point in the debate. Recent studies on the quarrel between 'true' and 'false' prophets have shown that, among the criteria allowing us to define the orthodoxy of a prophet, questions concerning the means of inspiration, or prophetic technique, were not of primary importance. It was shortly before, in the course of the eighth century BCE, under the impulse of Deuteronomic legislation, that a distinction between divination and prophecy, that is to say between deductive and spontaneous divination, first took shape. However, if by reason of the technicality of divination—and therefore the professionalism of its practitioners—the distinction between the art of diviners and prophecy became more and more apparent, this does not mean that the latter became entirely indifferent to practices designed to favour inspiration.

Dreams are to be found at the join where these two modes of inspiration meet, in so far as the divine message that they transmit may come spontaneously to a passive sleeper, or else may be solicited by one of the practices related to incubation. The oneiric message may also either be immediately intelligible, or on the contrary require recourse to the practical know-how of oneirocritics. In Israel, therefore, given the recognized diversity of oneiric states and related practices, everything predisposes the *ḥ^{a}lōmôt* to figure among experiences that were considered suspect and practices that were forbidden, while at the same time they were recognized as an incomparable means of communication with God.

In the search for criteria allowing one to discern true from false prophecy, the question of the authenticity of the inspiration is naturally essential. In Israel, however, we find none of the divinatory practices designed to test the oracular value of prophetic dreams, such as are mentioned in the Mari texts. The rejection of such practices, parallel to the development of a form of prophetic orthodoxy, forbade their use, or perhaps simply filtered any memory of them. The traditional way of proving the authenticity of an oracle was to wait and see whether it was realized in concrete terms (cf. Deut. 18.21-22; 1 Kgs 22.28). Even the miracle accompanying the prophetic word was in time considered a doubtful sign of authenticity, and Deuteronomy set against it the obligation for this word to conform to faith in Yahweh (Deut. 13.2-4).

In line with the Deuteronomistic definition of the true prophet as someone in whose mouth God puts his words and who proclaims them faithfully (Deut. 18.18), Jeremiah, followed by Ezekiel (ch. 13) initiates a psychological reflection on the problem. False prophets are not only people who speak in the name of Baal, nor those who are led astray by the spirit of Yahweh, but people who, in Yahweh's name, do no more than simply use their imagination: *tarmit libbām*, 'the affabulations of their hearts', becomes the equivalent of *šeqer*, 'lie' (Jer. 14.14; 23.26). Lying prophets are those who 'speak visions of their own mind, not from the mouth of the Lord' (Jer. 23.16b: *ḥ*^{a}*zôn libbām y*^{e}*dabb*^{e}*rû lo' mippî yhwh*). The distinction between what comes from God and what belongs to the prophets' imagination does not succeed in generating objective criteria for discernment, for it remains above all a polemical argument. In its formulation, however, an effort is made to situate the cleavage between false and true prophecy in relation to anthropology. Indeed, previously, apart from those who prophesied in the name of foreign gods, false prophets were essentially characterized as people who offered accommodating oracles to those who solicited them and paid them for their services (cf. Mic. 3.5-7; Isa. 30.10). It was still only the moral and sociological dimensions of the problem that were considered.

It is in the context of the problems rapidly summarized here that questions concerning prophetic dreams arise. It should be pointed out that, during this crisis, the 'vision' *(ḥāzôn)* underwent similar criticism: allusions to 'delusive visions' (sing. *ḥ*^{a}*zôn šāw*^{e}*'*) appear from Isaiah and Micah onwards in polemical texts long before dreams, which only enter the ring with Jeremiah. Identical terms are found by Ezekiel, who accuses certain prophets of having had delusive visions (Ezek. 13.6, 7, 23; 21.34; 22.28), while he himself makes no other allusion to dreams. It seems, therefore, that the question of dreams is but a very limited aspect of a much larger problem and that the difficulties did not concern all oneiric phenomena.

Jeremiah 23.25-31 is the most explicitly negative passage as regards its attitude towards dreams, though we are unable to say with any accuracy what is behind the criticism of the prophet's *ḥ*^{a}*lôm*. The unit 'concerning the prophets' (23.9-40) gathers together several elements of a polemic found in numerous other passages in the book,[1] but in which references to the question of dreams are rare and treat different aspects (Jer. 27.9; 29.8). Moreover, the passage appears to be composite, made up of a collection of oracles (some of which are in prose), grouped

1. 2.8; 5.13, 31; 6.13; 8.10; 14.13-15; 27.9, 14-18; 28; 29.8-9, 15.

together by the Deuteronomistic redactors of the book. Neither is the redactional unity of vv. 25-32 beyond question: the lengthy period constituted by v. 32 is clearly a recapitulatory conclusion for which a Deuteronomistic redactor is responsible. On account of the shift to the singular in 28a and to a poetic form in 28b, the authenticity of v. 28 is contested; moreover, vv. 28 and 29 together constitute a block that comes between the accusation formulated in vv. 25-27 and the sentence in v. 30. These two verses could well be a redactional addition.

In its present form, the unity constituted by vv. 25-32 concludes an argument begun in v. 16 and that comprises two sections: (1) these prophets 'speak visions of their own minds, not from the mouth of the Lord' (v. 16b: *ḥ*^{a}*zôn libbām y*^{e}*dabb*^{e}*rû lo' mippî yhwh*); (2) they are not sent by God (v. 21a). From v. 25 onwards, the passage attacks a precise element in the prophets' teaching, an element related not to the contents of the visions but to their form: their oracles are presented as *dreams*.

The solemn exclamation *ḥālāmtî ḥālāmtî* introduced in v. 25b would seem to indicate the presence of an oracle, just as the expression *ina šutiya*, 'in my dream', introduces oracles described in some Mari letters. This suggests that dreams could be a credible source of oracles. Leaving aside vv. 28-29, 32, Jeremiah's criticism is not of dreams as such; his point is that reference to this type of inspiration—and probably also to the contents of the oracles themselves—can lead to forgetting the name of Yahweh. The rereading proposed by vv. 28-29 redirects his attack in such a way as to disqualify dreams entirely by contrast with the divine word. The reason why criticism of dreams becomes so radical may lie in the reaction of Deuteronomistic redactors to a situation that developed during the exile.

The question of dreams does in fact reappear in two other passages in the book, both of which are Deuteronomistic: Jer. 27.9 and 29.8.

The oracle in Jer. 27.9 is supposedly addressed to the ambassadors of neighbouring kingdoms come to Jerusalem to negotiate a coalition against Babylon. In v. 14, the same oracle is addressed to Zedekiah and to the people of Judah: 'Do not listen to the words of your prophets who are saying to you…' In this version, the redactor is careful to mention 'prophets' only; he makes no allusion to the other specialists in divination enumerated in v. 9 and who seem thus to be the voluntary reserve of foreign peoples. Among these specialists are 'dreamers', if we emend the form *ḥ*^{a}*lōmôtêkem* in the MT to *ḥolmêkem*, which is found in the versions. All the divinatory functions mentioned here are also present in the list of forbidden practices in Deut. 18.10-11, except for 'dreamers'. Consequently, we may suspect that the reason why dream specialists have found a place in the stereotypical list of the multiple forms of Syro-Canaanite divination in Jer. 27.9 is to disqualify dreams by associating them explicity with pagan techniques of divination. In the time that lapsed between the redaction of Deuteronomy 18 and that of Jeremiah 27, divination by means of dreams had been integrated into the list of practices that were preferably only associated with pagans. The reason for this was probably not their newness but rather the particular circumstances that drew attention to them. Without being directly engaged in the polemic, this pericope thus testifies to the radical mistrust of one of the redactional layers of the book of Jeremiah as regards dreams.

In the letter addressed to them, the exiles are warned against prophets, diviners and 'the dreams which you cause to dream' (Jer. 29.8). Unlike Jeremiah 23, which is concerned with prophets' dreams and incubation as practised by diviners, here it is the use of dreams in general as a means of knowing the future that is called into question. It seems, therefore, that the exilic community had allowed itself to be seduced by the highly developed oneiromancy of Babylon, and that the latter could not but attract this demoralized population.

It is understandable, therefore, during the exile, and in a Babylonian context where so much attention was paid to the ominous value of dreams, that the Deuteronomistic redactors of the book reacted with an attempt to force certain of the prophet's words, the addition constituted by Jer. 23.25-32, for example. The result was to associate dreams in general with a number of forbidden divinatory practices, and posthumously to make them the privileged instrument of false prophecy, no doubt because they offered the clearest illustration of 'affabulations of the heart', in contrast to the authentic word of God.

As we have just suggested, the legislation in Deuteronomy 18 concerning those who mediate the word of God makes no allusion to dreams in its list of forbidden practices. Over and above child sacrifice by burning, vv. 10-11 mention no less than seven different forms of divination or magic, in a list that grew with successive additions. The original text of these verses taken up by the Deuteronomistic author seems only to have concerned those who consult oracles (*qosem* *q*^{e}*sāmîm*), those who cast spells (*ḥober ḥāber*) and necromancers (*dorēš 'el hammētîm*). A Deuteronomistic redaction added soothsayers (*m*^{e}*'ônēn*), augurs (*m^{e}naḥēš*) and mediums (*šo'ēl 'ôb w^{e}yid'onî*), while the mention of sorcerers (*m^{e}kaššēp*) is probably the addition of a glossator. In spite of the hypothetical character of the redactional reconstruction proposed here, the superabundant character of this list betrays a desire to be exhaustive on the subject; the diverse forms of sorcery and divination condemned by the law are thereby enumerated. The absence of dreams in this context is therefore highly significant.

Deuteronomy 13 records three ancient laws aimed at repressing those whose incite others to apostasy, the prophets being the first concerned (vv. 2-6). This is the only place in the Deuteronomic Code in which there is any allusion to dreams. In v. 2a the text proposes a doublet more or less synonymous with *nabî'* in the form of *ḥolēm ḥ^{a}lôm.* As such, the expression is a hapax; even if paranomasia is well-attested elsewhere as a way of introducing symbolic dream accounts, *ḥozēh* would have been a more usual parallel for *nabî.*

If we are to rely on the analysis of Merendino (1969) and Seitz (1971), the redactional stratigraphy of this text shows evidence of a development provoked by successive rereadings. The ancient legislation ran as follows: 'If a prophet arises among you, [or a dreamer of dreams] and if he says: "Let us go after other gods and let us serve them!", that prophet [or that dreamer of dreams] shall be put to death: you shall purge the evil from the midst of you!' On the basis of this terse utterance, successive additions contributed towards the development of a veritable argumentation on the subject of false prophecy, giving important criteria for discernment (vv. 2b-3) and an explanation of its origins (v. 4b) similar to that suggested in the narrative of 1 Kgs 22.19-23. Some of the key arguments forged in the controversy against false prophets have thus been grafted on to this ancient legal text.

The original text of the law did not, in its concision, require a synonym for *nabî,* (it being sufficiently clear by itself), and especially not such an unusual parallel. It is therefore highly probable that the syntagm *ḥolēm ḥ^{a}lôm* was added by a Deuteronomistic redactor, and that it refers to the controversy that set Jeremiah against certain prophets who were also likely to incite the people to apostasy 'by their dreams which they tell one another' (Jer. 23.27). This way of glossing *nabî* adds nothing to the intelligibility of Deut. 13.2-6, but accentuates its polemical character by actualizing it in terms of a specific situation.

Zechariah 10.1-2 echoes the prophetic controversy about dreams one last time. However, as in Jer. 29.8, the expression 'the dreamers tell false dreams' (*ḥ^{a}lōmôt haššāw' y^{e}dabb^{e}rû*) would seem to refer to oneiromancy rather than to the dreams of false prophets. The latter are mentioned in the preceding verse, 'the diviners see lies' (*haqqôs^{e}mîm ḥāzû šeqer*). Verse 2a synthesizes the entire range of forbidden divinatory practices by referring to the archaic *t^{e}rāpîm*, to diviners and to dreams.

The question of dreams, therefore, at first absent from the prophetic polemic—absent even from Deuteronomic legislation—suddenly appears in Jeremiah, who speaks out against prophets who refer to dreams as the source of their oracles. Without directly challenging this form of inspiration, which had long belonged to the panoply of divinatory techniques, Jeremiah does however sow the seeds of suspicion as regards dreams by contesting the authenticity of *the word* of prophets who use them. The resurgence of oneiromancy in the context of the Jews' exile in Babylon had the effect of hardening the criticism directed against dreams in Deuteronomistic texts, since it provoked the amalgamation of techniques that by right were distinct. Criticism of dreams is therefore not so radical as is often suggested, and the literary cliché that associates dreams with lies (cf. Zech. 10.2) is not representative of the general or undivided attitude of prophecy to them, far from it.

2. *Dreams and Visions: Distinction and Confusion*

If dreams appear to be absent from the prophetic books, apart from the cases studied above, the same is not true of *visions*, whose relationship with the oneiric world is always complex and subtle, as the redactional history of Gen. 31.10-13 demonstrates. The question tackled here, therefore, is the relationship between dreams and visions, in so far as the former is sometimes described as a 'night vision' (*ḥāzôn/ḥizzāyôn lay^{e}lāh),* and that certain visions are supposed to have been seen during the night (those of Proto-Zechariah).

The prophetic corpus contains 24 accounts of visions, if we include the two visions of Michah ben Yimla (1 Kgs 22.17, 19-23). On the whole, these accounts are identical in structure, a structure that differs from that of symbolic dreams in so far as they comprise not only the actual vision, but also a dialogue between the visionary and God (or an angel) and a word of prophecy. While dream accounts treat symbolic visions and words of prophecy separately and differently (hence the distinction between symbolic dreams and message-dreams), the 'prophetic vision' genre combines what is seen and what is heard in the same narrative, that is the visual allegory, its interpretation and the message. In spite of these differences, the formal and stylistic analogies between accounts of dreams and those of visions have encouraged certain critics to suggest that the prototype of the vision narrative consisted of 'dream + interpretation'.

Num. 12.6-8, a short poem presented as an oracle, appears in the pericope in which Myriam and Aaron oppose Moses. Literary criticism of this chapter is renowned for its difficulty, and even if the documentary theory is no longer applied, current research is obliged to disentangle at least two strata in this text. It is obvious that vv. 6-8 do not fit easily into a narrative in which Moses is criticized for his unsuitable marriage to a Cushite woman, and if v. 2 introduces the theme of the primacy of Moses, it still does not constitute the beginning of an autonomous narrative. The text of vv. 6-8 is very well constructed; it is poetic in form and has a concentric structure:

6a. *šim'û nā' debārāy*
6b. *'im yihyeh nābî' bākem*[2]
bammar'āh 'ēlāyw 'etwadā'
baḥalôm 'adabber bô:
7a. *lo' kēn 'abdî mošeh*
7b. *bekol bētî ne'emān hû':*
8a. *peh 'el peh 'adabber bô*
ûmar'eh welo' beḥîdot
< *ûtemunat yhwh yabbîṭ* >
8b. *ûmaddûa' lo' yerē'tem*
ledabbēr be'abdî bemošeh:

It should be pointed out that this structure leaves aside v. 8aγ, long thought to be a gloss. The inclusion constituted by vv. 6abα and 8b integrates the poem into its context, and at the same time sets the word of Yahweh (6a) against that of Moses' critics (8bβ) and 'a prophet among you' (6bα) against 'my servant Moses' (8bβ). Moses predominates owing to his position at the centre of the poem (v. 7a), and to the recurrence of the expression 'my servant Moses' at the conclusion of each half of the poem. The poem responds to the question introduced in v. 2, and if we remove the unity constituted by vv. 2, (3), 6-8 from ch.

2. The MT *nebî'akem* should be emended according to the Latin versions.

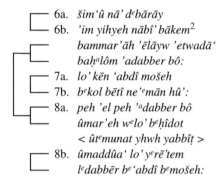

12, the meaning of the latter remains unchanged. On the contrary it is enhanced, for the distortion created by the repeated motif of a complaint made against Moses disappears. These verses would thus appear to be a redactional addition, which was polemical in tone, and the intention of which was apparently to correct Num. 11.24-30 in which the prophets are placed at Moses' side. Indeed, when stylistic features are also taken into account, it is likely that these verses are the addition of an exilic or immediately postexilic Deuteronomistic redactor, writing at a time when it was important to affirm the primacy of the Torah over the prophets.

The chiasmus that frames v. 7ab contrasts the direct knowledge which God gives of himself to Moses with the mediated knowledge which the prophets have of him through *dreams* and *visions,* both considered as *ḥîdôt*, 'enigmas'. Noteworthy is the insistent presence of the root *dbr* in the poem, and the meaning of *ḥîdah,* which is not normally used of images, but only of a type of speech, wisdom or prophetic (cf. Ezek. 17.2). The allusion here is therefore as much to a visionary and enigmatic form of prophetic *speech*, as opposed to the clarity of the word transmitted by the Torah, as to *perception* of the divine word in dreams and visions.

On the other hand, and in spite of the parallelism with *mar'āh*, it is not necessary to understand *ḥ^{a}lôm* as a symbolic dream. On the contrary, it is probable that the author made use of a certain structural parallelism to mention two complementary forms of prophetic inspiration, the one nocturnal and 'auditory', the other diurnal and 'visual'. It is not certain that such rational distinctions were really pertinent in the context of prophetic practice, but another important text indicates that a real effort was in fact made to analyse the processes of inspiration.

We now turn to Numbers 22–23. The tradition on which the Balaam pericope depends is now well known, and the importance of this text for a book about dreams stems from the fact that Balaam has one characteristic in common with the prophet of Deïr 'Alla: he converses with the gods at night. This point is all the more remarkable given that, in spite of his foreign origin, Balaam is presented in the biblical story as a prophet of exemplary obedience to the divine word.

Recent criticism has given up trying to argue for two parallel narratives behind the text of these chapters. The episode with the donkey (22.22-35a) apart, it is my opinion that 22.4b–23.26; 24.11, 25 constitute a homogeneous narrative composition; the doublets are a literary device and are essential to the very tight structure of the story. The compositional unity of the story stems from the unity of theme that runs throughout the prose and the two first oracles: the first theme is founded on the contrast, curse–blessing, a theme that first appears in 22.6 and reappears in 22.11-12; 23.7b-8, 11, 20, 25. The narrative is constructed around this theme and the oracles develop it in complementary fashion: 'do not curse' in the first (23.7b-8), 'bless' in the second (23.20).

The second theme, that of the unconditional submission of the prophet to the word of Yahweh, constitutes the theological dimension of the story. It first appears in 22.8, is taken up in 22.13, reaffirmed more forcefully in 22.18, 20, and is invoked in the conclusion (23.26). Balaam will speak the words 'which Yahweh will put in his mouth' (22.38b; 23.5, 12, 16a), he will speak or act according to 'what Yahweh tells him' (22.8, 20, 35; 23.3b, 26). Thanks to the remarkable variety of expressions under the guise of which these formulae appear, the reader is given to understand that the author wanted to present this foreign diviner as a model *nabî*, faithful to Yahweh, such as we find in Deut. 18.18.

Besides, the narrative develops and comes to a climax around the mounting tension beween the will of the king and that of Yahweh, both of whom lay claim to the prophet: the latter is solicited by contradictory desires, either to bless or to curse. Balaam must choose between pleasing the king who pays him and being faithful to Yahweh, a situation analogous to the one in the narrative about Michah ben Yimla (1 Kgs 22), who reacted in the same manner (1 Kgs 22.14). All these observations suggest that the Balaam narrative is a text engaged in a polemic against false prophets and that it was composed from the perspective of Deuteronomistic theology.

The narrative appears to be well-constructed, with an introduction (22.4b-6), a main part composed of two sections (22.7-21; 22.36–23.24) and a conclusion (23.25-26; 24.11, 25). The diptych formed by the central part is constituted on the one hand by the two diplomatic missions, each followed by a consultation with the divinity, and on the other by two oracles, each preceded by a sacrificial scene. Verses 22.36-40 handle the change of scene and of speaker between the two sections.

The way in which the narrative is constructed highlights two kinds of prophetic activity: on the one hand consultation of the divinity by night, and on the other ritual invocations and visionary oracles by day. Two ways of consulting the divinity, fulfilling two apparently distinct purposes. In the first part, the diviner must decide how he is to react to the solicitations of Balak; in order to clarify his decision, he makes the emissaries wait until the next day, confident that God will come and speak to him during the night. This is an obvious allusion to a technique enabling the diviner to provoke a nocturnal discussion with the divinity. If the narrative is clearly fictitious, the necessity for it to be intelligible to the reader and its source tradition at Deïr 'Alla suggest that these nocturnal dialogues reflect genuine prophetic experience. Even if the term *ḥ^a^lôm* does not appear in the text, these dialogues may be termed oneiric, if we take into account the possibility of a form of dream experience proper to the prophetic movement. This is an hypothesis that I will develop a little later.

By contrast with visionary oracles proclaimed during the day in the official exercise of a diviner's duty, we should note the confidential, personal character of the nocturnal dialogues between Balaam and God. The message received concerns the attitude of the prophet alone, it is not the object of any proclamation.

When placed in the context of the prophetic quarrel, and more especially in the debate about the value of dreams, the response of the Balaam story seems to be the following: God may certainly speak to a prophet in a dream, but the message will concern the one who receives it only. He may then take account of it for his own benefit, but should not make an oracle out of it! If the ideal prophet depicted in Numbers 22–23 and in the Deuteronomistic tradition allows God to speak directly, his capacity to interfere with the divine message is considered void. From this perspective, the prophet who formulates in plain language a more or less enigmatic message previously received in a dream or vision is suspicious *a priori*, for the mediation of the divine message that this necessitates is in great danger of altering it.

Here we return to some of the questions underlying the text of Num. 12.6-8, as well as to the distinction between dreams and visions, though considered a little differently. It seems that the debate about false prophets, which raised numerous theoretical questions concerning the authenticity of the prophetic word, led to an attempt to rationalize the relationship between dreams and visions in this sphere. In so doing, night-time was reserved for dreams and day-time for visions, the former being concerned with regulating the prophet's personal conduct, and the latter being the direct expression of the word of God. In the Balaam pericope, the very precise distinction made between dream and vision does not yet result in denigrating the former, but attempts simply to limit its importance in prophetic practice. The desire of groups sympathetic to Deuteronomy to create such norms did not have any lasting effect, as far as we can see. The oracle that opens the second part of the book of Joel (Joel 3.1) once more places dreams and visions parallel to one another, as typical manifestations of the prophetic spirit:

> And it shall come to pass afterward,
> that I will pour out my spirit on all flesh;
> your sons and your daughters will prophesy,
> your old men shall dream dreams *[ḥᵃlōmôt yaḥᵃlōmûn]*
> and your young men shall see visions *[ḥezyōnôt yir'û]*.

We certainly find in this text an echo of Num. 12.6-8, but here dreams and visions are no longer presented as enigmatic ways of knowing God. On the contrary, they appear to be characteristic of an intimacy with him made possible by the pouring out of his spirit. Use of the expression *ḥezyōnôt yir'û* to designate the visionary experience is a little unexpected, for visions such as those described in Amos, Jeremiah, Ezekiel or Zechariah are designated by the term *mar'ôt,* while the root *ḥzh*, in the biblical corpus, generally signifies a perception without any image. In fact, the technical vocabulary of Joel 3.1 strays from the usages of classical prophecy and already reflects those of the apocalyptic writers. In the Hebrew text of Daniel, 'to see' is exclusively rendered by *r'h*, while in Dan. 8 (vv. 1, 2, 15) the word for a symbolic vision is *ḥāzôn,* found in the same expression as noted above, *ḥāzôn rā'āh*, 'to see a vision'.

Joel 3.1 therefore evokes symbolic visions after the manner of apocalyptic writers. It is possible that dream and vision are no longer as distinct here as they were in Num. 12.6-8, and that the poetic parallelism is much more strictly synonymic. We saw above, as regards the narratives of Daniel 1–7, that from the very first manifestations of the apocalyptic movement—visionary by definition—dreams served as a means of expression for experiences that only literary fiction allows one to call oneiric. The definitive assimilation of dreams with visions takes place at the beginning of the apocalyptic part of the book (Dan. 7.1), where Daniel's vision is presented as a dream; after which, *ḥēlēm*, is discarded from the vocabulary of visions like a worn-out rag.

The identification of dreams with visions at a late period confirms the observations we made as regards the literary evolution of Jacob's dreams (Gen. 28; 31). It remains difficult, for want of documents, to know exactly how the relationship between the two was perceived before the exile, but Zech. 1.8 presents the eight visions of the book as nocturnal experiences without ever speaking of dreams, and the literary form still remains strictly that of the vision (introduced by the formula *wā'ēre' w*e*hinnēh*). It seems likely that, in classical prophecy, dreams and visions are two distinct phenomena, although visions can *also* take place at night.

3. *A Particular Kind of Oneiric Experience*

The texts presented up till now vouch for the fact that dreams did play a part in the prophetic office, in spite of the discretion of the prophetic scrolls in this respect. In order to explain this apparent contradiction, we may venture to suggest that specifically prophetic oneiric experience, previous to and up till Jeremiah, was clearly distinguished from the general experience of dreams (*ḥ*a*lôm)*, and was designated by a special term, *ḥāzôn.*

Mic. 3.5-8 records an oracle of judgment condemning false prophets who mislead the people of Israel by uttering oracles to suit themselves; the attack is neither directed at the quality of their prophetic experience nor at their capacity to consult Yahweh, but at their readiness to be open to bribery, by means of which the truth of their oracles is distorted. It is by reason of this crime that they are to be punished by being deprived of further visions: 'there is no answer from God' (7b: *kî 'ēn ma'*a*nēh '*e*lohîm*). The very type of punishment meted out to them vouches for the fact that up till then the visions of these prophets had been considered authentic. Verse 6 suggests that they occurred during the night:

> Therefore it shall be night to you, without vision,
> and darkness to you, without divination.

The text is susceptible to two interpretations, depending on whether one understands the *min* before *ḥāzôn* and *q*e*som* to be privative in meaning (as it is translated here) or whether it should be understood in terms of substitution, giving 'it is night for you *rather than* a vision, etc.'. These two meanings are not contradictory, and it is probable that the Hebrew played on this amphibology.

The vision designated by *ḥāzôn* is not of the same sort as that described in the vision narratives of Amos, Isaiah, Jeremiah, Ezekiel and *Zechariah*. In these texts, visual perception is exclusively denoted by the root *r'h* and its derivatives; *ḥzh* never appears, in spite of the fact that it is common in a prophetic context where it more often signifies the perception of something *spoken*. The use of *ḥzh* in the edition of prophetic collections, notably in their titles, testifies to the completion of a process that ended up making *ḥāzôn* into the equivalent of *dābār* (Obad. 1; Nahum 1.1), and at the term of which the spoken word, and oracles (*maśśa*) too, were 'seen' (*ḥzh*). In other words, it came to describe any object of revelation that had no specifically visual element (Amos 1.1; Hab. 1.1; Mic. 1.1; Isa. 1.1; 2.1; 13.1).

This particular meaning of *ḥzh* is observed in other languages apart from Hebrew. Indeed, we have already seen that, in the Deïr 'Alla inscription, if Balaam 'had a vision, like an oracle of El' (*wyḥz mḥzh / kmś' 'l*: DAPT I: 1-2), this vision in fact consisted of words: 'and they said to Balaam…' (*wy'mrw lbl'm*: DAPT I: 2). There are also a number of allusions to the fact that prophets receive a *word* from God during the night: Samuel (1 Sam. 15.16), Nathan (2 Sam. 7.4) and, more unexpectedly, Jeremiah (Jer. 31.26):

> Thereupon I awoke and looked,
> and my sleep was pleasant to me.

From this we may conclude that the preceding oracle of salvation was received during the prophet's sleep.

The so-called *vocation narrative* of Samuel is a perfect illustration of how the word of God may be heard in the night. 1 Sam. 3.1-20 is a well-constructed narrative composed of a double introduction (vv. 1+2-3), of a first part divided into three small units (vv. 4-5, 6-7, 8-9) and of a second part composed of two sections (vv. 10-14, 16-18) followed by a conclusion (vv. 19-20). In the first part, Yahweh calls Samuel three times though the young boy is unable to identify the voice. In the second part, once Samuel has been shown how to listen to this particular voice, there is a diptych constituted by two dialogues, each introduced by a call addressed to Samuel (the verb *qr'* is one of the key words of the text): one by night between Yahweh and Samuel, the other in the morning between Eli and Samuel. Verse 15 makes the transition between the two. The symmetry we previously noted between a nocturnal or oneiric dialogue and its daytime counterpart is evident again here.

The oracle in vv. 11-14, does not constitute the centre of gravity of the narrative. The threefold call of Samuel is not a literary device designed to highlight it, but is intended to illustrate, by means of dramatic progression, the laborious appearance of the divine word in the heart of darkness. This becomes obvious if we take into account the structure of the text, the inclusion formed by vv. 1b ('and the *word* of the Lord was rare in those days...') and 20, and the manner in which thirteen occurrences of the root *dbr* are distributed: three in vv. 1-9 and ten in vv. 10-20, of which six fall between 17 and 18a. This layout echoes the narrative development and theological intention of the text very closely.

The decisive point in the narrative is v. 8b where the elderly Eli, in spite of his blindness, has still enough understanding to discern what is happening to the young Samuel *and to explain it to him*. What marks out this text from other prophetic vocation narratives, in addition to God's call, is the place accorded to knowledge passed on from one individual to another. Verse 9 constitutes, from a structural point of view, the central axis of the narrative and signifies, according to the theological perspective of the narrative, the transfer of power from the then decadent and worn-out Silo priesthood to a new form of prophetism. The conciseness of the narrative does not give any details, but clearly suggests that the charismatic powers of the future prophet might be accompanied by more practical teaching about how the word of God might be heard. Verse 9, therefore, should be seen as an allusion to a kind of initiation of the young *nazir* into the prophet's savoir-faire, and the words 'speak, Lord, your servant is listening' could refer to a technique whereby the prophet conditioned himself to receive an oracle during sleep. This 'initiation', begun in the night, ends in the morning when Eli obliges Samuel to speak without holding anything back (v. 16). The neophyte is thus guided through the two phases of the prophetic process, hearing–proclaiming, and in so doing takes on the role of mediator.

As we would expect, given the background outlined above, no mention is made of dreams in this text, but insistence is made upon the nocturnal character of the event, and *dābār* parallels *ḥāzôn* in v. 2. The experience as a whole is described as a *mar'āh* in v. 15, even though there is no visual element in it; but then the expression *b^{e}mar'ot hallay^{e}lāh* designates Jacob's oneiric experience in Gen. 46.2. Besides, the appearance of Yahweh in v. 10, 'and the Lord came and stood forth' (*wayyābō' yhwh wayyityaṣṣab*), is typical of an oneiric theophany, and the hitp. form of *yṣb*—of which this is the only example with Yahweh as subject—recalls an analogous formula in Jacob's dream in Gen. 28.13a: *w^ehinnēh yhwh niṣṣāb 'ālāyw.*

It has been much debated whether Samuel is awake when he hears the oracle or whether he hears it in his sleep. Numerous critics draw attention to the fact that, since he gets up to go to Eli, the call necessarily wakens him each time. This apparently logical interpretation is not as obvious as it seems. When he is called a fourth time, there is no mention of the boy going anywhere, but only of a response on his part, indicating his attentiveness (v. 10b). We have seen above that it is a characteristic of oneiric theophanies that the god appearing in the dream 'wakens' the dreamer. This does not mean that the latter comes out of his sleep, but that he accedes to a specific state of *consciousness in his sleep*. To conclude, it is the explanation of the old priest that allows the young *nazir* to identify the true origin of the voice heard, and which introduces him to this particular form of consciousness during sleep, an experience no doubt close to what one calls a *lucid dream*.

In texts such as these, this form of consciousness in sleep is given literary form by means of imaginary dream dialogues between the dreamer and the divinity appearing in the dream. If we take this idea a little further, we might ask ourselves whether it is not precisely this experience of a special kind of consciousness on the occasion of certain dreams that has made people describe them as 'divine'. In other words, could not the vision of the divinity, or the experience of his presence in a dream, be a way of indicating that the dreamer has acceded by means of a special form of wakefulness during sleep to a consciousness experienced as divine, because it opens him up to a realm other than the external human world?

Chapter 10

DREAMS AND WISDOM

Wisdom literature is thought to have regarded dreams with some scepticism, or even with irony, as is proper to the enlightened. In reality, however, this literature is so diverse that it is impossible to define a general tendency on the basis of a few quotations. It is during the Persian period that the developments in wisdom thinking that led to their writings being more outrightly theological took place. Characteristic of this trend is the increasing importance of the Torah and of the fear of God as the source of true wisdom. No less characteristic, and more significant for us, is the recourse made to divine inspiration in order to authenticate wisdom thinking. Traditionally, it was the teaching of the elders, the observation of nature and experience that were the sages' authorized sources of knowledge. With the book of Job, however, there apppears a form of wisdom that in addition, dares to claim divine inspiration or even a form of prophetic revelation for itself, and in which dreams may have a mediating role.

Finally, we must take into consideration the echoes or influences of wisdom upon texts outwith the body of wisdom literature as such. Relevant here is Solomon's dream at Gibeon, the figures of Joseph and Daniel, and more unexpectedly Abimelech's dream in Genesis 20.

1. *An Unbiased Attitude*

The collections of maxims gathered together in the book of Proverbs make no reference to dreams, but it is hazardous to interpret their absence as a sign of disdain. We might suspect that the sages' pragmatism might make them wary of onciromancy. They were not wary enough, however, to consider it necessary to warn their disciples against the practice, unlike Ben Sira, who did so later. Noteworthy is the fact that the 'instructions' of the sages of Egypt are equally discreet on the subject. There, however, the science of dreams was never the object of polemic.

In Job 20.8, on the other hand, where the brevity of the wicked's triumph is under discussion, Zophar says of the ungodly, 'He will fly away like a dream, and not be found; he will be chased away like a vision of the night.' Similarly, in Isa. 29.5-7, the enemies of Jerusalem will disappear like a dream the moment Yahweh intervenes. The metaphor depends on the dream belonging to the night world, an inference underlined each time by the parallelism *ḥēzyôn layᵉlāh.* The darkness that accompanies night is the accomplice of hostile forces, of wicked people and evil spirits (Ps. 91.5-6); it occasions all kinds of dangers and reprehensible deeds. But this world of shadows, of terrors and of evildoers is destroyed with the coming of daylight (Job 24.14-17; 38.12-15), and is consequently associated with the reality of the dream world that disappears in the morning:

> Like a dream when one awakes, oh Lord,
> on awaking you despise their phantoms (Ps. 73.20).

The expression here is bold, for it attributes the success of the ungodly to a sort of sleep on the part of Yahweh, during which they rise up and flourish like images in a bad dream.

The background to this metaphor does not therefore specifically belong to wisdom literature, but is part of the *Weltanschauung* of the Semites in general, in which the darkness of the night is associated with the forces hostile to the equilibrium of the cosmos and of society. By virtue of belonging to the night, dreams in general are marked by the same ambiguity as the latter, which is not only the moment when the dark forces in the world make themselves busy, but also the moment when God makes his most decisive interventions. The metaphor used in the three texts cited does not therefore reveal so much an attitude derisory of dreams as the more or less conscious fear that they arouse, by virtue of their nocturnal, strange, elusive and sometimes even truly frightening character. Mesopotamian documents show that the fear that dreams provoke, in so far as they are experienced as the activity of a malevolent force upon the dreamer until they have been intepreted and thereby in some way have been exorcized, is not contradictory to the attention they command in other respects.

Other texts, already referred to in the introduction, use dreams as a point of comparison in an ironic context. First of all, there is the rest of the oracle in *Isaiah* mentioned above, in which v. 8, probably an addition, picks up the theme of the dream that vanishes upon awakening; it is, however, developed differently: 'As when a hungry man dreams he is eating and awakes with his hunger not satisfied, or as when a thirsty man dreams he is drinking and awakes faint, with his thirst not quenched' (Isa. 29.8). Here, the enemies of Jerusalem are no longer compared to a dream, but to the dreamer, deceived by the dream in the realization of his desire. Eccl. 5.2 refers to the experience we all have of how our daily preoccupations provide the material for our dream life and sometimes even disturb our sleep (see also Eccl. 2.23). That there is a link between the psychosomatic state of the sleeper and the contents of his or her dreams seems therefore to be an observation unanimously accepted. These passages are in no way hostile to dreams, but simply testify to the recognized diversity of oneiric experiences.

Siracide: Ben Sira states a doctrinal position concerning the value of dreams, which is not lacking in ambiguity, in spite of the fact that it is voiced with vehemence. Sir. 34 (= 31).1-8 is a long tirade about the vanity of dreams (ἐνύπνια) and the risk one runs in paying attention to them. The entire passage is tightly constructed: in the first part, he enumerates over the space of ten verses (vv. 1-5), and in a measured fashion, all the arguments that denigrate dreams: they are 'vain hopes' (v. 1), comparable to shadows (v. 2) or to reflections (v. 3), assimilated with lies (v. 4), associated with divination and with augurs, with the 'fancies' of 'a woman in travail' (v. 5). The second part comprises five verses (vv. 6b-8) and constitutes an exhortation not to pay any attention to them.

The arguments are not new; over and above the illusory aspect of the dream world, *Siracide* picks up (v. 5b) the expression coined by Jeremiah, the 'imagination of the heart', which he associates with illicit divinatory practices (v. 5a). As we have seen above, this is something that the Deuteronomic code never did. On the other hand, he is in line (v. 8) with the Deuteronomists' final work of redaction, which placed the revelation of the Law well above prophetic techniques, dreams included (cf. Num. 12.6-8). Furthermore, ἐνύπνια in v. 5a should be understood to designate oneiromancy, mentioned after the consultation of oracles in general (μαντεῖαι) and presages based on the observation of birds (οἰωνισμοί) in particular. This last form of divination is not of Mesopotamian origin, but seems to have been rather more specific to Asia Minor, to Assyria and to Syria. One senses, behind this last charge against divination, characterized here by its most popular forms, *Siracide*'s constant preoccupation with preserving Jewish identity in a context impregnated by Hellenistic culture.

In a text that resurrects old elements of polemic, it is important to note the contents of v. 6a, situated at the join between the first and second part: 'Unless they are sent from the Most High as a visitation…' (ἐὰν μὴ παρὰ ὑψίστου ἀποσταλῇ ἐν ἐπισκοπῇ). Its position and function as a means of transition between two sections mean that this eventuality is evoked with a remarkable concern for discretion. Nevertheless, the attitude of the author is clear: rejection of oneiromancy should not lead one to deny that God may also speak through dreams. In the language of the Septuagint, the terms ἐπισκοπή, ἐπισκέπτω denote a 'visit' from God, that is, intervention on his part in order to save (Gen. 21.1; 50.24, 25; Exod. 3.16; 13.19, etc.) or to judge (Isa. 10.3; Jer. 6.15; 10.15-16, etc.); we will soon see that this corresponds to an important aspect of the function of dreams in the postexilic wisdom tradition. The expression ἐν ἐπισκοπῇ is also intended to remind the reader that in dreams such as these it is God himself who takes the initiative to come and visit the sleeper. This is not insignificant given the influence of Hellenistic culture on precisely this point, an influence perceptible in apocalyptic literature, where the visionary's journey, in spirit, through the heavens is a well-known motif.

Siracide thus appears to be relatively conservative by comparison with the general trend as regards this issue, but his attitude towards dreams is representative of an opinion that will gradually became normative in Judaism.

2. *Nightmares and the Sages*

As we noticed regarding Mesopotamia, disagreeable or frightening dreams are never recounted in the texts for apotropaic reasons. Nevertheless, the effect they have upon the dreamer became a literary cliché. Sir. 40.1-11 picks up the theme, often developed in wisdom literature, of the misery of human beings in this world: among the ills that afflict humankind, those one experiences by night in dreams (ἐν ὕπνοις) and 'in visions of the mind' (ἐν ὁράσει καρδίας αὐτοῦ) are not the least (vv. 5-7). In this text, Ben Sira fuses elements from two different thematic sources: the misery of humankind during his sojourn on earth and the cry of those who suffer unjustly. It is to the latter that the descriptions of terrifying dreams usually belong:

When I say, 'My bed will comfort me,
 my couch will ease my complaint',
then thou dost scare me with dreams
 and terrify me with visions (Job 7.13-14).

Neither Akkadian nor Hebrew have a specific term for a bad dream or nightmare, but the context indicates clearly that this is what *ḥ*^{a}*lôm* means here. From a literary point of view, these two verses play on the contrast between the relief that rest should bring and the torment that is occasioned by the subject's dreams. This theme is already present in *Ludlul bēl nēmeqi* (I: 54): 'When I sleep at night, my dream terrifies me.' In a Mesopotamian context, nightmares are thought to be provoked by the nocturnal dream gods, *Zaqīqu* or AN.ZA.QAR, who belong to a band of innumerable evil spirits that attack their victims and assail their bodies.

In Job's speeches, even more striking than the obvious inadequacy of the retribution theory is the fact that Yahweh alone is held responsible for the origin of evil. This poses a problem in itself, all the more so when it is the innocent who suffer. We know that one of the essential arguments of his friends in response to this question is the educative value of suffering for someone who is wise enough to allow himself to be taught. Elihu's speeches return to this point with even more regularity. In Job 33.13-18, Elihu presents a veritable theory as regards nightmares when responding to Job as to the grounds of his revolt: God addresses man in two ways to turn him away from evil, through dreams (vv. 15-18) and suffering (vv. 19-22). Verses 15-16 describe how God appears during sleep, in dreams:

In a dream, in a vision or the night,
when deep sleep falls upon men,
 while they slumber on their beds,
then he opens the ears of men,
 and terrifies them in warning them (Job 33.15-16).

In these two verses, there is a discreet echo of Job 7.14, cited above. It comes by way of chiasmus:

7.14 *w*^{e}*ḥittattanî baḥ*^{a}*lomôt ûmēḥezyonôt t*^{e}*ba'*^{a}*tannî:*
33.15a *baḥ*^{a}*löm ḥezyön lay*^{e}*lah...*
16b *ûb*^{e}*mosārām yaḥtōm:*

This parallel allows us to resolve the problem posed by v. 16b, probably corrupt in the MT. On correcting the vocalization, we read: *ûb*^{e}*musārām y*^{e}*ḥittem*: 'and with the warnings (addresssed) to them, he terrifies them'. In place of the faulty vocalization of the Hebrew *yaḥtom*, there should be, as in 7.14, a piel form of the root *ḥtt*, 'to be terrified'.

The comparison of these two verses is not just of philological interest but helps us to put Elihu's argument into context. The author's intention in recalling Job 7.13-14 in Elihu's speech is to respond to the entirely traditional complaint: if God terrifies someone with nightmares, it is not for nothing and for no other reason than to increase his torment, but in order that this reprimand (*mûsār*) might serve as a warning shot. Elihus response is not therefore intended only for Job; through him, he addresses the tradition of the righteous sufferer as a whole, which conveys the motif of night terrors resulting from nightmares.

The educative function of this kind of oneiric divine intervention is emphasized by the vocabulary of v. 16 and vv. 17-18 as a whole. *Mûsār* (an emendation of the vocalization in the MT), meaning 'instruction, warning, punishment' is a term characteristic of the instructions of the sages. The expression 'to open one's ear' *(gālāh 'ōzen)* usually means 'to announce, spread news', but when God is the subject, it designates a particular kind of revelation, one in which there is confidentiality between God and man (cf. 1 Sam. 9.15; 2 Sam. 7.27). Elihu uses it again twice in his fourth speech (36.10, 15), where his argument is the same: if the just succumb to pride, God puts them on their guard by enchaining and thereby humiliating them (36.5-15). Acting thus, 'he opened their ear to instruction' (v. 10: *wayyigel 'oznām lammûsār*). The idea that a vigorous education, accompanied by blows if need be, will turn the disciple away from perdition is widespread in wisdom texts, hence it is not surprising that we find it here. It is neither evil spirits nor some kind of perversity in the divine will that is responsible for making nightmares scary, therefore, but rather God's educative concern. Their ferocity translates the vigour and efficaciousness of a master who is all the more strict on account of the great love he has for his disciple.

According to this explanation, in which we notice a real evolution in thinking between the composition of the dialogues of Job and the later addition of Elihu's speeches, bad dreams are exempt, at least partially, from the category of demoniacal dreams or those of psychosomatic origin. A nightmare may also be a message-dream, but a particular type of message-dream, accompanied by an emotional intensity foreign to other dreams of this kind; it is a veritable 'judgement dream'. It should be remembered that the oneiric theophanies in message-dreams arouse neither fear nor terror in the dreamer. It is not therefore the appearance of God that is terrifying in judgment dreams, but rather the conditions and contents of this type of oneiric experience. Elihu's speeches give no details of their contents, but simply say that they are terrifying. But when Ben Sira defines a real dream as a 'visit' from the Most High (Sir. 34.6a: ἐπισκοπή), he is probably thinking of a form of divine intervention that transposes into the life of individuals, the characteristic pattern of those key moments in history when God intervenes to save his people or judge the nations.

As we have seen, Abimelech's dream (Gen. 20) develops a dialogue between the king and God that reproduces a tribunal scene. By means of this oneiric dialogue, which initially terrifies the dreamer, he is warned by Yahweh himself of the moral seriousness of having abducted Sarah and of the punishment that awaits him. Thus, by becoming aware of his guilt, which was previously unknown to him, he is led to change his behaviour. Behind this very theological narrative in Gen. 20, we find the same idea as in the speeches of Elihu, according to which dreams may be the occasion for divine judgment and for an exhortation to change one's conduct. We have underlined, as regards this text, the essential role of the dream in the theological argument presented there. Clearly, however, this argument can only function if nightmares are interpreted in the manner outlined above. The dream account in Genesis 20 is a typical example, and indeed the only example, of a judgment-dream, of a nightmare rehabilitated (Husser 1991a).

In a late wisdom text, Wis. 18.17-19, we find again the idea that dreams can bring about awareness of divine judgment. This *midrash* of Exodus 12 associates in the course of the same night both aspects of the 'visit': salvation brought to the saints and judgment to the ungodly, the latter pronounced in terms of dreadful dreams. At the very moment when 'the all powerful Word' strikes the sleeping first-born dead, they hear in a dream the announcement of the divine verdict that merits their sudden death:

> Then at once apparitions in dreadful dreams [φαντασίαι μὲν ὀνείρων δεινῶν] greatly troubled them, and unexpected fears assailed them; and one here and another there, hurled down half dead, made known why they were dying, for the dreams [ὀνείροι] which disturbed them forewarned them of this, so that they might not perish without knowing why they suffered (Wis. 18.17-19).

Here it is no longer really a question of a warning shot or of an admonition, for the judgment once passed leaves no place for an appeal or for conversion. However, what is common to these diverse representations of nightmares is the idea that this type of dream does not announce a future event, but brings to mind and elucidates an event in the dreamer's past. Whether judged or severely reprimanded by God, we are not very far from a psychological or moral interpretation of nightmares as a painful way of coming to terms with some cause of remorse.

3. *Dreams as a Source of Wisdom*

The silence of sentential collections and the discretion of the other books in the corpus of wisdom literature on the subject of dreams is to an extent counterbalanced by the tradition that places most of these writings under the authority of Solomon, and that makes him out to be the wisest of sages. Even if this paternity as regards wisdom is the result of a progressive rehabilitation of Solomon and of an idealization of his reign after the return from exile, it seems to have had an important consequence, that of attributing the origin and source of the wisdom tradition in Israel to an oneiric revelation.

Solomon's dream at Gibeon—a typical royal dream—belonged to the propagandist literature of his reign, but the Deuteronomistic redaction of the present text prevents us from discerning what the contents of the pre-Deuteronomistic text might have been. As suggested above, it is likely that the request for wisdom already belonged to the pre-Deuteronomistic version. Taking into account the note in 1 Kgs 11.41, which indicates that the Acts of Solomon also speak of his wisdom, we may suppose that the wealth and glory of his reign were already celebrated there and were set in relation to the latter. If the Deuteronomistic redactor considers the wealth and glory of Solomon as Yahweh's free gift in reward for the piety of his request (1 Kgs 3.13), there is no doubt that they were originally considered to be the fruit and consequence of the king's wisdom. This is a well-known trait of royal ideology, attested in several eighth-century west Semitic inscriptions.[1]

In the royal ideology of the ancient Near East, if the king is the wisest of the wise—as is evident from the very first collections of Egyptian wisdom literature—it is by reason of his participation in divine kingship. There is thus an almost prophetic, inspired aspect to royal wisdom

1. See the Aramean Zenjirli inscription (*KAI* 215: 10-11), the bilingual Phoenician–Hittite Karatepe inscription (*KAI* 26 A: i 11-13).

that fits in naturally with the king's other privileges, among which there is that of oneiric meetings with the gods. It is because all the charismatic powers and attributes associated with the royal function form a homogenous whole, that nobody, it seems, has ever drawn the restrictive conclusion that if the king was wise it was because he had dreams. His wisdom did not come from his dreams, although they confirm it, for both are signs and consequences of his belonging to the world of the divine. That is why none of the wisdom texts that pseudepigraphy attributes to Solomon makes the slightest allusion to the dream at Gibeon. This is not a late form of repudiation, but simply an indication that dreams and wisdom should not be perceived in a relationship of cause and effect, but rather as complementary.

Eliphaz's first speech introduces a gripping description of an oneiric revelation as the core to his argument: Job 4.12-16. The text is very well constructed; it advances according to a dramatic progression that has the effect of presenting v. 17 as an oracle. Here, we are outwith the context of royal wisdom, and the nocturnal experience is more akin to a prophetic dream experience than to a typical message-dream. Besides, the term used is not *ḥ^a^lôm* but the plural 'visions of the night' (*ḥēzyōnôt lay^e^lāh*). This is not the only occasion in Job's friends' speeches where a form of divine inspiration is presented as a source of knowledge (cf. Job 11.5-6; 15.8; 32.8); we have here a clue to the marked evolution in wisdom thinking that took place after the exile.

Recent studies attempt to demonstrate the ironic character of the text, for, as in other passages, the author seems to seek to ridicule Job's friends. This reading depends on a particular interpretation of the book as a whole, a reading that assumes that Job expresses the position of the author of the dialogues (though this is far from being certain), as opposed to the attitude of his friends, which is deliberately caricatured. Without entering into a general discussion of the book, there is in fact nothing in Eliphaz's first speech (Job 4–5) to suggest a rigid or retrograde attitude. Nor is there, in the words of vv. 4.7-21, any remark that deserves to be thus disqualified.

One thing we can be sure of is that this text is woven from references to different forms of famous theophanies, trace of which lingers in a few allusive terms. In v. 13 there is an allusion to the torpor and fear that seized Abraham in Gen. 15.12. The distich in v. 15 completes that of v. 14 in the description of inner dread (and not of a tempest, as the Targum, followed by several scholars who emend *śa'arat*, 'hair', to *śeʿārāh*, 'tempest', suggests); the author uses a well-attested literary cliché in magical Akkaddian literature to evoke a spirit (*eṭemmu*) 'which made the hair of my head stand up' *(ša šârat muḫḫiya uzanaqqapu).* The vision described in v. 16a picks up the terms *mar'eh* and *tᵉmunāh* that in Num. 12.8 describe the immediacy of Moses' contact with God. In v. 16b finally, 'there was silence, then I heard a voice' recalls the theophany at Horeb where Yahweh appears to Elijah in 'the voice of thin silence' (v. 12b: *qôl dᵉmāmāh daqqāh*). As in 1 Kgs 19.9-18, the author plays on the contrast between turbulence and sudden silence to highlight the words that follow. By accumulating these references, Eliphaz situates himself in the line of none other than Abraham, Moses and Elijah. But despite this undeniably artificial aspect, the 'vision' attributed here to Job's interlocutor does genuinely attempt to describe a type of experience to which some sages claimed to refer in order to authenticate their knowledge, and in which the specifically prophetic form of dream experience presented above may be recognized: an absence of scenario and of precise visual images, but on the other hand an auditory perception and a strong impression of a presence.

No other text is as precise and as detailed as the latter as regards the psychosomatic reaction of the individual subject to such an experience. We find something similar, however, in a late text in Isaiah, the famous 'oracle concerning the wilderness of the sea' (Isa. 21.1-4), whose literary links with Ezekiel, Second Isaiah and Job have been demonstrated. The prophet receives a 'stern vision' (v. 2a: *ḥāzût qāšāh huggad lî*) by night (after dark, v. 4b), which paralyses him with terror: 'I am bowed down so that I cannot hear, I am dismayed so that I cannot see' (v. 3b: *naʿᵃwêtî miššᵉmoaʿ nibhaltî mērᵉʾôt*). According to the context—the announced fall of Babylon—it is not the contents of the vision that provokes this unhinging of the psyche, but the visionary experience itself, experienced as oppressive *(qašāh)* and accompanied by convulsions (v. 3a: *ṣîrîm*).

This parallel suggests that the author of the dialogues of Job drew on similar prophetic experiences to describe his character's 'night' vision. Eliphaz represents a category of sages who, in aligning themselves with the tradition of the ancients, do not hesitate to have recourse to a form of inspired knowledge, and appropriate for themselves techniques that up to then had been the sole reserve of the prophets.

Moreover, this type of sage is also represented by such characters as Joseph in Genesis 40–41 and Daniel in the narratives of Daniel 1–6.

Recent studies have limited the wisdom characteristics recognized in the Joseph story by von Rad to a few passages only, including chs. 40–41. It is noteworthy that in these chapters Joseph's wisdom is demonstrated in a rather unexpected way for the wisdom tradition by his ability to interpret dreams, and by the fact that this capacity is inspired by God. By contrast with learned specialists, who have a bookish knowledge of sacred things, Joseph is the humble and docile mediator of knowledge that comes directly from God. His companions in misfortune have already been told this (40.8b): ‘Do not interpretations belong to God?’ The idea is formulated a little differently in 41.16: ‘It is not in me; God will give Pharaoh a favorable answer.’ Although he is the necessary interpreter of a message that otherwise would remain enigmatic, Joseph knows that he is not able to decipher the dream by virtue of his own knowledge or savoir-faire, but entirely thanks to divine revelation. This is what Pharaoh says in v. 38b: ‘Since God has shown you all this, there is none so discreet and wise as you are.’

The same pattern reappears in chs. 1–6 of Daniel. The portrait of Daniel painted there is of the wise courtier; indeed ch. 1 describes in rather minute detail the natural qualities, physical and intellectual, of young men such as him, and their training over a period of three years. To this profane, courtly education, the narrative adds an exemplary religious attitude on the part of the young Hebrews, an attitude in conformity with the idea that true wisdom consists in observance of the law of Moses. Their faithfulness to the Law means that they surpass their colleagues, even in secular sciences (Dan. 1.18-20), for ‘God gave them learning and skill in all letters and wisdom’ (1.17). Finally, the text specifies that ‘Daniel had understanding in all visions and dreams’ (1.17b: *w^{e}dānîyē’l hēbîn b^{e}kol ḥāzôn waḥ^{a}lōmôt*), a remark that introduces the special role he will have in the following chapters. From ch. 2 onwards, there is no more mention made of the secular knowledge of these sage courtiers; the group seems to be essentially composed of diviners and of magicians, and it is above all in the realm of divination that Daniel will employ his skill. Like Joseph, he is a specialist in the inspired interpretation of dreams, and even if he does not himself dream (in chs. 1–6), it is in a ‘night vision’ that the mystery of the king's dream is revealed to him (2.19: *b^{e}ḥezwâ dî lêlyâ rāzāh g^{a}lî*). Each narrative insists, sometimes excessively, upon the eminent qualities of Daniel, upon his intelligence and wisdom, owing to the presence of the divine spirit within him: 4.5, 6, 15; 5.11-12 (MT).

In Dan. 5.12 three of Daniel's aptitudes are enumerated: his ability to interpret dreams (*m^{e}paššar ḥelmîn*), to explain riddles (*wa'aḥ^{a}wāyat '^{a}ḥîdān*), to undo spells (*ûm^{e}šārē' qiṭrîn*); this is the description of someone whose knowledge pertains at once to the realms of wisdom, to oracles and to magic. It also makes a discreet allusion to Num. 12.6-8: without usurping Moses' privilege to dialogue face to face with Yahweh, 'clearly and not in dark speech', and using the prophetic modes of revelation (dreams and visions) Daniel appears to be more able than the prophets in so far as he knows how to interpret dreams and solve enigmas.

We must take into account here the taste that these tales had for the fantastic, and the exaggerations that appear as a consequence, just as we should not forget the ambient pre-apocalyptic atmosphere into which they are born. By embodying wisdom and prophetic qualities, Daniel is only an enhancement of what is already present in Joseph. The works of Müller (1969; 1972) have drawn attention to the resurgence after the exile of a form of wisdom qualified as 'mantic and divinatory', attested in the most ancient texts of all the Near East. Very different from the didactic wisdom of proverbs, *ḥokmāh* here designates the knowledge and skill of someone expert in the handling of magical techniques or in the knowledge of things hidden, either past or future.

It is owing to the exile and in the communities of the Diaspora that this form of wisdom rediscovered its rightful place in the literary tradition of Israel. The Joseph and Daniel narratives clearly testify to this, as does the postexilic origin of several texts that make allusion to it (Isa. 44.25; 47.10; Jer. 50.35-36). Although one part of the wisdom movement remained attached to the ancient didactic tradition (e.g. Ben Sira), it is certain that the convergence of prophetism with a form of wisdom that claimed a certain degree of inspiration, and which was very keen on the interpretation of dreams and mysterious writings (cf. Dan. 5), played an important part in the emergence of the apocalyptic movement. The above-mentioned texts testify to the place held by dreams in this form of wisdom, both as a source of wisdom, but also as the object of interpretation. It is probable that, if we are to discern any irony in the description of Eliphaz's oneiric experience (Job 4.12-16), it is at this new category of sages that it is directed.

Chapter 11

PRACTICES ASSOCIATED WITH DREAMS

As we said in the introduction, a certain number of ritualized practices take shape around oneiric experiences. They do so according to the ominous or genuinely oracular value attributed to dream experiences in certain cases. In so far as the study of the comparative history of religion allows us to itemize them, the aim of these practices was essentially to provoke dream experiences, to interpret their contents or to protect oneself against their harmful consequences. They therefore belong to the realm of divination or to magic.

The biblical corpus does not transmit any ritual of this kind, nor indeed anything resembling a dream book. If the question of the existence of such practices in Israel may be legitimately posed, it is only on the basis of the comparative study of religion. This discipline enables us, due precautions taken, to make explicit certain scattered allusions, or to confirm some hints yielded by the internal examination of the texts. We come back, therefore, in this last chapter, to a certain number of texts studied previously to examine them in this particular respect only. Some have been the object of much debate (e.g. 1 Kgs 3.4-15; 1 Sam. 3); to these we will attempt to bring not so much a solution as perhaps a new way of tackling the question. It is beyond doubt that dreams belonged to the panoply of divinatory techniques authorized in Israel, even if the latter decreased considerably in number under the pressure of successive legislations. The episode in which Saul consults the witch of En Dor is revelatory of this situation.

In this narrative (1 Sam. 28), Saul only decides to have recourse to necromancy—which he himself would have abolished—after having exhausted the resources of legal divination: 'And when Saul inquired of the Lord, the Lord did not answer him, either by dreams, or by Urim, or by prophets' (v. 6: *wayyiš'al šā'ûl byhwh w*^{e}*lō' 'ānāhû yhwh gam baḥ*^{a}*lōmôt gam bā'ûrîm gam bann*^{e}*bî'im*). The narrative contrasts a series of silent oracles with Saul's illicit consultation of a deceased prophet who gives him the answer he was looking for. The insertion of this episode (28.3-25, less vv. 17-19a) in this particular context is attributed to a Deuteronomistic prophetic redactor (dtrP), but it is probable that he reworked an older autonomous tradition. Whatever the case, Saul is once more presented as the transgressor of divine law (cf. Deut. 18.10-11, to which the text seems to refer), even if the text insists more on the human drama than on this legal aspect.

Authorized divination takes three main directions: it makes use of dreams, *'ûrîm* and the prophets. The verb here is *š'l*, the equivalent of *drš* in other contexts, but which seems usually to designate more specifically the consultation of priestly oracles, in which the reply given is either 'yes' or 'no' (*ṭôb–ra'*). There are other examples of this kind of 'divinatory trivium' outside Israel, namely among the Hittites (p. 54), and in Homeric literature (p. 79), where priests, diviners and dream specialists sum up all aspects of mantic science. In 1 Samuel 28, reference is made to a war oracle, solicited through the intermediation of a prophet (cf. 1 Sam. 23.2, 4; 2 Sam. 2.1; 5.19, 23), and the *'ûrîm* designate the kind of divination proper to priests (cf. 1 Sam. 14.36-42; 22.10-15). On the other hand, it is more difficult to decide to what sort of divination the expression *baḥ^{a}lōmôt* refers.

If it is agreed that *'ûrîm* and *n^{e}bi'îm* refer to the mediators constituted by priest and prophet, we might be tempted to assume that *ḥ^{a}lōmôt* refers to dream specialists or oneiromancers. In actual fact, the literary expression is more flexible and seems to denote in succession, a 'natural' phenomenon (the dream), an instrument of divination (the *'ûrîm*) and a person (the prophet). It is certain that it is a stylistic effect that is desired here, and the example constitutes a salutary warning against being too systematic in our deductions. On the other hand, the context clearly indicates that different forms of *deductive* divination are referred to here: God is solicited or questioned in diverse ways. This being so, the *ḥ^{a}lōmôt* may also allude to a specific technique enabling one to receive God's response in a dream, an incubatory practice in other words. Nothing indicates that Saul himself had the dreams; he could just as easily have had recourse to a specialist in *directed dreams*. There is no detail in this allusive text that permits us to be more precise. The only element of which we are certain is that oneiric experiences are numbered among divinatory techniques, a fact that the Deuteronomistic redactor seems neither to contest nor to criticize.

1. *Oneiromancy*

It would be good to be able to treat deductive and inspired oneiromancy separately, for this distinction would allow us to assess whether the difference we observe in Mesopotamia between the technique of the *bārû* and the science of the *šā'ilu* also exists in Israel. Unfortunately, the nature of the texts is such that it is almost always difficult to know to which of the two allusion is made. We should remind ourselves that the first denotes the interpretation of dreams by specialists in possession of scholarly knowledge, using collections itemizing the greatest possible number of dream types. The second is an interpretation dependent upon the intuition, or even inspiration of the interpreter, without the aid of any systematic technique. Although no collection of Hebrew presages, however fragmentary, has ever been found by archaeology, a certain number of allusions allow us to affirm that one or other form of dream interpretation was practised, more or less legally.

For example, Jeremiah's letter to the exiles warns the latter (Jer. 29.8) not to allow themselves to be deceived by prophets or diviners, and he adds 'do not pay attention to your dreams' (*w^{e}'al tišm^{e}'û 'el ḥalōmōtêkem*). The expression gives the reader to understand that the prophets and diviners (*qos^{e}mîm*) in question occasionally acted as dream interpreters for the community. The Babylonian context of those for whom the letter was written leaves one question unanswered: was it the oneiromancy of the *bārû* or the inspired interpretation of the *n^{e}bî'im* that was practised? Is it the legitimacy of dream interpretation or is it the quality of the intepreter that is contested? The same uncertainty hangs over the oracle in Zech. 10.2 where the three aspects of divination, broadly summed up by the headings *terapîm*, diviners and dreams are this time referred to in negative terms.

I have already summarized Richter's argument in his study of *Formgeschichte*: the recurrence of the same grammatical form in all the symbolic dream accounts, whatever their origin, invites us to suppose that this is the mark of an institutionalized practice of oneiromancy and the confirmation of its *Sitz im Leben*. Richter also draws attention to the fact that all these accounts speak of or imply an interpretative phase, and that a good number present an interpreter of undisputable Yahwistic orthodoxy. Despite the weaknesses of his historical reconstitution deduced from these observations, recourse to form criticism is nevertheless one of the only ways of gaining any light on the subject.

However, the clues contained in these accounts orient us in two different directions:

1. The structure of the accounts (dream + interpretation), as well as numerous details observable in Genesis 40–41 and in the narratives of Daniel 1–6, do indeed present figures practising a form of inspired oneiromancy that is completely different from the deductive interpretation of professional oneiromancers. We have seen how the texts emphasize forcibly the superiority of these heroes over the colleges of Egyptian or Chaldean *ḥarṭummîm* and insist upon the inspired character of this particular kind of sage. They accede, like Daniel, to the status of prophet precisely by virtue of their capacity to interpret dreams. Admitted into the realm of prophecy, this particular form of wisdom also evolves in such a way as to find a place in the apocalyptic movement, thanks to the conviction that the true sage is aided by the *ruaḥ* of God, which reveals to him the hidden relationship between events in the world and the designs of God. In order to decipher the prophetic signs contained in oneiric visions or in the sacred writings, the sage must be granted the same spirit that brought them about. The interpreter is not just someone who can undo the oppressive bonds of dreams (e.g. Gen. 40.6; 41.8; Dan. 2.1), but he becomes the necessary mediator without whom the divine word would remain trapped in enigmas. Consequently, he is its true messenger.

Besides, the inspired interpretation of dreams is well attested in Judaism from the beginning of the Christian era. When Archeläus, Herod's son, is upset by a dream, Simon the Essene is sent for to interpret it (Josephus, *Ant.* 17.345-48; *War* 2.112-13). Josephus emphasizes the prophetic gifts of certain Essenes (*Ant.* 15.373-79) judged to be expert in the interpretation of the holy books (*War* 2.159). He himself sees dreams as a sign of the providential intervention of God in the history of mankind (*Life* 208-209; *War* 2.114-16) and he likes to think he can interpret them (*War* 3.351-54) (see Gnuse 1989). According to the Talmud (*b. Ber. 55b*), there were twenty-four dream interpreters in Jerusalem who were remunerated for their services and seem to have constituted a professional group. *b. Ber.* 55a compares an uninterpreted dream to a sealed letter. Among the *Tannaïm*, three benefit from a special reputation in this domain: R. Ishmaël b. Yosé, R. Yosé b. Halafta and R. 'Akiba (*y. M.Š.* 4.8). In spite of a notable diversity of opinion among the experts (cf. *b. Ber.* 55a), the relatively numerous pieces of evidence in ancient rabbinic literature show that inspired oneiromancy was not the exclusive reserve of apocalyptic milieux.

Some kind of intuitive dream intepretation had probably always existed in Israel. The Joseph story presupposes that this practice existed as early as the beginning of the Persian period, in the same wisdom movement that initiated the evolution described above. Before that, the only written sources that refer to it are Joseph's dreams (Gen. 37) and the dream of the Midianite soldier (Judg. 7.13-15); as we have seen, these accounts describe a spontaneous, non-institutionalized kind of interpretation, which is little concerned with theory, both as far as the aetiology of the dreams and the charism of the interpreter is concerned.

2. Given the absence of any *dream book*, traces of deductive oneiromancy may also be found in the grammatical form of the dream accounts in the Joseph story. The interpretative part, sometimes introduced by the formula 'This is its interpretation' (*zeh pitrōnô*: Gen. 40.12, 18), always begins by giving an explanation of the symbolic elements in the dream: 'the three branches are three days' (40.12b: *š^elošet haśśārigîm š^elošet yāmîm hēm*); 'the seven good cows are seven years' (41.26a: *šeba' pārōt haṭṭobōt šeba' šānîm hēnnāh*), etc. In each case, the sentence consists of short nominal clauses set in juxtaposition. The interpretation is then developed by verbal clauses in the *yiqṭol* and *w^eqaṭal* form.

The systematic nature of Joseph's deductions is intended to give the impression of a rational procedure, as if inspired dream interpretation gained even more authority by being dressed up in the formulae of the interpretative science of diviners. Indeed, behind these nominal clauses in juxaposition we recognize the stereotyped expression of *dream books*, which organized each presage around protasis ('if someone dreams that...') and apodosis ('it is/means...'). The survival of this formulaic style in these chapters perhaps bears witness to the prestige that deductive oneiromancy, based upon lists of presages, enjoyed, and thus to the existence of this kind of divination in Israel. The evidence is slender and does not permit us to advance any firm conclusions on the subject. Besides, it is possible, given the relative silence of Ugaritic sources on this subject, that the absence of presage lists in Israel is not only the result of theological censure, but of a general tendency in the west Semitic world to prefer inspired divination to deductive inspiration, in direct contrast with Mesopotamia.

2. *Incubation*

As in the case of oneiromancy, incubation is not easily discernible in ancient Israel, and many authors have been tempted, in the face of texts always suspected of bowdlerization, to fill out the slender indices that might allude to it. There is no certainty as to the existence of such a rite, and even less as to the details of how it was practised. Caution, however, must not lead us to become radically sceptical, for there are other ritual practices which are equally poorly known in any detail, but whose existence is beyond doubt (ordeals, priestly oracles, for example). Besides, the texts concerned do not all seem to refer to the same type of incubation and a distinction should be made between royal, cultic and popular practices.

Among all the texts of the Old Testament, it is Solomon's dream at Gibeon (1 Kgs 3.4-15) that has provoked the most discussion on the subject. For Ehrlich (1953: 19-26) it is the only biblical text to attest indubitably to the existence of such a rite in Israel, in spite of the corrections made to the original text by a Deuteronomistic redactor in order to efface all trace of it. Referring to the model of incubation such as it is described in Greek sources, he claims to find all the constituent elements in this passage: a sanctuary, a sacrifice, night, sleep and finally a dream accompanied by a divine revelation.

Ehrlich, followed by numerous authors, is of the opinion that the MT made one last attempt to camouflage the incubation rite by making a correction at the join between vv. 4 and 5. The Greek version, he argues, is the more authentic textual tradition, in so far as it places the separation between verses *after* the complement designating the place 'at Gibeon' (and not before as in the MT). In so doing the rather unfortunate layout of the MT, which places the demonstrative pronoun at the end of the verse, is avoided: *'al hammizbēaḥ hahû'*. It is true that the LXX is more satisfying stylistically at this point: (4) χιλίαν ὁλοκαύστωσιν ἀνήνεγκεν Σαλωμων ἐπὶ τὸ θυσιαστήριον ἐν Γαβαων. (5) Καὶ ὤφθη κύριος κτλ...

According to these authors, although the text transmitted by the LXX does not speak explicitly of incubation, there are hints in it that the sacrifices offered by Solomon at Gibeon and the apparition of Yahweh in Solomon's dream are somehow related in terms of cause and effect. If we content ourselves with the Greek model of incubation, then it is indeed important to establish this point. Ehrlich claims to find confirmation of this reading of the LXX in Josephus's version of the event (*Ant*. 8.2):

> He decided to go to Gibeon to make a sacrifice to God on the altar of bronze built by Moses, and he offered a thousand victims as a burnt offering. In so doing, it appears that he honored God greatly; indeed God appeared to him that very night in a dream.

Josephus puts together pieces of information from 1 Kings 3 and 2 Chron. 1.3-13. It is certain that, without insisting any further, this text would have evoked the practice of incubation for a first or second century reader CE. However, it simply testifies to Josephus's rhetorical skill in expressing the way he himself understood the biblical passage, but cannot claim greater 'historical authenticity' than the MT.

It is certain that the Greek depends upon an original Hebrew different from that of the MT, but that does not of itself suffice to make it more 'authentic'. In these two verses, which are characterized by a certain awkwardness of expression, it is the MT that presents the *lectio difficilior*; the textual tradition on which the Greek depends seems in fact to have been the object of corrections intended to eradicate the identification, in v. 4, of the altar with the high place. Indeed, the association of *habbāmāh hagg*^{e}*dôlāh* with *hammizbēaḥ hahû'*, given that the demonstrative pronoun has no other antecedent, had become embarrassing ever since the Chronicler identified the altar at Gibeon with the bronze altar of the sanctuary in the desert (1 Chron. 1.5-6). Moreover, in Hebrew as well as in Greek, the syntax of v. 4b indicates that the evocation of 'a thousand burnt offerings' is introduced in parenthesis, and that the *yqṭl* form of the verb is to be understood frequentatively: 'Solomon will offer a thousand burnt offerings on this altar.' There is not even in Greek, therefore, any direct relationship between the sacrifices and the dream.

Seen in this light, the question of incubation does not make much sense here, on the one hand because reference is made exclusively to the Greek model of the ritual, and on the other hand because it means reading the text as if it were a faithful chronicle of events. It is obvious that the text does not describe an incubation ritual, even though an effort is made to discern the latter behind the present text, as if it were an albeit allusive record of hard historical facts. Scholars then invoke censure, put in place at diverse moments in the redaction in order to camouflage an 'historical truth' that has never at any time been questioned. Logically enough, those who consider this passage to be an entirely Deuteronomistic compostition reject any reference to incubation, since, according to this hypothesis, the entire narrative is fictitious.

We explained above why the hypothesis of a pre-Deuteronomistic document remains the most likely, and how the latter has the function of legitimizing a reign by illustrating an important theme in royal ideology: that of the royal privilege of making a free wish before the dynastic god. This theme is well attested in Aramaic inscriptions and in the psalms, but always by way of allusion. The *Keret Epic* and 1 Kings 3 are the only literary descriptions to develop the way in which this privileged relationship between king and his god was lived out. As it happens, and quite independently, these narratives both situate the meeting in which the god proposes and the king makes his request *in a dream*. If we were to advance the hypothesis that dreams were generally and habitually the context in which this exchange took place, then we might conclude that a habitual form of incubation, perhaps linked to the rites of enthronement, also existed.

These indices do not permit us to affirm that Solomon really did undergo an incubation ritual in order to receive a dream in the sanctuary at Gibeon, but they do imply that the legitimation narrative based its argument upon a known and perhaps institutionalized practice of incubation in a royal context. For a dream to function as a legitimation narrative, there must by implication have been a common belief in the possibility of such an oneiric meeting, and recognition of a ritual specially designed to provoke such an encounter. It is impossible, however, on the basis of 1 Kings 3, to say any more on the subject or to try to reconstitute any such ritual.

A certain number of verses in the Psalms are sometimes thought to allude to incubation practices, which might be qualified as cultic. Mowinckel (1961) forwards this interpretation systematically, though with certain reservations: 'Finally, there are a few places, which perhaps point to an incubation oracle' (p. 145). Among these passages is Ps. 3.5-6 (MT):

> I cry aloud to the Lord,
> and he answers me from his holy hill. Selah.
>
> I lie down and sleep;
> I wake again, for the Lord sustains me.

Most critics, and among them Gunkel, refuse to see any allusion to an oracle received in the course of incubation in this passage. They point out that there is no mention either of a dream or of sleep in a sanctuary. This objection is in fact as fragile as the argument they seek to counter, for (1) it takes as its reference the Greek model of incubation, and (2) it demands of a psalm, which is a prayer, the same degree of concrete detail as regards its *Sitz im Leben* as that which is normally expected of a ritual text. Other passages allude to sleep under Yahweh's (4.9) or Shaddaï's (9.1) protection, others mention meditation in the night (63.7) or evoke a vision of God on 'waking up' (17.15). All have been the object of the same debate.

In fact, the whole problem of using psalms to restitute an incubation practice lies in none other than the absence of precise details concerning the liturgical act with which we presume they were associated, *whatever it was like*. If some of them accompanied the ritual watch of an incubant, or his prayer of thanksgiving on awakening, they did not necessarily include an explicit reminder of the night spent in the sanctuary or of the incubant's sleep, or of his dream. Thus nothing prevents us from supposing that the oracle of salvation, which is thought to be the background to several psalms of supplication, including Ps. 3, was *heard in a dream*, and not from the lips of a priest (who is also absent from the text of the psalm), for example, Psalms 6, 13, 22, etc. But this is a hypothesis that is definitively unverifiable.

Psalm 155, up till now only known in the Syriac version (*5 Apoc. Syr. Ps.* 3), and which the Hebrew text, found at Qumran (11QPs[a] = 11Q5: xxiv.3-18), revealed to be an alphabetic psalm, has a passage in it that might possibly contain an explicit allusion to incubation:

> My trust is in you, YHWH.
> I called 'YHWH', and he heard me
> [and healed] my broken heart.
>
> Now I slumbered and slept;
> I dreamt and, well: [woke up!]
>
> (11Q5: xxiv.15b-17; Garcia Martinez 1994: 308)

We can restore the end of v. 17 with the help of the Syriac. The psalm was not composed at Qumran, and probably dates between the fifth and second century BCE. The study of its structure and of the deficiencies in its alphabetic form seems to indicate that it is the result either of a combination of two psalms, or the secondary extension of an acrostic poem. Its structure is that of an individual lamentation psalm and it is very close in style to Ps. 22. The three last verses (lost in the Hebrew text) contain the thanksgiving of the supplicant after he has been healed. The allusion to incubation falls precisely at the join between supplication and thanksgiving, at the very point where it is generally agreed that the oracle of salvation was pronounced.

Finally, an allusion to a popular form of incubation is to be found in an oracle often attributed to Third Isaiah, which enumerates pagan practices still current in Israel:

> They sacrifice in gardens
> and burn incense upon bricks;
> they sit in tombs,
> and spend the night in caves [Greek];
> they eat swine's flesh,
> and broth of abominable things is in their vessels (Isa. 65.3b-5).

Verse 4a mentions necromancy, which we know was strictly forbidden (cf. Deut. 18.11; Lev. 19.31; 20.6, 27; 1 Sam. 28; Isa. 8.19). It is set in parallel with incubation 'in caves',[1] 'in order to have dreams', as the Greek specifies (καὶ ἐν τοῖς σπηλαίοις κοιμῶνται δι' ἐνύπνια). Unlike necromancy, incubation was never explicitly forbidden, perhaps because it was very infrequently practised in ancient times in the form that is envisaged here. In his commentary, St Jerome makes the allusion in this passage explicit on the basis of what he knew of the practice in his day:

> Sitting down or living in the tombs and sanctuaries of idols, where they were in habit of lying down on the skins of sacrificed animals, in order to know the future by means of dreams, an abomination which is practiced in the temple of Esculap even to this day (*PL* 24.657A).

3. *The Prophets and Directed Dreams*

We have seen above (pp. 151-54) that if dreams *(ḥ^alôm)* are apparently absent from prophetic texts, the prophets' nights were sometimes rich in 'visions' *(ḥāzôn)*. We have also noted that a hypothesis concerning a specific kind of dream experience relative to their particular function may be advanced. In addition to what we have already said on this subject as regards 1 Samuel 3, we should add here that one of the particularities of prophetic dream experience was that it responded to a conscious prompting: the prophet could provoke, or even direct his

1. BHS proposes to emmend the MT according to the Greek so that we read *ûbên ṣôrîm* (instead of *ûbann^{e}ṣûrîm*) *yālînû*.

'dream', using techniques that escape us. The narrative that describes Samuel's call seemed to contain a precise allusion to the transmission of knowledge from master to disciple (1 Sam. 3.9), based upon a technique of self-conditioning permitting the disciple to perceive a divine word 'heard' in the night. Samuel's response, 'Speak Lord, your servant is listening,' is the literary expression of an awakening to a particular form of consciousness *in sleep*, permitting the *nabî'* not only to listen to an oneiric oracle but also to solicit it.

This hypothesis has nothing improbable about it from the standpoint of modern science, as we noted in the introduction: cases of lucid dreams observed in the laboratory, and therapies using daydreams among their techniques, can supply us with similar indicators. If we avoid speaking of incubation here, it is only to dispel any confusion with the generally received model. In a prophetic context, in fact, it is useless to try to be sure of the use of a precise ritual—perhaps there never was one—for we are no doubt much nearer what we call today a directed dream in a shamanic sense than what is generally described as incubation.

Several authors, however, have argued that 1 Samuel 3 contains a description of incubation, and Oppenheim has addressed the subject of 'involuntary incubation' (!). To my mind, the reason why Samuel slept in the sanctuary was not so as to provoke a divine revelation, for his nearness to the ark, in the minds of the Deuteronomistic redactors of the narrative, was none other than expressly to place the future prophet in the line of Moses, the first mediator of the *dābār*. However, the initiatory value of this first nocturnal revelation and of the prophetic knowledge transmitted by the elderly Eli suggests that it is henceforth by means of nocturnal, oneiric conversations such as this that the prophet will hear the word of God (1 Sam. 3.21). Thus, if the narrative does not describe an incubation as such, it allows us to suppose that a *nabî'* like Samuel knew how to control a form of dream experience that favoured contact with the world of the divine.

Another illustration of dream experiences directed by the prophets is evident in the story of Balaam (Num. 22–24) studied above. We have seen how the narrative is structured in such a way that the prophets' two nocturnal conversations with God parallel the two visionary oracles that take place during the day. The fact that God comes to visit Balaam during the night already belongs to the Transjordanian tradition of Deïr 'Alla, but the way in which the event is presented in Numbers 22, shows that the diviner himself knew how to enter into contact with the divinity by night: Balaam makes each of the embassies wait until the following morning for his reply. The allusion is clearly to a professional know-how that allows the prophet to provoke nocturnal conversations with the divinity, in the same manner as the oneiric dialogues (Num. 22.8-13, 19-20) evoke a form of 'lucid dream'.

However fictitious the narrative, its active involvement in the struggle against false prophets and the effort made to make it correspond to certain theological norms give this piece of evidence special weight. Even if, owing to a concern to clarify the process of inspiration in theoretical terms, and in reaction to certain deviations, the author attempts to subordinate oneiric experience to visionary oracles, the former nevertheless appears to be one of the major aspects of prophetic practice. We have no option here but to suspect the existence of a specifically prophetic form of incubation whose technical aspects will no doubt always escape us, but which encourage us to keep our options open when defining incubation.

BIBLIOGRAPHY

Alster, B.

1972 *Dumuzi's Dream: Aspects of Oral Poetry in a Sumerian Myth* (Mesopotamia, 1; Copenhagen: Akademisk Forlag).

Asher-Greve, J.M.

1987 'The Oldest Female Oniromancer', in J.-M. Durand (ed.), *La femme dans le Proche-Orient antique* (XXXIIIe Rencontre Assyriologique Internationale, Paris: Recherches sur les civilisations): 27-32.

Assmann, J.

1978 'Eine Traumoffenbarung der Göttin Hathor', *RE* 30: 22-50.

Badawi, A.M.

1943 'Die neue historische Stele Amenophis' II', *Annales du Service des Antiquités de l'Egypte* 42: 1-23.

Balmary, Marie

1986 *Le sacrifice interdit* (Paris: Grasset).

Barguet, P.

1953 *La stèle de la famine à Séhel* (Bibliothèque d'Etudes, 24; Cairo: IFAO).

Bergmann, E., G. Botterweck and Ottosson

1980 '*ḥālam*/*ḥ^{a}lôm*', *TDOT*, VI: 421-32.

Beyerlin, W.W.

1978 *Near Eastern Religious Texts Relating to the Old Testament* (OTL; London: SCM Press).

Bonechi, M., and J.-M. Durand

1992 'Oniromancie et magie à Mari à l'époque d'Ebla', *Quaderni di Semistica* 18: 151-59.

Bottéro, J.

1974 'Symptômes, signes, écriture en Mésopotamie ancienne', in J.-P. Vernant *et al.*, *Divination et rationalité* (Paris: Le Seuil): 70-197.

1987 'L'oniromancie en Mésopotamie ancienne', in J. Bottéro, *Mésopotamie, l'écriture, la raison et les dieux* (Paris: Gallimard): 133-56.

Bouché-Leclercq, A.

1963 *Histoire de la divination dans l'Antiquité* (4 vols; Brussels: Culture et civilisation [1879–82]).

Brekelmans, C.H.W.

1982 'Solomon at Gibeon', in W.C. Delsman (ed.), *Von Kanaan bis Kerala* (Festschrift J.P.M. van der Ploeg; AOAT, 211; Neukirchen–Vluyn: Neukirchener Verlag): 53-59

Butler, S.A.L.

1998 *Mesopotamian Conceptions of Dreams and Dream Rituals* (AOAT, 258; Münster: Ugarit Verlag).

Byl, S.

1979 'Quelques idées grecques sur le rêve, d'Homère à Artémidore', *EC* 47: 107-23.

Cagni, L.

1969 *L'epopea di Erra* (Studi Semitici, 34; Rome: Università di Roma).

Caillois, R., and G.E. von Grunebaum (eds.).

1966 *The Dream and Human Societies* (Berkeley: University of California Press).

Caquot, A.

1959 'Les songes et leur interprétation selon Canaan et Israël', in *Les songes et leur interprétation* (Sources Orientales, 2; Paris: Le Seuil): 99-124.

Casevitz, M.

1982 'Les mots du rêve en grec ancien', *Ktema* 7: 67-74.

Cavalletti, S.

1959 'Sogno e profezia nell'Antico Testamento', *RivB* 7: 356-63.

1960 'L'incubazione nell'Antico Testamento', *RivB* 8: 42-48.

Cooper, J.S.

1985 'Sargon and Joseph: Dreams Come True', in A. Kort (ed.), *Biblical and Related Studies Presented to Samuel Iwry* (Winona Lake, IN: Eisenbrauns): 33-39.

1986 *Sumerian and Akkadian Royal Inscriptions.* I. *Presargonic Inscriptions* (AOS Translation Series; New Haven: Yale University Press).

Cooper, J.S., and W. Heimpel

1983 'The Sumerian Sargon Legend', *JAOS* 103: 67-82.

Couffignal, R.

1977 'Le songe de Jacob. Approches nouvelles de Genèse 28, 10-22', *Bib* 58: 342-60.

Dalley, S.

1989 *Myths from Mesopotamia* (Oxford: Oxford University Press).

Dietrich, M. and O. Loretz

1990 *Mantik in Ugarit* (ALASP, 3; Münster: Ugarit Verlag).

Dray, J.D.

1976 *The Archive of Hor* (Texts from Excavations, 2; London: Egypt Exploration Society).

Drewermann, E.

1984 'Die Wahrheit der Formen. Traum, Mythos, Märchen, Sage und Legende', in *Tiefen Psychologie und Exegese*, I (Olten-Freiburg im Br.: Walter Verlag).

Dunand, F.

1997 'La consultation oraculaire en Egypte tardive: l'oracle de Bès à Abydos', in J.-G. Heintz (ed.), *Oracles et prophéties dans l'Antiquité* (Actes du Colloque de Strasbourg, 15–17 juin 1995; Strasbourg: Université des Sciences humaines): 65-84.

Durand, J.-M.

1988 *Archives épistolaires de Mari* 1.1 (Paris: Recherches sur les civilisations).

Ehrlich, E.L.

1953 *Der Traum im Alten Testament* (BZAW, 73; Berlin: Alfred Töpelmann).

Falgayrettes, C.
1988 *Supports de rêves* (Paris: Fondation Dapper).
Falkenstein, A.
1966 'Wahrsagung in der sumerischen Überlieferung', in *La divination en Mésopotamie ancienne et dans les régions voisines* (XIVe Rencontre Assyriologique Internationale; Paris: Presses Universitaires de France): 45-68.
Festugière, A.J.
1975 *Artimédore: La clef des songes* (Paris: Belles Lettres).
Finkel, A.
1963–64 'The Pesher of Dreams and Scriptures', *RevQ* 4: 357-70.
Fishbane, M.
1985 'The Mantological Exegesis of Dreams, Visions and Omens', in M. Fishbane, *Biblical Interpretation in Ancient Israel* (Oxford: Clarendon Press): 447-57.
Follet, R.
1954 'Šunatua damqa', *VD* 32: 90-98.
Foster, B.R.
1993 *Before the Muses: An Anthology of Akkadian Literature*, II (Maryland: Bethesda Press).
1995 *From Distant Days: Myths, Tales and Poetry from Ancient Mesopotamy* (Bethesda, ML: CDL Press).
Gadd, C.J.
1958 'The Haran Inscriptions of Nabonidus', *AnSt* 8: 35-92.
Garcia Martinez, F.
1994 *The Sead Sea Scrolls Translated* (Leiden: E.J. Brill).
Gardiner, A.H.
1935 *Hieratic Papyri in the British Museum.* III. *Chester Beatty Gift* (London: British Museum).
Gibert, P.
1990 *Le récit biblique de rêve: Essai de confrontation analytique* (Lyon: Profac).
Gnuse, R.
1984 *The Dream Theophany of Samuel: Its Structure in Relation to Ancient Near Eastern Dreams and its Significance* (Lanham, MD: University Press of America).
1989 'Dream Reports in the Writings of Flavius Josephus', *RB* 96: 358-90.
1995 'Dreams in the Night—Scholarly Mirage or Theophanic Formula? The Dream Report as a Motif of the so-Called Elohist Tradition', *BZ* 39: 28-58.
Goedicke, H.
1996 '*ḥartummîm*', *Or* 65: 24-30.
Goetze, A.
1925 *Hattušiliš: Der Bericht über seine Thronbesteigung nebst den Paralleltexten* (MVAG, 29.3; Leipzig: Hinrichs).
Gordon, C. H.
1953 'Sabbatical Cycle or Seasonal Pattern?', *Or* 22: 79-81.

Green, C.
1989 *Lucid Dreams* (Institute of Psychological Research; Oxford: Whitaker).

Griffith, F.L.
1900 *Stories of the High Priests of Memphis: The Sethon of Herodotus and the Demotic Tale of Khamuas* (Oxford: Clarendon Press).

Guillaume, A.
1938 *Prophecy and Divination among the Hebrews and Other Semites* (London: Cassell).

Hark, H.
1982 *Der Traum als Gottes vergessene Sprache* (Olten-Freiburg im Br.: Walter Verlag).

Hermann, A.
1938 *Die ägyptische Königsnovelle* (LÄS, 10; Glückstadt: Augustin).

Herrmann, S.
1953–54 'Die Königsnovelle in Ägypten und in Israel', *WS(L).GS* 3: 52-62.

Hobson, J.A.
1988 *The Dreaming Brain* (New York: Basic Books).

Hoftijzer, J., and G. van der Kooij (eds.)
1989 *The Balaam Text from Deïr 'Alla Re-evaluated* (Leiden: E.J. Brill).

Hout, Th. P.J. van den
1994 'Träume einer hethitischen Königin: KUB LX 97 + XXXI 71', *Altorientalische Forschungen* 21.2: 305-27.

Husser, J.-M.
1991a 'Le songe comme procédé littéraire: à propos de Gn 20', *RevScRel* 65: 157-72.
1991b 'Les métamorphoses d'un songe. Critique littéraire de Genèse 28,10-22', *RB* 98: 321-42.
1994 *Le songe et la parole: Etude sur le rêve et sa fonction dans l'ancien Israël* (BZAW, 210; Berlin: W. de Gruyter).
1996 'The Birth of a Hero: Form and Meaning of KTU 1.17 i-ii', in Wyatt, Watson and Lloyd 1996: 85-98.

Israelit-Groll, S.
1985 'A Ramesside Grammar Book of Technical Language of Dream Interpretation', in S. Israelit-Groll (ed.), *Pharaonic Egypt, the Bible and Christianity* (Jerusalem: Magnes Press; Hebrew University): 71-118.

Jacobsen, T.
1976 'The Stele of the Vultures, Col. I-X', in B.L. Eichler (ed.), *Kramer Anniversary Volume* (AOAT, 25, Neukirchen–Vluyn: Neukirchener Verlag; Kevelear: Verlag Butzon): 247-59.
1987 *The Harps That Once... Sumerian Poetry in Translation* (New Haven: Yale University Press).

Jaroš, K.
1982 'Die Träume', in *idem*, *Die Stellung des Elohisten zur kanaanäischen Religion* (OBO, 4; Göttingen: Vandenhoeck & Ruprecht): 31-50.

Jeffer, A.
1990 'Divination by Dream in Ugaritic Literature and in the Old Testament', *IBS* 12: 167-83.

Jouvet, M.
1992 *Le sommeil et le rêve* (Paris: O. Jacob).

Kammenhuber, A.
1976 *Orakelpraxis, Träume und Vorzeichenschau bei den Hethitern* (Texte der Hethiter, 7; Heidelberg: Carl Winter).

Kenik, H.E.
1983 *Design for Kingship: The Deuteronomistic Narrative Technique in 1 Kings 3,4-15* (SBL, 69; Chico, CA: Scholars Press).

Kessels, A.H.M.
1969 'Ancient Systems of Dream-Classification', *Mnemosyne* 4: 389-424.
1978 *Studies on the Dream in Greek Literature* (Utrecht: Hes).

Killborne, B.
1987 'Dreams', in M. Eliade (ed.), *The Encyclopedia of Religions*, IV (New York: Macmillan): 482-92.

Köcher, F., and A.L. Oppenheim
1957–58 'The Old-Babylonian Omen Text VAT 7525', *AfO* 18: 62-77.

Kramer, S.N.
1944 'The Death of Gilgamesh', *BASOR* 94: 2-12.

Kühlewein, J.
1980 'Gotteserfahrung und Reifungsgeschichte in der Jakob-Esau-Erzählung', in R. Albertz (ed.), *Werden und Wirken des Alten Testament* (Festschrift C. Westermann; Neukirchen–Vluyn: Neukirchener Verlag): 116-29.

La Berge, S.
1985 *Lucid Dreaming* (New York: J.P. Tarcher).

Lambert, M.
1947 'Le rêve de Gudea et le cylindre BM.N 89115', *RA* 41: 185-200.

Lambert, W.G.
1960 *Wisdom Literature* (Oxford: Clarendon Press).

Lebrun, R.
1980 *Hymnes et prières hittites* (Louvain-la-Neuve: Centre d'Histoire des religions).

Leibovici, M.
1959 'Les songes et leur interprétation à Babylone', in *Les songes et leur interprétation* (Sources Orientales, 2; Paris: Le Seuil): 63-86.

Levine, B.A.
1964 'Notes on an Aramaic Dream Text from Egypt', *JAOS* 84: 18-22.

Levy, E.
1982 'Le rêve homérique', *Ktema* 7: 23-41.

Lieshout, R.G.A. van
1980 *Greeks on Dreams* (Utrecht: Hes).

Malinine, M
1960 'Texte démotique relatif à un accident de travail', *AcOr* 25: 250-265.

Margalit, B.
1989 *The Ugaritic Poem of AQHT: Text, Translation, Commentary* (BZAW, 182, Berlin: W. de Gruyter).

McAlpine, T.H.
1987 *Sleep, Divine and Human, in the Old Testament* (JSOTSup, 38; Sheffield: JSOT Press).

Merendino, R.P.
1969 *Das deuteronomische Gesetz: Eine literarkritische, gattungs- und überlieferungsgeschichtliche Untersuchung zu Dt 12-26*, (BBB, 31; Bonn: Hanstein).
Miller, J. E.
1990 'Dreams and Prophetic Visions', *Bib* 71: 401-404.
Mowinckel, S.
1961 *Psalmenstudien* (2 vols.; Amsterdam: Schippers).
Müller, H.-P.
1969 'Magisch-mantische Weisheit und die Gestalt Daniels', *UF* 1: 79-94.
1972 'Mantische Weisheit und Apokalyptik', in G.W. Anderson *et al.* (eds.), *Congress Volume: Uppasala, 1971* (VTSup, 22; Leiden: E.J. Brill, 1972): 268-93.
Niederland, W. G.
1954 'Jacob's Dream', *Journal of Hillside Hospital* 3.
Oberman, J.
1946 *How Daniel Was Blessed with a Son: An Incubation Scene in Ugarit* (JAOSSup, 6; New Haven: American Oriental Society).
Oepke, A.
1967 'Οναρ', *TDNT*, V: 220-38.
Olmo Lete, G. del
1984 'Antecedentes cananeos (ugariticos) de formas literarias hebreo-biblicas', *Simposio Biblico Español, Salamanca, 1982* (Madrid: Universidad Complutense): 84-114.
Oppenheim, A.L.
1956 *The Interpretation of Dreams in the Ancient Near East* (Transactions of the American Philosophical Society, 46.3; Philadephia: American Philosophical Society: 179-373.
1964 *Ancient Mesopotamia. Portrait of a Dead Civilization* (Chicago: University Press): 206-27.
1966 'Mantic Dreams in the Ancient Near East', in R. Caillois and G.E. von Grünebaum (eds.), *The Dream and Human Societies* (Berkeley: University of California Press): 341-50.
1969 'New Fragments of the Assyrian Dream-Book', *Iraq* 31: 153-65.
Pardee, D.
1986 'The Ugaritic *šumma izbu* Text', *AfO* 33: 117-147.
Parlebas, J.
1982 'Remarques sur la conception des rêves et sur leur interprétation dans la civilisation égyptienne antique', *Ktema* 7: 19-22.
Pedersen, J.
1926 *Israel, its Life and Culture*, I–II (London: Cumberledge; Copenhagen: Bramer): 133-45.
Perdrizet, P. and G. Lefèbvre
1919 *Les graffites grecs du Mnemonion d'Abydos* (Nancy: Garis).
Priest, J.F.
1970 'Myth and Dream in Hebrew Scripture', in J. Campbell (ed.), *Myths, Dreams and Religion* (New York: Dutton): 48-67.

Quaegebeur, J.
1987 'La désignation (P*ꜣ*-)ḤRY-TP: phritob', in J. Osing and G. Dreyer (eds.), *Form und Mass* (Festschrift G. Fecht; ÄAT, 12; Wiesbaden: Otto Harrassowitz): 368-94.

Rachet, G.
1962 'Le sanctuaire de Dodone, origine et moyen de divination', *BAGB*, IV: 86-99.

Rad, G. von
1958 'Das judäische Königsritual', in *idem*, *Gesammelte Studien* (Munich: Chr. Kaiser Verlag): 205-13.
1985 *Genesis: A Commentary* (Minneapolis: Augsburg).

Reiner, E.
1960 'Fortune-Telling in Mesopotamia', *JNES* 19: 23-35.

Resch, A.
1964 *Der Traum im Heilsplan Gottes* (Freiburg: Herder).

Richter, W.
1963 'Traum und Traumdeutung im Alten Testament', *BZ* 7: 202-220.
1966 *Traditionsgeschichtliche Untersuchungen zum Richterbuch* (BBB, 18; Bonn: Peter Hanstein).

Roeder, G.
1960 *Kulte, Orakel und Naturverehrung im alten Ägypten* (Die Bibliothek der alten Welt; Zürich: Artemis Verlag).

Saporetti, C.
1995 'Paronomasia nell'oniromanzia assira', *Egitto e Vicino Oriente* 18: 193-211.

Sasson, J.M.
1983 'Mari Dreams', *JAOS* 103: 283-93.

Sauneron, S.
1959 'Les songes et leur interprétation dans l'Egypte ancienne', in *Les songes et leur interprétation* (Sources Orientales, 2; Paris: Le Seuil): 18-62.

Schenkel, W.
1975 'Die Bauinschrift Sesostris I. im Satet-Tempel von Elephantine', *MDAI* 31: 109-58.

Seitz, G.
1971 *Redaktionsgeschichtliche Studien zum Deuteronomium* (BWANT, 5; Stuttgart: W. Kohlhammer).

Schmidtke, F.
1967 'Träume, Orakel und Totengeister als Künder der Zukunft in Israel und Babylon', *BZ* 11: 240-46.

Silva, A. da
1993 'Dream as Demonic Experience in Mesopotamia', *SR* 22: 301-10.
1994 *La symbolique des rêves et des vêtements dans l'histoire de Joseph et de ses frères* (Héritage et Projet, 52; Montreal: Fides)

Stahl, W.H.
1952 *Macrobius. Commentary on the Dream of Scipio* (New York: Columbia University Press).

Tait, W.J.
1977 *Papyri from Tebtunis in Egyptian and in Greek* (Texts from Excavations, 3; London: Egypt Exploration Society).

Tfinkdji, J.
1913 'Essai sur les songes et l'art de les interpréter (onirocritie) en Mésopotamie', *Anthropos* 8: 505-25.

Thomson, J.G.
1955 'Sleep: An Aspect of Jewish Anthropology', *VT* 5: 421-33.

Tigay, J.H.
1982 *The Evolution of the Gilgamesh Epic* (Philadelphia: University of Pennsylvania Press).

Tropper, J.
1996 'Ugaritic dreams. Notes on Ugaritic *ḏ(h)rt* and *hdrt*', in Wyatt, Watson and Lloyd 1996: 305-14.

Vergote, J.
1959 *Joseph en Egypte* (OBL, 3; Louvain: Publications universitaires): 46-86.

Vernus, P.
1986 'Traum', *Lexikon der Ägyptologie* 5: 745-49 (in French).

Vieyra, M.
1959 'Les songes et leur interprétation chez les Hittites', in *Les songes et leur interprétation* (Sources Orientales, 2; Paris: Le Seuil): 87-98.

Vinagre, M.A.
1996 'Die griechische Terminologie der Traumdeutung', *Mnemosyne* 49: 257-80.

Volten, A.
1942 *Demotische Traumdeutung (Pap. Carlsberg XIII und XIV verso)* (Analecta Aegyptiaca, 3; Copenhagen: Akademisk Forlag).
1962 'Das demotische Ostracon im Brooklyn-Museum (Inv. No. 37.1821 E)', *AcOr* 26: 129-132.

Waerden, B.L. van der
1953 'History of Zodiac', *AfO* 16: 216-30.

Wente, E.F.
1975–76 'A Misplaced Letter to the Dead', in P. Naster, H. de Meuleuaere and J. Quaegebeur (eds.), *Miscellanea in honorem J. Vergote* (OLP, 6.7; Leuven: Department Oriëntalistiek): 595-600.

Westermann, C.
1985 *Genesis: A Commentary* (3 vols.; Minneapolis: Augsburg).
1986 'Der Traum im Alten Testament', in *idem* (ed.), *Traüme verstehen—Verstehen durch Traüme* (Munich: Schnell & Steiner): 8-23.

Wikenhauser, A.
1948 'Doppeltraüme', *Bib* 29: 100-11.

Wilken, U.
1927 *Urkunden der Ptolemäerzeit* (Berlin: Akademie-Verlag).

Wilson, E.J.
1996 *The Cylinders of Gudea: Transliteration, Translation, Index* (AOAT, 244; Neukirchen–Vluyn: Neukirchener Verlag; Kevelaer: Verlag Butzon).

Wyatt, N.
1998 *Religious Texts from Ugarit: The Words of Ilimilku and his Colleagues* (Sheffield: Sheffield Academic Press).

Wyatt, N., W.G.E. Watson and J.B. Lloyd (eds.)
1996 *Ugarit, Religion and Culture: Proceedings of the International Colloquium, Edinburgh, July 1994* (UBL, 12; Münster: Ugarit Verlag).

Zeitlin, S.
1975–76 'Dreams and their Interpretation from the Biblical Period to the Tanaanite Time: An Historical Study', *JQR* 66: 1-18.

Zibelius-Chen, K.
1988 'Kategorien und Rolle des Traumes in Ägypten', in H. Altenmüller and D. Wildung (eds.), *Studien zur altägyptischen Kultur*, XV (Hamburg: Buske-Verlag): 277-93.

Indexes

Index of References

Bible

OTHER ANCIENT REFERENCES

Index of Authors